The Activist's Handbook

26 in 26
Neighborhood Resource Centers
26 Neighborhood Strategies in a 26 month time frame
A Grant Funded by the LSTA
(Library Services & Technology Act)

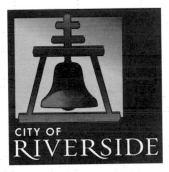

CITY OF
RIVERSIDE

Riverside Public Library

The Activist's Handbook

Winning Social Change in the
21st Century

Second Edition

Randy Shaw

UNIVERSITY OF CALIFORNIA PRESS

Berkeley • Los Angeles • London

University of California Press, one of the most distinguished university presses in the United States, enriches
lives around the world by advancing scholarship in the
humanities, social sciences, and natural sciences. Its
activities are supported by the UC Press Foundation and
by philanthropic contributions from individuals and
institutions. For more information, visit www.ucpress.
edu.

University of California Press
Berkeley and Los Angeles, California

University of California Press, Ltd.
London, England

Library of Congress Cataloging-in-Publication Data

Shaw, Randy, 1956–.
  The activist's handbook : winning social change in the
21st century / Randy Shaw.
      p.   cm.
  Includes bibliographical references and index.
  ISBN 978-0-520-27405-1 (cloth : alk. paper)
  ISBN 978-0-520-95699-5 (ebook)
  1. Social action—United States. 2. Community
organization—United States. 3. Political activists—
United States. 4. Political participation—United
States.5. Social reformers—United States. I. Title.
  HN65.S48   2013
  303.480973—dc23   2013012617

Manufactured in the United States of America

21 20 19 18 17 16 15 14 13

10 9 8 7 6 5 4 3 2 1

In keeping with a commitment to support environmentally responsible and sustainable printing practices, UC
Press has printed this book on Rolland Enviro100, a
100% postconsumer fiber paper that is FSC certified,
deinked, processed chlorine-free, and manufactured with
renewable biogas energy. It is acid-free and EcoLogo
certified.

To Erik Schapiro

Contents

Acknowledgments

I have learned much about social change from my fellow activists. Whether through one-time meetings or common struggles, my discussions with activists have been essential to the insights expressed in this book. I have been particularly inspired in writing this new edition by the young activists whose struggles are described in the pages that follow. From the DREAM Activists to those battling sweatshop labor, to the students fighting for the environment and against rising college tuition costs, it is heartening to see new generations working for greater social and economic justice.

The Tenderloin Housing Clinic, which I cofounded in 1980 and have headed since 1982, has provided me with a perfect vehicle for implementing my ideas for achieving social change. When I wrote the original edition of this book, we had roughly twenty full-time staff; we now have closer to 250. I would not have had the mental energy to write this new edition without the strong, skillful leadership of Deputy Director Krista Gaeta, who administers much of the Clinic's daily operations. This edition has greatly benefited from my discussions of activist strategies with other current and former Clinic staff. This group includes Tim Lee, Sam Dodge, Jeff Buckley, Dean Preston, Pratibha Tekkey, Jamie Sanbonmatsu, Paul Hogarth, and Clinic cofounder Chris Tiedemann. Mercy Gonzalez provided important clerical assistance.

Leroy Looper, owner of the historic Cadillac Hotel who died in 2011, offered me a model of integrity and street-smart strategic savvy that I have benefited from for over thirty years. He and his wife, Kathy, became great friends, and I have always tried to live up to Leroy's ideals. I barely knew Sister Bernie Galvin when the original version of this book was published, but soon after we became close confidants and friends. We have talked regularly for over a decade to plan activist strategies for local and national affordable-housing campaigns. Fred Ross, Jr., whom I got to know well when writing my prior book on the farmworkers movement, has also proved a valuable strategic sounding board.

This new edition is dedicated to my longtime friend Erik Schapiro. Our early work in the Tenderloin and our collaboration during his days as a supervisor's aide and in the Agnos administration still reverberate in my thinking about activism today.

I am fortunate to have Naomi Schneider of UC Press as my editor. It was Naomi's idea for me to write a new edition of this book, and she expressed continual confidence in its development.

My children, Anita and Ariel, were young kids when I wrote the first edition of *The Activist's Handbook*. Both are now out of college and working in public schools to assist low-income students. Their personal experiences have added to the concern over testing-driven education "reform" that I discuss in this new edition. My late grandmother Hylda Levin was a New Deal Democrat and McGovern supporter who always vowed she would take me to Canada, if necessary, to avoid the draft. Although she died in 1975, her spirit lives on.

Finally, I am most indebted to Lainey Feingold, my wife and best friend since 1977. Lainey helped make me an activist and provided me with important and enthusiastic editorial assistance. This book could not have been written without her.

Introduction

When I wrote the original version of *The Activist's Handbook* in the early 1990s, activists faced a very different social landscape. "Online activism" and "social media" were still in the future, and the potential of email and the Internet to boost activist campaigns was untapped. Americans got their news solely from television, radio, and daily newspapers. Campaigns for marriage equality were off the political radar, and a powerful national immigrant rights movement did not exist. We heard little about growing inequality between "the 99 percent and the 1 percent," and few imagined the election of the nation's first African American president in 2008.

These and other changes in the past two decades require a completely new version of the original book. This second edition examines new strategies, tactics, issues, and grassroots campaigns, and revisits whether activists have learned from past mistakes. It allows me to describe how activists should harness social media and other new tools to achieve their goals, and how new media can be best connected to traditional organizing and "old media" strategies. Student activism, at a low point when the original book came out and little mentioned, has since surged and is now the subject of an entirely new chapter. I have expanded my discussion of direct action activism to include additional campaigns and groups, and I explain why greater innovation is needed in response to opposition tactics. Since the original book, activists have become far more engaged in electoral politics, and the new book enables me to discuss how new media tools have enabled activists to increase assistance to progressive campaigns nationwide.

The times have changed, as have many of the issues, campaigns, and activist tools. But the fundamental rules for winning struggles for social change still apply. In fact, the strategies and tactics that brought activists success in the past provide valuable guidance to us today. For example, in Montgomery, Alabama, in December 1955, a seamstress named Rosa Parks was arrested for refusing a driver's order to move to the back of the bus. Her arrest spurred a citywide bus boycott that brought national attention to Parks and a young minister named Martin Luther King, Jr. Although it took another decade of struggle before state-imposed segregation laws were eliminated, Rosa Parks's courageous act stands as the symbolic start of the modern civil rights movement.

The civil rights movement comprised thousands of heroic acts, but even after her death Rosa Parks's story resonates long after other events of the period have been forgotten. When, forty years after her legendary act, Parks held a book signing in a small bookstore in Oakland, California, thousands of people waited in line for hours merely for the opportunity to see her up close.

Rosa Parks's stature, along with that of Cesar Chavez, Rachel Carson, and other activist icons, has grown rather than diminished over the years. I believe it is because people today have nostalgia for a seemingly bygone era when individuals at the grassroots level could initiate campaigns that made a difference in the world. Underlying the reverence for Parks is the common perception that today's political climate is so dominated by big money and so burdened by institutional barriers (e.g., the Supreme Court, filibusters) that campaigns for significant social change cannot prevail.

We saw a break in this cynicism in 2008 when millions of Americans, and particularly young people, put their hopes, dreams, and time into Barack Obama's presidential campaign. Although Obama achieved some major goals in his first term, many of his supporters were left disappointed. They saw his failure to accomplish more as signaling the inability of the nation's political system to accept transformative change. This feeling was bolstered when the Supreme Court's *Citizens United* ruling struck down hard-won restrictions on campaign financing. This left many convinced that the system was rigged and that activists could never win real change against corporate and wealthy interests.

In this book I flatly reject the widely held notion that current political conditions have confined social change activism to the history books.

The civil rights, farmworker, environmental, and other social movements all faced seemingly insurmountable barriers, yet all used the right combination of strategy and tactics to prevail. Their success shows that today's activists can use strategy and tactics to triumph in their own campaigns for change. As difficult as the path to progressive change in the United States appears in the second decade of the twenty-first century, activists in prior generations have overcome far greater institutional and cultural obstacles.

The critical impact of strategy and tactics on the outcome of social change campaigns is often overlooked. One reason is that most analyses of U.S. politics are not written by activists. People who participate in social change activism recognize that the chosen tactics or strategies often spell the difference between victory and defeat; outside commentators, however, evaluate actions by what *did* happen, not by what alternative strategy or tactic might have brought a better result. Moreover, the value of tactics and strategies is best demonstrated at the local level, but most accounts of institutional barriers to political change focus exclusively on Washington, D.C.

In the following pages I detail the strategies and tactics that activists in diverse fields have found necessary for success. I focus on winning campaigns and show how efforts that lost might have been victorious had the proper tactics and strategies been used. I also analyze why a particular tactic was successful and why it was preferable to other approaches. By discussing the strategic and tactical choices faced by activists, I take the reader inside the thought processes of experienced activists in the midst of their struggles.

Central to all social change activism is the need to engage in proactive strategic and tactical planning. Activists must develop an agenda and then focus their resources on realizing it. Unfortunately, many activists have failed to establish and implement their own agendas and instead have focused on issues framed by their opponents. Although the contemporary political environment frequently requires activists to respond to threats or defend past gains, these defensive battles cannot be waged at the expense of proactive campaigns for change. Social change activists can avoid fighting battles on their opponents' terms by establishing a broad, realizable program for fulfilling their goals. The means of carrying out the program are often the subject of lengthy meetings and internal debate. Once they have agreed upon an agenda and endorsed tactics and strategies, activists should expend their energy primarily on implementation, responding to the opposition's campaign solely within the framework of furthering their own programs. This proactive approach ensures that the social change organization sets the public debate, forcing the opposition to respond to the unceasing drive for progressive reform.

Against the backdrop of proactive agenda setting, particular tactics and strategies have consistently maximized the potential for achieving social change. These tactics include creating what prominent Texas community organizer Ernesto Cortes, Jr., has described as a "fear and loathing" relationship with elected officials to ensure political accountability; forging coalitions with diverse and even traditional opposition groups; harnessing the mainstream and alternative media to the social change agenda; and using sit-ins, "die-ins," and other forms of direct action.

Through a discussion of current political issues and events, I analyze the impact of particular strategies and tactics on the outcome of campaigns centered on neighborhood preservation, immigrants' rights, homelessness, economic inequality, crime, tenants' rights, sweatshops, the environment, AIDS policies and programs, student battles against tuition hikes, disability rights, gay and lesbian rights, and school reform. These issues serve to illustrate the diverse avenues activists may take to achieve social change: state and local ballot initiatives, electoral politics, grassroots lobbying and advocacy, direct action, media events, and litigation. Participants in these struggles range from the ACT UP activists of New York City to young DREAM Activists and undocumented Latino families across the nation. They include the urban poor of San Francisco, blue-collar and radical environmentalists, and teachers challenging the corporate takeover of public schools. These diverse constituencies have not always fit the popular chant that activists are involved in the "same struggle, same fight," but they have used similar tactics and strategies to achieve their goals.

My analysis covers local, state, and national battles. I have placed greater emphasis on national campaigns in this new version of the book, for two reasons. First, the rise of the Internet and social media has made it easier for activists to participate in national struggles. Second, activists are working in many areas—immigration, education, economic fairness, health care, public transit—where key decisions are made in the national arena. Most progressive activists remain primarily involved in struggles in the geographic area in which they live, and I discuss many local campaigns that have made a real difference in people's lives. New media tools have expanded national activism without detracting from local campaigns, and activists can now think and act both nationally and locally.

Bookstores and libraries contain dozens upon dozens of business-oriented how-to books. There exists a virtual industry of works designed to assist people in developing skills in management, negotiation, sales, communications, networking, and media relations. These volumes emphasize the tactics necessary to defeat in-house competitors, overseas competitors, and any other competitor who stands in the way of business success. People in the business of seeking social change, however, have few such resources to turn to for guidance. This book is meant to provide such guidance, particularly to a younger generation that has exhibited strong interest in fights for social and economic justice.

Although the media will never promote young people's activism as it did in the 1960s, when it was "new," the eighteen-to-thirty-four-year-old generation has demonstrated a tremendous desire to work for progressive change. We see this in many of the social justice struggles discussed in this book, and it was prominently demonstrated in the 2008 Obama presidential campaign. Today's young people want to address poverty, the environmental crisis, and other forms of social and economic injustice, but most are graduating from college thousands of dollars in debt. They need paid jobs that enable them to work full-time for social change. Obama's 2008 campaign could have offered such opportunities by retaining its best-trained young organizers to boost the president's agenda after the election, but this did not occur. With foundation and government support for community organizing having sharply declined in the past decade, idealistic young people face greater challenges than prior generations did in securing full-time, paid jobs working for change. As a result, new generations of activists often lack organizational mentors who can train them in the skills of creating and winning social justice campaigns. This book helps to fill that void.

President Obama's reelection creates enormous opportunities for activism. As I discuss in the context of the immigrant rights, environmental, and gay marriage movements, activists' response to the president has proved determinative for their movement's success. The Republican Party's obstructionism is a major challenge, as are corporate and big-money interests at the local level. All of these obstacles have been overcome in the past, and can be defeated in the future.

But make no mistake: while having President Obama or another Democratic president in the White House, or a sympathetic mayor in City Hall or progressive ally as governor, opens the door to opportunities, only grassroots activism can translate this into meaningful change. From the Freedom Rides of the civil rights movement, to the "no business as usual" actions of ACT UP, to young DREAM Activists risking deportation to gain a legal path to the American Dream, grassroots activism has been the driving force for change. To paraphrase Mark Twain, reports of the demise of progressive social change have been greatly exaggerated. A generation of activists who understand the tactics and strategies essential for success can bring greater social and economic justice to the United States in the twenty-first century.

1

Don't Respond, Strategize

In a previous era, social change activists were guided by the immortal words of Mary "Mother" Jones: "Don't mourn, organize." These words, spoken following the murder of a union activist, emphasized the value of proactive responses to critical events. Although American activists today face less risk of being killed, they still must heed Mother Jones's command. A political environment hostile to progressive change has succeeded in putting many social change activists on the defensive, and the need for proactive planning—what I like to call tactical activism—has never been clearer.

Unfortunately, proactive strategies and tactics for change all too frequently are sacrificed in the rush to respond to the opposition's agenda. Of course, activists must organize and rally to defeat specific attacks directed against their constituencies; if a proposed freeway will level your neighborhood, preventing the freeway's construction is the sole possible strategy. I am speaking, however, of the far more common scenario where the opposition pushes a particular proposal or project that will impact a constituency without threatening its existence. In these cases, it is critical that a defensive response also lays the groundwork for achieving the long-term goal.

The best way to understand tactical activism is to view it in practice. The Tenderloin neighborhood of San Francisco, where I have worked since 1980, is a virtual laboratory demonstrating both the benefits of tactical activism and the consequences of its absence. The Tenderloin won historic victories using proactive strategies in response to luxury tourist developments threatening its future, but had less success in responding defensively to crime. This chapter also discusses how the Occupy movement used proactive activism to reshape the national debate about inequality, and how activists played into their opponents hands by allowing homelessness to be reframed from a socially caused housing problem to a problem of individual behavior.

THE TENDERLOIN: TACTICAL ACTIVISM AT WORK

The Tenderloin in San Francisco lies between City Hall and the posh downtown shopping and theater district of Union Square. Once a thriving area of bars, restaurants, and theaters, the Tenderloin gave birth to the city's gay and lesbian movement and was long home to thousands of merchant seamen and blue-collar workers living in the neighborhood's more than one hundred residential hotels. When I arrived in the Tenderloin in 1980, it was often described as San Francisco's "seedy" district—a not entirely inaccurate depiction. For at least the prior decade, the Tenderloin had more than its share of prostitution, public drunkenness, and crime. It was notorious for its abundance of peep shows, porno movie houses, and nude-dancing venues; the high profile of these businesses and their flashing lights and lurid signs fostered the neighborhood's unsavory reputation.

The Tenderloin's location in the heart of a major U.S. city distinguishes it from other economically depressed neighborhoods. Many people who spend their entire lives in Los Angeles or New York City never have cause to go to Skid Row or the South Bronx; Bay Area residents can easily avoid the high-crime area of East Oakland. However, most San Franciscans are likely to pass through the Tenderloin at some point—to visit one of the city's major theaters or the Asian Art Museum, to see a friend staying at the Hilton Hotel or Hotel Monaco (both located in the Tenderloin), to conduct business at nearby City Hall, or to reach any number of other destinations. San Franciscans have firsthand experience with the Tenderloin that is highly unusual for low-income neighborhoods.

The thirty-five blocks at the core of the neighborhood constitute one of the most heterogeneous areas in the United States, if not the world. The Tenderloin's 20,000 residents include large numbers of senior citizens, who are primarily Caucasian; immigrant families from Vietnam, Cambodia, and Laos; a significant but less visible number of Latino families; perhaps San Francisco's largest concentration of single African

American men, and a smaller number of African American families; one of the largest populations of gays outside the city's Castro district; and a significant number of East Indian families, who own or manage most of the neighborhood's residential hotels. The Tenderloin's broad ethnic, religious, and lifestyle diversity has held steady as the rest of San Francisco has become more racially segregated over the past decades.

With government offices and cultural facilities in the Civic Center to the west, the city's leading transit hub on Market Street to the south, the American Conservatory and Curran Theaters to the north, and Union Square (one of the most profitable shopping districts in the United States) to the east, in the late 1970s the neighborhood's economic revival was said to be just around the corner. This widespread belief in the imminent gentrification of the Tenderloin profoundly shaped its future. During that time, Tenderloin land values rose to levels more appropriate to the posh lower Nob Hill area than to a community beset with unemployment, crime, and a decrepit housing stock. Real estate speculators began buying up Tenderloin apartment buildings, and developers began unveiling plans for new luxury tourist hotels and condominium towers.

Further impetus for the belief in imminent gentrification came from the arrival in the late 1970s of thousands of refugees, first from Vietnam, then from Cambodia and Laos. The Tenderloin was chosen for refugee resettlement because its high apartment-vacancy rate made it the only area of the city that could accommodate thousands of newly arrived families. The refugees' arrival fostered optimism about the Tenderloin's future in three significant ways. First, the refugees filled long-standing apartment vacancies and thus raised neighborhood property values and brought instant profits to Tenderloin landowners. Second, many in the first wave of refugees left Vietnam with capital, which they proceeded to invest in new, Asian-oriented businesses in the Tenderloin. These businesses, primarily street-level markets and restaurants, gave the neighborhood a new sense of vitality and drove up the value of ground-floor commercial space.

Third, and perhaps most significant, those eager for gentrification expected Southeast Asian immigrant families to replace the Tenderloin's long-standing population of seniors, merchant seamen, other low-income working people, and disabled persons. The families, it was thought, would transform the neighborhood into a Southeast Asian version of San Francisco's popular Chinatown.

My introduction to the Tenderloin came through Hastings Law School, another significant player in the Tenderloin development scene.

In 1979, when I was twenty-three, I enrolled as a student at Hastings, a public institution connected to the University of California. During the 1970s, Hastings had expanded its "campus" by vacating tenants from some adjacent residential hotels. Until 2006, its relationship to the low-income residents of the Tenderloin was based on the perspective of territorial imperative, one shared by urban academic institutions such as Columbia and the University of Chicago. Hastings was aptly described during its expansion phase as the law school that "ate the Tenderloin."

I became involved in trying to help Tenderloin residents soon after starting at Hastings. My personal concern was tenants' rights, an interest developed when I lived in Berkeley while attending the University of California. On February 1, 1980, I joined fellow law students in opening a center to help Tenderloin tenants prevent evictions and assert their rights. Our center, called the Tenderloin Housing Clinic, started with a budget of $50, and our all-volunteer staff was housed in a small room at Glide Memorial Church, in the heart of the neighborhood.

When we opened the Clinic, the Tenderloin did not appear to be on the verge of an economic boom. Some thriving Asian markets had opened, and nonprofit housing corporations had begun to acquire and rehabilitate some buildings, but the dominant impression was of an economically depressed community whose residents desperately needed various forms of help. The inhabitants of the Tenderloin, unaware of the agenda of those predicting upscale development, would have laughed at anyone proclaiming that neighborhood prosperity was just around the corner. How quickly everyone's perspective would change in the months ahead!

Almost immediately, I found myself plunged into what remains my best experience of how tactical activism can transform a defensive battle into a springboard toward accomplishing a significant goal. In June 1980 I was invited to a meeting at the offices of the North of Market Planning Coalition (NOMPC). NOMPC initially comprised agencies serving the Tenderloin population. In 1979, however, it obtained enough staff through the federal VISTA program (the domestic incarnation of the Peace Corps) to transform itself into a true citizen-based organization. The VISTA organizers were like me: recent college graduates from middle-class backgrounds excited about trying to help Tenderloin residents. The convener of the June 1980 meeting, Richard Livingston, had secured the VISTA money for NOMPC with the vision of getting neighborhood residents involved in planning the community's future.[1]

Livingston revealed that three of the most powerful hospitality chains in the world—Holiday Inn, Ramada, and Hilton—had launched plans to build three luxury tourist hotels in the neighborhood. The three towers would reach thirty-two, twenty-seven, and twenty-five stories, respectively, containing more than 2,200 new tourist rooms. The news outraged us; the encroachment of these big-money corporations would surely drive up property values, leading to further development and gentrification and, ultimately, the obliteration of the neighborhood. Fighting construction of the hotels, however, presented mammoth difficulties. None of the hotels would directly displace current residents, so the projects could not be attacked on this ground, and zoning laws allowed for the development of the proposed luxury high-rise hotels, which removed a potential legal barrier.

The situation seemed hopeless. The Tenderloin's residents were entirely unorganized, NOMPC's newly hired VISTA organizers were energetic but inexperienced, and our opponents were multinational hotel corporations in a city where the tourist industry set all the rules. How could we succeed in preserving and enhancing the Tenderloin as an affordable residential community for the elderly, poor, and disabled in the face of this three-pronged attack? The answer lay in tactical activism.

Prior to the threat of the hotels, NOMPC's central goal for the Tenderloin was to win its acceptance as an actual neighborhood worthy of assistance from the city. The lack of participation by Tenderloin residents and agency staff in the city's political life had led to a consensus, accepted even by progressive activists, that a viable neighborhood entity north of Market Street did not exist. The hotel fight gave NOMPC the opportunity to educate the rest of the city about the state of affairs in the Tenderloin. As the Coalition organized residents to fight the hotels, the overall strategy became clear: first, to establish that the Tenderloin was a residential neighborhood and, second, to insist that, as such, it was entitled to the same zoning protections for its residents as other San Francisco neighborhoods. If NOMPC could force City Hall and the hotel developers to accept the first premise, the second premise—and NOMPC's strategic goal—would follow.[2]

The attempt to rezone the neighborhood in response to the hotel development threat was certainly not inevitable; it was the result of carefully considered tactical activism. Instead of using the hotel fight as a springboard for change, the organization could have made the usual anti-development protests, then sat back and awaited the next development project in the neighborhood. The organizational identity could have been that of a fighter of David-and-Goliath battles pitting powerless citizens against greedy developers. Livingston, NOMPC organizer Sara Colm, and other Tenderloin organizers understood, however, that development projects are rarely stopped and are at best mitigated. This is particularly true where development opponents are primarily low-income people and where the local political leadership—as is true for most cities, large and small—is beholden to developers and real estate interests.

The organizers foresaw that a succession of fights against specific development projects would destroy the residential character of the neighborhood they wished to strengthen. A rezoning of the community, in contrast, would prevent all future development projects without directly attacking the financial interests of any particular developer. A proactive battle for neighborhood rezoning was thus both the most effective and the most politically practical strategy. "No hotels" was not a solution to the neighborhood's problem—rezoning was.

In concert with the local chapter of the Gray Panthers, many of whose senior activist members lived in the Tenderloin, NOMPC unified residents by forming the Luxury Hotel Task Force. The Task Force became the vehicle of resident opposition to the hotels, but it had a greater and more strategic importance as a visible manifestation that the Tenderloin was a true residential neighborhood. Although most Task Force members had lived in the Tenderloin for years, they were invisible to the city's political forces. Suddenly, hotel developers and their attorneys, elected officials, and San Francisco Planning Department staff were confronted with a group of residents from a neighborhood whose existence they had never before recognized. The Tenderloin residents' unified expression of concern over the hotels' possible impact on their lives permanently changed the political calculus of the neighborhood. Once the developers' representatives and city officials encountered the Task Force, NOMPC's strategic goal of establishing the Tenderloin as a recognizable residential neighborhood was achieved.

The battle against the hotels was short and intense. After learning of the proposal in June, we held two large community meetings in July. More than 250 people attended the meetings, a turnout unprecedented in Tenderloin history. The formal approval process for the hotels began with a Planning Commission hearing on November 6, at which more than 100 residents testified against the project. Final commission approval came on January 29, 1981, in a hearing that began in the afternoon and ended early the next morning.

The projects clearly had been placed on the fast track for approval; the city was in the midst of "Manhattanization," a building boom during which virtually no high-rise development project was disapproved. This made the accomplishments of the Luxury Hotel Task Force that much more astounding. As a result of residents' complaints that the hotels would have a "significant adverse environmental impact" on rents, air quality, and traffic in the Tenderloin, the commission imposed several conditions to mitigate these effects. The hotels had to contribute an amount equal to fifty cents per hotel room for twenty years for low-cost housing development (about $320,000 per hotel per year). Additionally, each hotel had to pay $200,000 for community service projects, sponsor a $4 million grant for the acquisition and renovation of four low-cost residential hotels (474 units total), and act in good faith to give priority in employment to Tenderloin residents.

Such "mitigation measures" are now commonplace conditions of development approval in U.S. cities, but they were unprecedented in January 1981. In the view of local media and business leaders, that a group of elderly, disabled, and low-income residents had won historic concessions from three major international hotel chains in a pro-development political climate was an ominous precedent. *San Francisco Chronicle* columnist Abe Mellinkoff weighed in strongly against "the squeeze" in two consecutive columns following the Planning Commission vote. Referring to the mitigations as a "shakedown" undertaken by "bank robbers," Mellinkoff urged the business establishment to publicly protest this "rip-off of fellow capitalists." As Mellinkoff saw it, Luxury Hotel Task Force members were "crusaders" and "eager soldiers" whom City Hall had allowed to prevail in "a war against corporations." Clearly, NOMPC's strategy had worked. The hotel fight had made the Tenderloin a neighborhood to be reckoned with.[3]

The decision to use this defensive battle to achieve a critical goal resulted entirely from continual discussions of strategy and tactics among the thirty to forty residents who regularly attended Luxury Hotel Task Force meetings. A good example of the group's extensive tactical debates arose when the Hilton Hotel offered to provide lunch at a meeting to discuss its project. Gray Panther organizer Jim Shoch, whose tactical insights were critical to the Task Force's success, made sure that every facet of the Hilton offer was analyzed for its implications. Some Task Force members felt that lunch should be refused so the Hilton couldn't "buy us off." The majority wanted to take advantage of a high-quality lunch, recognizing it as a vast improvement over their normal fare. Ultimately, the group went to the lunch but gave no quarter to the Hilton in the meeting that followed.

These time-consuming and often frustrating internal discussions enabled residents to understand that they did not have to accomplish the impossible (i.e., prevent approval of the towers) to score a victory. Without this understanding, the city's ultimate approval of the hotels could have been psychologically and emotionally devastating. Instead, the Planning Commission's approval did not diminish residents' feelings that they had achieved a great triumph in their own lives and in the neighborhood's history.

With city officials having recognized the Tenderloin as a viable neighborhood, the Task Force turned to the second half of NOMPC's agenda: establishing the Tenderloin's right to residential rezoning. In 1981, San Francisco residents could initiate the rezoning process by circulating petitions in the neighborhood in question. NOMPC began its rezoning campaign immediately after the city's approval of the luxury hotels. The rezoning proposal affected sixty-seven square blocks overall, with the strictest downzoning proposed for the thirty-five-square-block heart of the Tenderloin.

In this central area, the new zoning prohibited new tourist hotels, prevented commercial use above the second floor, and imposed eight- to thirteen-story height restrictions. The strategy succeeded largely because of its timing: on the heels of the Planning Commission's approval of the hotel towers, even the pro-growth local political leadership felt the neighborhood should not be required to accept additional commercial high-rise development. But the city's sense of obligation to residents of a low-income community might quickly evaporate in the face of a new high-rise development proposal; quick action was necessary to prevent new projects from emerging as threats.

The wisdom of the strategy was confirmed in 1983, prior to the city's approval of the rezoning. A one-million-square-foot development that included hotels, restaurants, and shops was proposed for the heart of the Tenderloin. The project, "Union Square West," effectively would have destroyed the affordable residential character of a major portion of the neighborhood. Clearly, Union Square West conflicted with the fundamental premise of the rezoning proposal; the project included three towers ranging between seventeen and thirty stories, a 450-room tourist hotel, and 370 condominium units. Would the pro-growth Planning Commission turn its back on the neighborhood and support the project? In the absence of the rezoning campaign, and despite the "obligation" incurred to the community after approval of the luxury hotels, San Francisco's Planning Commission undoubtedly would have authorized the project. The tactical activism of NOMPC, however, preempted the mammoth proposal. When Union Square West went for approval on June 9, 1983, the ardently pro-growth Planning Commission chairman strongly chastised the developer. The rezoning process had gone too far for the city to change its mind. A project that would otherwise have been approved was soundly defeated.

The Tenderloin rezoning proposal was signed into law on March 28, 1985. Its passage culminated nearly five years of strategic planning that had involved hundreds of low-income people in ongoing tactical discussions. The rezoning enabled the Tenderloin to avoid the gentrification that occurred in virtually every other central-city neighborhood across the nation in the following three decades. Today, thirty-one blocks of the still-low-income neighborhood constitute the nationally recognized Uptown Tenderloin Historic District, listed on the National Register of Historic Places. The North of Market Planning Coalition's transformation of a major threat into a springboard for achieving long-sought goals stands as a shining example of what can be accomplished through tactical activism.

THE OCCUPY MOVEMENT: WE ARE THE 99 PERCENT

Tactical activism is also vital in national campaigns. Activists seeking to implement a proactive agenda must overcome corporate and wealthy interests that not only spend billions to frame issues in their preferred terms but also have strong media allies to further their goals. That's why Occupy Wall Street's success in the fall of 2011 is so impressive. Occupy activists reframed a complex series of economic and social forces into a bumper sticker paradigm: the 1 percent versus the 99 percent. And after creating a new way for understanding inequality, Occupy trusted its instincts and avoided arcane policy debates and pressure to submit a list of "demands." While some Occupy activists later became reactive, and the movement's growth did not meet the expectations of its most enthusiastic backers, the Occupy movement reshaped the nation's political dialogue in its first two months alone. Occupy also shows the grassroots energy that can be tapped when activists aspire to transcend conventional wisdom about what is politically possible.

Occupy Emerges

On July 13, 2011, the anti-capitalist Vancouver-based online publication *Adbusters* called for "20,000 people" to "flood into lower Manhattan, set up tents, kitchens, peaceful barricades and occupy Wall Street for a few months." The protest was set to begin on September 17. While gathering 20,000 protesters in New York City is not difficult, the plan was for people to "occupy" a park for not just a night or a weekend, but for "a few months." *Adbusters* had no idea how many would respond to its call. Some activists were mobilizing. A group known as US Day of Rage was organizing actions that day in New York City, Austin, Los Angeles, San Francisco, and Seattle, and the protests were promoted on websites and tweets put out by the Internet hacktivist group Anonymous; and local activists associated with the newly formed New York General Assembly were committed to the plan. But labor unions, churches, and other large institutions whose outreach is often necessary to generate major turnouts were not involved. Nor was there an official website, commonly used to mobilize mass events.[4]

On September 14, Nathan Schneider wrote on *Adbusters*' website: "Not only will this weekend be a test of Americans' readiness to resist, but of whether an idea lobbed into the internet by Adbusters, then grabbed by artists, students, Twitter hashtags, and a shadowy network of hackers (and hacker wannabes), can really turn into a 'flood,' a show of meaningful political force, a new way forward."[5] Many would have questioned whether the *Adbusters* network and its anarchist allies could create a viable "test of Americans' readiness to resist," given their lack of connection to mainstream progressive organizations.

Nevertheless, as many progressives despaired over President Obama's failure and/or inability to implement his 2008 campaign vision, *Adbusters* and its initial allies saw an opportunity to tap grassroots discontent that nearly everyone else missed. Occupy's call revived demands to address Wall Street abuses, rising income and economic inequality, and the inability of the U.S. political system to address either. Occupy also provided activists with an organizational vehicle to pursue this agenda. By offering both a vision and a vehicle, the Occupy movement became a case study in the power of proactive grassroots activism.

Redefining the National Agenda

Occupy's very first protest showed that when activists take the initiative, it can cause strategically wrong responses on the part of government or other power centers that help expand the movement. The New York City Police Department made two early decisions that fueled Occupy's growth.

First, the September 17 occupation was originally planned for 1 Chase Plaza, the site of the "Charging Bull" sculpture symbolizing nearby Wall Street. But this was a public space. Police fenced it off after learning of the planned takeover. The occupation then shifted to Zuccotti Park, which was private property. This meant that police could not force protesters to leave absent the property owner's request. Zuccotti was a far better site for pitching tents, setting up tables, holding meetings, and attracting people to Occupy Wall Street. Not recognizing that the city had given a great gift to Occupiers by shifting the protest to a private site, New York City mayor Michael Bloomberg told a September 17 press conference that "people have a right to protest, and if they want to protest, we'll be happy to make sure they have locations to do it."[6]

The September 17 protests included about one thousand people, only 5 percent of the number that organizers projected. It received little media attention. Follow-up protests were also ignored. Keith Olbermann observed on his MSNBC show *Countdown* on September 21, 2011, that "after five straight days of sit-ins, marches, and shouting, and some arrests, actual North American newspaper coverage of this—even by those who have thought it farce or failure—has been limited to one blurb in a free newspaper in Manhattan and a column in the *Toronto Star*." He noted that, in contrast, "a tea party protest in front of Wall Street about [Federal Reserve chief] Ben Bernanke putting stimulus funds into it, it's the lead story on every network newscast."[7]

The lack of media coverage obscured the fact that activists were still learning about the occupation. As more visited Zuccotti Park and came away impressed, Occupy's message expanded. Many got their first opportunity to join an Occupy protest on Saturday, October 1. This rainy day became a significant turning point for the Occupy movement. Once again, a proactive move by Occupy triggered a counterproductive police response that helped build the campaign. In this case, when Occupy protesters began walking across the Brooklyn Bridge—a very common New York City activist tactic—more than seven hundred were arrested. The protesters were apprehended despite having engaged in no violence, vandalism, or civil disobedience. Nor were they trying to block traffic. In fact, Occupy had tried to avoid conflicts with police.

The huge number of arrests made headlines. It also put the Occupy movement on the national map. Media coverage of the mass arrests necessarily reported Occupy's arguments about inequality, boosting plans already in the works to expand local Occupy actions nationwide.

Occupy now attracted support from labor unions and other more mainstream progressive groups. The symbolism of the arrests could not have been more effective: the same police force that protected Wall Street was used to arrest Occupy protesters, with many assuming that the NYPD had acted at the behest of the 1 percent. To top it off, the media sided with the marchers' version of events. As the *New York Times* put it, "Many protesters said they believed the police had tricked them, allowing them onto the bridge, and even escorting them partway across, only to trap them in orange netting after hundreds had entered."[8]

The Brooklyn Bridge arrests turned Occupy into a national story. Reporters unable pre-Occupy to convince editors to cover rising economic inequality were now given space to address the issue. Republican presidential front-runner Mitt Romney then added fuel to the growing media fire by criticizing the Occupy protests as "class warfare"; this comment effectively turned income inequality into a partisan issue. When thousands took to the streets in New York City to express solidarity with Occupy, President Obama said he "understood" the protesters' concern: "It expresses the frustrations that the American people feel that we had the biggest financial crisis since the Great Depression, huge collateral damage all throughout the country, all across Main Street. And yet you're still seeing some of the same folks who acted irresponsibly trying to fight efforts to crack down on abusive practices that got us into this problem in the first place." For many who were disappointed with Obama's aligning with Wall Street after taking office, such words meant that the president clearly saw Occupy's agenda as reshaping the national debate.[9]

Proactively Framing the Movement

Only two weeks after occupying Zuccotti Park on September 17, the Occupy movement was a national phenomenon. But activists took nothing for granted, including their ability to continue camping in the private park. Mayor Bloomberg's assurance that the city would provide Occupiers with locations to protest meant that a quick eviction would appear hypocritical; nonetheless, activists took a number of proactive steps to protect the occupation by framing it as a political gathering rather than a squatters' encampment.

To this end Occupy maintained a library of progressive books, many donated by publishers and authors eager to connect their works with the emerging movement. Activists also launched the *Occupied Wall*

Street Journal newspaper, whose 50,000 press run was funded by the crowd-funding site Kickstarter. Adding to the sense that this was a political movement and not simply a homeless tent city were publicly posted agendas for each day's activities, including training sessions, educational events, and the General Assembly meetings that became widely identified with the movement.

Since city restrictions banned electrical amplification at Zuccotti Park, speakers relied on a call-and-response system known as human microphones. Speakers' words were repeated by the entire assembly, including each meeting's starting call for a "mic check." Richard Kim described a meeting on October 6, 2011: "The overall effect can be hypnotic, comic or exhilarating—often all at once. As with every media technology, to some degree the medium is the message. It's hard to be a downer over the human mic when your words are enthusiastically shouted back at you by hundreds of fellow occupiers, so speakers are usually pretty upbeat (or at least sound that way). Likewise, the human mic is not so good for getting across complex points about, say, how the Federal Reserve's practice of quantitative easing is inadequate to address the current shortage of global aggregate demand . . . so speakers tend to express their ideas in straightforward narrative or moral language."[10]

The call-and-response approach replicated a vision of grassroots democracy harkening back to the New England town meeting. This turned the General Assembly at Zuccotti Park into a model for the type of democratic system in which the people rather than big-money interests rule—a model to which Occupiers wanted the nation to return.

New York City activists had spent months preparing for September 17 and its aftermath. The structure, design, and agenda of the Zuccotti Park occupation were no accident. When Mayor Bloomberg announced that authorities would "clean the park" and evict Occupy on October 14, all believed that the mayor was calling the shots on behalf of Brookfield Properties, the private owner, and public sympathy toward the Zuccotti campers was strong. In fact, it was so strong that Bloomberg withdrew the planned eviction rather than face thousands of sympathizers planning to descend on Zuccotti Park on the morning of the 14th to save Occupy. The response to the possible shutdown of the encampment showed that Occupy had created a remarkable sense of community built along class lines. From activists wearing buttons to signs displayed in retail businesses, a new sense of unity emerged around Occupy's slogan, "We Are the 99%."

From the October 1 Brooklyn Bridge arrests to the October 14 planned eviction, media coverage of the movement increased exponentially. Although activists had long decried the widening gap between the rich and everyone else, Occupy's 1 percent–versus–99 percent rallying cry publicized economic inequality in a way not seen since the New Deal. It was as if a big curtain titled "American Dream" had been pulled away, exposing a system rigged for the rich against the middle class and the rest of the 99 percent. The traditional media, rarely aligned with progressive attacks on the wealthy, provided surprisingly favorable coverage in Occupy's first weeks. Rather than profile young anarchists expressing contempt for capitalism—the standard media image for anti-globalization protests—Occupy stories focused on hardworking, down-on-their-luck Americans who simply wanted a job, a roof over their heads, or a living wage.

These positive media stories were no accident. The Occupy movement relied on hard economic facts to make its case, and maintained an intellectual integrity that swayed mainstream reporters. The media portrayed the movement as more than angry youth acting out against authority. An online survey of traffic to the OccupyWallStreet website on October 5, 2011, found that Occupiers reflected the diversity of the nation. The report "Main Stream Support for a Mainstream Movement: The 99% Movement Comes from and Looks Like the 99%" revealed a surprisingly broad consensus that Occupiers were regular folks. This sharply contrasted with the way protesters challenging corporate power are often portrayed in the United States.[11]

A Demand for Demands

Although Occupy was growing and creating a national debate about class and income inequality, some began questioning the movement's alleged lack of specific demands. At one level, the idea that a movement demanding greater economic fairness and increased restrictions on Wall Street somehow lacked demands made no sense; politicians certainly knew how to address these concerns. Yet for some activists, issuing a list of specific demands to those in power was part of Organizing 101. They argued that absent demands, politicians would co-opt the movement, those in power would be under no pressure to acquiesce, and the movement would even become "a joke."[12]

These critics misunderstood the Occupy project. Occupy sought to propel a political and cultural shift toward redistributing the nation's wealth. Occupy was not akin to a neighborhood group pressuring a politician to clean up a park, or a national campaign pushing the president or Congress to stop construction of a pipeline. Occupy was also very different from previous high-profile anti-corporate campaigns against Gallo Wine, J.P. Stevens, and Nike, all of which addressed a specific set of abuses. Occupy captivated the public by offering a systemic challenge to a political and economic structure that had proved impervious to piecemeal reforms. Furthermore, the notion that Occupy's relatively small base in October 2011 gave it authority to issue specific demands on behalf of "the 99 percent" would have mocked its own critiques of the democratic process. Rather than squander time and effort debating demands, Occupy needed to continue expanding its base.

Formalizing demands would also have been a mistake because it would have shifted Occupy's struggle to Wall Street and its political opponents' favored turf: Congress and banking regulators. Once Occupy became yet another Beltway lobbying force, it would have no energy left for tactics that could really shake up the system. Occupy wisely recognized that the 1 percent and Congress would not agree to any meaningful "demands." Pursuing and then failing to achieve legislative changes would simply allow critics to quickly declare the movement's failure.

The Movement Grows

On October 25, 2011, hundreds of police officers wearing gas masks and riot gear, firing rubber bullets, and using tear gas stormed Occupy Oakland's base in a public plaza. The police assault left Scott Olsen, a twenty-four-year-old marine, in critical condition after a blow to his head from a tear gas canister fired by police fractured his skull and led to swelling of the brain. Footage of the police violence played on television for days. The dominant theme was that Olsen had survived two tours of duty in Iraq but was nearly killed while peacefully protesting in Oakland. Nobody defended the police actions, and even media generally sympathetic to law enforcement condemned the excessive force.

The attacks gave the Occupy movement more positive national publicity than ever before. Many activists saw the Oakland police response as evidence that Occupy's message was unhinging the elite, who could defend their greed only through violence. The media saw Iraq War veteran Olsen, who was working in the computer industry at the time, as the type of "mainstream" supporter the Occupy movement had attracted.

Olsen's biography forced the media to acknowledge that a struggle initiated by anarchists and anti-establishment forces now extended beyond the traditional activist base.

On November 2, Occupy Oakland held a "General Strike" that brought more than 10,000 protesters marching through the city. This tremendous display of nonviolent unity was enormously empowering for many of those involved. While late-night vandalism by black-clad anarchists drew attention, the media went out of their way to distinguish this behavior from Occupy's daytime protesters. Many participants saw the General Strike as just the beginning, creating momentum for a broader movement for change.

But the mass strike would instead prove Occupy Oakland's high point. Occupy Oakland did no systematic recruitment on November 2, and those coordinating the General Strike failed to get email, phone, or other contact information helpful for enlisting activists for future protests. Nor was a follow-up event announced that would have left protesters feeling that the General Strike was not a one-shot deal but was part of a larger strategy. Instead of affirmatively mobilizing hundreds of new activists to be centrally involved in a broader movement, Occupy coordinators apparently assumed that they could use the same turnout tactics in future actions that they had used for the General Strike. But many labor unions and other groups that had mobilized for the strike could not devote similar resources toward building future large Occupy turnouts. Occupy Oakland missed a great opportunity in not building upon the General Strike, and as a result, thousands departed the spectacular one-day protest without ever returning to the movement.

Going Off Message

The October 25 police attacks and November 2 General Strike gave Occupy Oakland a high national profile. But the group soon shifted its focus from "the 1 percent" to challenging Oakland mayor Jean Quan and insisting on its right to continue camping in the public plaza that had been the site of the attacks. Occupy Oakland never recovered from this shift from targeting income inequality to challenging misconduct by Oakland public officials. To be sure, Oakland activists had long battled police misconduct, and many Occupiers saw reclaiming public spaces (or "the commons") as a central movement goal. But neither Quan nor any other urban mayor had the power to rectify staggering national income inequality, and targeting wayward Oakland officials got the once-promising local Occupy movement off track.

Following the police attacks, Occupy Oakland continued to generate publicity. But now it was about confrontations with Oakland's mayor and police chief, and fights over the right to camp in a public plaza. Occupy Oakland's activities soon had little direct connection to Wall Street or the financial sector. There were major confrontations with police over occupying a vacant city building and blocking the Oakland port. Meanwhile, Occupy's image as representing a truly democratic, grassroots decision-making process came under scrutiny. A process that required people to attend meetings deep into the night did not work for those with family responsibilities or other work commitments. In fact, it skewed decision making to a small segment of "the 99 percent" that had time to attend hours of outdoor evening meetings on work nights. A process claiming to be truly democratic effectively excluded many of those who might have become heavily involved in the movement following the General Strike.

Occupy Oakland was only one branch of a national movement, but its ongoing confrontations with police greatly raised its national profile. When a small number of protesters associated with Occupy Oakland engaged in vandalism against downtown businesses, defenders of this tactic correctly argued that it was sanctioned by Occupy. By refusing to reject violence, Occupy Oakland marginalized itself. In debating between violent and nonviolent resistance, the movement showed how far it had strayed from the 99 percent it claimed to represent.

When Oakland officials cleared Occupy Oakland's encampment and arrested dozens on the morning of November 14, one activist told the media, "I don't see how they're going to disperse us. There are thousands of people who are going to come back." But thousands did not come back. Occupy Oakland's focus on police misconduct, occupying public buildings, public camping, and vandalizing property had alienated it from "the 99 percent." The thousands who had joined the November 2 Oakland General Strike wanted to target Wall Street and "the 1 percent," not Mayor Quan. Many would have stayed involved had Occupy Oakland not strayed from its original course.[13]

Police were also clearing out Occupy encampments in other cities. Many longtime supporters publicly questioned the Occupy movement's direction, and a poll taken November 11–13, 2011, by the progressive organization Public Policy Polling appeared to confirm these doubts. The poll found that more respondents opposed (45%) than supported (33%)

"the goals of the Occupy Wall Street movement." A month earlier, the same poll had found voters equally split about Occupy. Yet more important than these numbers was the overwhelming support among respondents to the November 2011 poll for raising taxes on those earning over $150,000 a year, and their strong backing for other measures addressing income inequality. Pollster Tom Jensen noted, "What the downturn in Occupy Wall Street's image suggests is that voters are seeing the movement as more about the 'Occupy' than the 'Wall Street.' The controversy over the protests is starting to drown out the actual message."[14]

Occupy's preoccupation with preserving its public encampments reflected its shift from a proactive to a defensive approach. Originally, the "occupying" of Zuccotti Park that launched the movement had created powerful visual imagery. Similar encampments in other cities created visibility and facilitated recruitment. But once local Occupy chapters were established, there was no reason to divert the focus from Wall Street abuses and income inequality to battling with local officials over the right to camp. These struggles muddied the movement's goals. Many Occupiers wanted to sleep in tents in public spaces because they lacked a place to live. But once the public saw Occupy camps as homeless encampments rather than as vehicles for economic justice, support fell. That "the 99 percent" did not support camping in public parks or plazas meant that Occupy had adopted a political position at odds with much of its purported base.

Prioritizing public encampments also caused other problems. First, it relegated those unable to live outdoors in tents to reduced roles in the movement. Second, it turned Occupy from being broadly inclusive into a group led by a small, unrepresentative fraction of "the 99 percent." Third, it raised questions about Occupy's moral authority to seize public plazas funded by taxpayer dollars for a sustained period, denying access to those among "the 99 percent" who wanted to use the space. No democratic process supported Occupy's ongoing seizure of public spaces, raising questions about its legitimacy that could have been avoided had private property been occupied instead.

The battles over public camping made even less sense considering that the arrival of winter would make Occupy's use of outdoor space as headquarters infeasible. Kalle Lasn, the founder of *Adbusters,* acknowledged this fact on November 14 when he wrote, "Now that winter is approaching, I can see this first wild, messy, crazy occupation phase kind of slowly winding down and the second phase will begin. Some people will continue to sleep in the snow and inspire all of us, but in the meantime many of us will go home and we will resurface next spring." Lasn suggested that December 17, the three-month anniversary of the Occupy movement, was a good time to begin planning a spring renewal: "We use the winter to brainstorm, network, build momentum so that we may emerge rejuvenated with fresh tactics, philosophies, and a myriad projects ready to rumble next Spring." Displaying his continued confidence in the movement's future, Lasn added, "Permit me to be grandiose for a moment, but I can feel it—I can feel this movement is the beginning of a deep transformation of capitalism. It's a game changer."[15]

Lasn's idea of declaring victory and regrouping for future struggles showed a strategic savvy that many Occupy activists by that time appeared to lack. When police cleared Occupy Wall Street from Zuccotti Park in an early-morning raid on November 15, they did the movement a favor; the activists' forced ouster avoided feelings of failed personal commitment that having to leave Zuccotti due to the cold would have caused. After completely changing the way politicians, the traditional media, and much of the public perceived and talked about inequality in the United States, the Occupy movement needed time to recharge its batteries and refocus its agenda.

Regaining the Offensive

Although 2012 began with high expectations for Occupy's resurgence, the movement faced a far more challenging political and media environment than it had when it emerged in the fall of 2011. Then, Occupy events were not competing with national or state elections for media coverage. And for activists eager to engage in social change struggles, Occupy was the leading game in town. But once 2012 began, the media began focusing on the November presidential race. Activist energies also moved to state and local primary campaigns, as well as to the June 5 recall election of Wisconsin's Republican governor, Scott Walker. Whereas Occupy had generated 14 percent of the reporting from U.S. news organizations in mid-November 2011, by December such coverage had slid to 1 percent and was virtually nonexistent in March. More than ever, Occupy needed to recruit new activists rather than relying on mobilizing those already politically involved.[16]

To this end, such mainstream progressive groups as MoveOn.org, Democracy for America, and labor unions helped recruit activists for training in direct action from April 9 to 15. Thousands of current and future Occupy activists were trained in preparation for a planned "99%

Spring." (Occupy had long identified with Egypt's 2011 Tahrir Square Uprising and the "Arab Spring" that overthrew long-standing dictatorships.) The established progressive groups sought to redirect the Occupy movement toward addressing bank abuses, foreclosures, tax breaks for the wealthy, student loan surcharges, and other core economic justice issues. The plan was for Occupy's resurgence to take the form of spring actions targeting corporate shareholders meetings, foreclosure actions, and legislation addressing income inequality. The training sessions and events would build up to nationwide protests on May 1 in which immigrant rights and labor activists would join Occupiers in a powerful display of the power of the 99 percent.

This was clearly a proactive strategy, and direct actions targeting all of the above issues occurred throughout the spring of 2012. But the same media that had covered every facet of Occupy the preceding fall were now preoccupied with election stories. While thousands turned out for Occupy's May 1, 2012, protests in New York City, Chicago, San Francisco, Oakland, and Seattle, the Occupy protests did not extend to smaller cities or rural areas, or outside traditional activist hotbeds. As a result, the May 1 Occupy protests got little coverage outside progressive media.

Ultimately, Occupy could not regain its past prominence in a presidential election year. As a non-electoral movement, Occupy was like a fish out of water in the national political scene of 2012. Its message did lead Democrats, from President Obama on down, to talk more about economic inequality and to strengthen opposition to tax breaks for the wealthy. But Occupy never aspired, as the Tea Party did for Republicans, to push the Democratic Party to the left by backing candidates in primaries or undertaking other electoral activism.

Measuring Occupy's Success

Occupy continues primarily in the form of multiple groups independently challenging foreclosures, banking policies, Wall Street practices, and other issues affecting income inequality and economic fairness. Identifying these diverse actions as part of the Occupy movement put these protests in a broader and more understandable context. But a social movement is more than independent groups acting independently, and some question whether the goal of building such a movement was ever feasible or even necessary.

Occupy brought discussions of class, income inequality, and corporate greed back into the national debate. A study by Fairness and Accuracy in

Reporting of leading newspapers and television news shows from the period of June–August 2011 (pre-Occupy) found the phrases "income inequality" and "corporate greed" barely mentioned; but uses of both phrases spiked dramatically after Occupy's emergence. Similarly, Think Progress found that in the last week of July 2011, the leading cable news networks overwhelmingly focused on the national debt, while barely mentioning unemployment or the unemployed. Yet in mid-October 2011, Occupy's emergence had made "jobs" and "Wall Street" far and away the top news media issues; the debt "crisis" barely registered. The Occupy movement clearly caused the media to shift coverage to job scarcity, Wall Street's wealth, and the underlying economic and class issues that it had previously downplayed.[17]

The Pew Research Center released a poll on January 11, 2012, that appeared to confirm that Occupy-generated media coverage of income inequality had influenced public attitudes. The study found that "in just two years the perceptions of class conflict have increased significantly among members of both political parties as well as among self-described independents, conservatives, liberals and moderates. The result is that majorities of each political party and ideological point of view now agree that serious disputes exist between Americans on the top and bottom of the income ladder." According to the study, 66 percent of the public believed that there are "very strong" or "strong" conflicts between the rich and the poor—an increase of 19 percentage points since 2009.[18]

Thanks to Occupy's proactive agenda setting, millions of Americans had gained a better sense of the nation's staggeringly unequal wealth and income distribution. And while the path toward reducing this disparity remains tortuous, Occupy activists have played an indispensable role in bringing public attention to this crisis. When Hurricane Sandy laid ruin to the Atlantic Coast and Northeast, Occupy activists created an "Occupy Sandy" campaign to mobilize and coordinate volunteer efforts by "the 99 percent." Using social media to secure resources for those in need, Occupy Sandy showed that the inspiration that launched the Occupy movement remains strong and that its activists still aspire to make a difference in the world.

HOMELESSNESS: THE FAILURE OF DEFENSIVE ACTIVISM

In comparison to the Occupy movement's far-reaching ambition to create a more just and equal society, the goal of ending homelessness in the

United States would appear much easier to achieve. After all, the United States has sufficient wealth to provide housing for all who need it, and Congress even passed a law in 1949 pledging housing for all. But as anyone walking the nation's streets knows, for more than two decades widespread visible homelessness has been a fact of life in the United States. Sadly, no presidential administration has called for allocating the money necessary to meaningfully reduce homelessness, even though its cause was the sharp decline in federal funding for affordable housing starting in the 1970s.

I was working in the Tenderloin when homelessness burst on to the local and national scene in 1982. I have spent three decades trying to reduce homelessness, and since 1988 my organization, the Tenderloin Housing Clinic, has created and run housing programs for homeless persons. At first, homelessness was overwhelmingly framed as a lack of affordable housing. Since the 1990s, homelessness has been associated in the public mind primarily with panhandling, public urination, "bums" sleeping on park benches, and other conduct lumped together as "problem street behavior." This reflects a tragic shift in perception. And its impact is stark: the United States has more homeless persons today than in 1982, the federal government has never tried to end the problem, and millions of Americans are no longer surprised to see homeless people in public plazas and other areas.

How did those unwilling to provide low-income people with a roof over their heads get so much of the public on their side? After the initial wave of sympathetic media stories, conservative think tanks, activists, and politicians got to work reframing homelessness as a problem of individual behavior rather than a social problem. Unfortunately, grassroots homeless activists accepted this reframing, zealously defending people's right to camp in public parks or panhandle on neighborhood streets. While homeless activists also advocated for more affordable housing, conservatives made sure that the "debate" about homelessness focused on camping and panhandling. And considering the number of homeless encampments and panhandlers in major cities, these issues easily overwhelmed discussions about homelessness as a housing problem. The public supported people getting affordable housing, but opposed camping and begging. Homeless advocates accepted the conservatives' redefinition of homelessness and fought the battle on their opponents' terms. It was a struggle they could not win.

San Francisco's Homeless Problem

San Francisco has been a national model for addressing homelessness, and its experiences from the 1980s through today both foreshadowed and mirrors that of other cities. San Francisco is the nation's most politically progressive city, a place where longtime Congress member Nancy Pelosi is more likely to be criticized from the left than the right. The successful reframing of homelessness from a lack of housing to a problem of individual behavior in progressive San Francisco explains why this strategy also found success elsewhere.

I head an organization that is San Francisco's leading provider of permanent housing for homeless single adults. I have crafted city homeless programs and believe San Francisco is the national leader in housing the population my organization serves. But I know that tourists view San Francisco as having the worst homeless problem they have ever seen. People feel this way not because they have any knowledge of the actual numbers of people who lack housing or shelter, but rather because of the visibility of panhandlers, people sleeping in doorways, and problem street behavior in Union Square, on Fisherman's Wharf, in UN Plaza, and along Market Street. These activities have come to define the city's homeless problem. And using that frame, many San Franciscans join tourists in equating "combating homelessness" not with getting people housed, but with pushing panhandlers and those involved in "problem street behavior" out of sight.

I saw this turn in the framing of homelessness firsthand after Art Agnos became mayor in 1988. Prior to his taking office, I was among a group of homeless advocates who created a consensus proposal for a new direction in city policy. Calling itself the Coalition on Homelessness, the group (which later became an independent nonprofit) offered a concrete and specific program to an incoming mayor who had vowed during his campaign to change how the city treated the homeless. The Coalition's proactive approach put Agnos in the position of having either to adopt a "ready to go" program or explain why it was inadequate. The group's tactical activism ensured that its consensus proposal would be the starting point for all future discussions about homeless policy.

Ultimately, the city adopted almost every component of the consensus proposal. Whereas homeless activists in most cities in 1988 were still fighting for more emergency shelters, the thrust of the Coalition's agenda was to divert funds from such stopgap measures toward transitional and permanent housing programs. The group's analysis was adopted in San Francisco's nationally acclaimed 1989 homeless plan, "Beyond Shelter," written by Robert Prentice (one of the formulators of the consensus proposal), who was hired by Mayor Agnos to serve as the city's homeless coordinator. President Bill Clinton's homeless plan, as set forth in 1994 by Housing and Urban Development (HUD) undersecretary and current New York governor Andrew Cuomo, was essentially a redrafting of "Beyond Shelter."

The Coalition's proactive approach proved so successful an example of tactical activism that many of the plan's authors, including me, became its implementers. I met with Agnos's new social services chief, Julia Lopez, to urge the adoption of a modified payment program that would enable General Assistance recipients to obtain permanent housing at below-market rates. Based on discussions with hotel operators, I believed they would agree to lower rents and allow welfare recipients to become permanent tenants if the risk of eviction for nonpayment of rent could be reduced. The modified payment plan lowered this risk by having tenants voluntarily agree to have their rent deducted from their welfare checks.

Lopez told me such a program sounded great but that it would succeed only if the Tenderloin Housing Clinic ran it. We had never sought to run homeless programs, but I had spent years fighting the city's practice of transforming single-room-occupancy (SRO) hotels into temporary lodging for poor people. We wanted to restore SROs to their historic status as homes for elderly, disabled, and low-income people and, not wanting to lose the opportunity to achieve this goal, we became a city-funded housing provider. As anticipated, landlords lowered rents so they could attract the formerly homeless tenants we could supply. The program was so successful that SRO rents fell significantly lower than they had been a decade earlier.

Agnos understood that homelessness was fundamentally a housing problem. But the city's business and real estate community never liked Agnos, and storm clouds were brewing. On May 29, 1989, the *San Francisco Examiner* ran a front-page story in which business leaders denounced Mayor Agnos for allowing camping in the park outside City Hall. In what many believed was the greatest political error of his term, Agnos had decided to allow camping in this park until his programs creating alternative sources of housing were in place. As public anger over "Camp Agnos" grew, the mayor decided in July 1990 to cut his losses and sweep the park of campers. The purge became a national media story, as reporters found interest in a self-described "progressive" mayor's cracking down on the homeless.

Because many of the campers had sought the now-independent Coalition on Homelessness's assistance to prevent the sweep, Coalition staff workers entered the national debate in opposition to Agnos's action, arguing that the mayor had caved in to political pressure and swept the park before his programs had become operational. The Coalition was correct about Agnos but failed to appreciate that his tolerance of camping had caused him serious political harm. The public never understood the rationale for allowing camping, and continuing the policy had become politically untenable. In their anger over Agnos's betrayal, the activists rushed to defend the campers without appreciating the risk that their fight for more low-cost housing and mental health services would be reduced to a dispute over the right to camp in a public park.

The Coalition's full-fledged attack on Agnos's action was an entirely defensive response on behalf of people whom the public saw as voluntarily homeless. The residents of Camp Agnos typically wore backpacks and had chosen to sleep outdoors rather than pay rent in residential hotels. The Clinic's outreach staff surveyed most of the campers and found that the majority received enough public assistance to pay rent if they so chose. In the public mind, people should be homeless only if they could not afford housing. Now the city's leading homeless advocacy group was arguing that people who could afford housing had the right to forgo this option and instead live under the stars outside City Hall until temporary shelter or permanent housing was available to everyone. The public and media rejected, even ridiculed, this notion; accustomed to viewing homeless people as victims of hard luck, they could not accept the idea that anyone should reject shelter.

Most believed that Agnos could fulfill his responsibility to the campers by ensuring that each received a shelter bed or hotel room. The Coalition countered by urging sympathizers to "storm the park" so there would be more park dwellers than Agnos could immediately shelter. This strategy, a sudden, defensive response, understandably backfired. The media, though long sympathetic to homeless activists, interpreted this move as a blatant attempt to inflate the number of homeless denizens of Camp Agnos. The activists were even seen as interfering with the government's effort to put a roof over people's heads.

Agnos's park sweep brought national attention unprecedented for a city homeless policy. From the *New York Times* to the *MacNeil-Lehrer*

News Hour, national observers were fascinated by this action, taken by a mayor viewed as one of the nation's most progressive. The publicity transformed San Francisco's public debate about homelessness and led to the emergence of an entirely new model in cities across the United States. The model, honed by ambitious politicians and their corporate and media allies, creates symmetry between repressive political agendas and homeless advocacy groups: a mayor calls for a crackdown on "aggressive panhandling" and public camping; homeless advocates object on civil-liberties grounds.

When Agnos sought reelection in 1991, he faced a runoff against a former police chief, Frank Jordan. Jordan attacked Agnos's "social worker" approach to homelessness and highlighted his own ability to get tough on individual homeless people by suggesting they be sent to work camps outside the city. Agnos got little political credit for providing thousands of housing units to the formerly homeless, and was instead condemned for allegedly allowing the homeless problem to get out of control. His defeat sent a powerful message to future San Francisco mayors: it's fine to house homeless people, but voters define success by stopping public camping and related "problem street behavior." Agnos laid the groundwork for the "housing first" approach to homelessness, which remains a national model, but some in San Francisco still believe he was a disaster in dealing with homelessness.

A Lost Opportunity

The 1990s proved an enormous lost opportunity for addressing homelessness. Bill Clinton's election in 1992 brought a Democrat to the White House for the first time since the homeless crisis had begun. The nation soon had a booming economy that could have built all the low-income housing needed, yet the public debate about homelessness had already shifted. Emotional battles were fought, not over the nation's affordable-housing shortage, but over the right to camp in parks and panhandle on city sidewalks. New York City mayor Rudy Giuliani won praise for reducing visible homelessness in his city, even though this "reduction" was achieved not by housing homeless people but by physically removing them from the areas of Manhattan frequented by tourists. San Francisco residents and politicians returned from Giuliani's city marveling at the reduction in homeless people and wondering why they could not do the same. People compared San Francisco's "failed" strategy with that of New York City's "successful" one, as the criterion was not housing homeless people but getting them out of sight. Although Giuliani acknowledged upon leaving office in 2001 that New York City's homeless numbers had risen during his eight-year tenure—despite great economic growth—his punitive methods became a "model" for other urban politicians.

By the 1990s, media sympathy for homeless persons had greatly declined. Media coverage of the homeless went from stories on recently unemployed middle-aged men to sound bites of long-haired, able-bodied young people confessing that they lie about being veterans so they can make more money panhandling. Panhandlers are no longer people trying to compensate for cuts in welfare checks; they are now drug addicts and alcoholics who use public charity to feed their habits. While positive stories are still reported about new housing and pro-grams for homeless persons, stories connecting homelessness to the inability of millions of Americans to afford rent are eclipsed by those that separate the homeless problem from housing needs.

In "The Year That Housing Died," the cover story of an October 1996 issue of the *New York Times Magazine,* author Jason DeParle claimed that "the Federal Government has essentially conceded defeat in its decades-long drive to make housing affordable to low-income Americans." The federal budget included no new housing subsidies that year, and the 1996 Republican platform sought to eliminate HUD.

Can Proactive Homeless Strategies Still Prevail?

Have activists missed their chance to mobilize the nation to finally end widespread visible homelessness? It is hard to see how this goal can be achieved if advocates continue to allow issues like panhandling and camping to frame the debate. For example, since 2010, voters in some of the nation's most progressive cities, including San Francisco, have enacted laws banning lying and sitting on commercial sidewalks. Opponents decry such "sit and lie" laws for "criminalizing homelessness," while pro-ponents argue that they target behavior, not homelessness. An October 19, 2012, *New York Times* story about a sit-lie ballot measure on Berkeley's November 2012 ballot ("Free Speech Is One Thing, Vagrants Another") profiled Chris Escobar, age twenty-three, "who left Miami five weeks ago" and "hitched a ride west with only a backpack, a yellow dog named Marley and a tiger striped kitten on a leash." Escobar resented the idea that he was not free to sit on the sidewalk with his pets, and said about the ballot measure, "This is not the Berkeley I came for."[19]

Young, able-bodied people like Escobar who spend their days sitting in front of small businesses and public buildings are not the part of the homeless population that most taxpayers desire to assist. They are perceived as choosing to be homeless and as hurting local commercial districts in the process. Unfortunately, this small segment of the homeless population continues to get much of the public and media attention. It does not represent the most vulnerable among the homeless; to the contrary, the young and able-bodied are often among the most self-sufficient. Yet activists continue to fritter away public support for helping the vast majority of homeless people, those desperate to obtain permanent housing, by defending a small subgroup that prefers to live under the stars.

Homeless advocates do not have to prioritize sit-lie, panhandling, and other quality-of-life issues. They do not have to be sidetracked from their core housing funding demand. Such issues can be addressed by civil liberties groups and legal organizations not involved in direct political advocacy for increased low-cost housing funds.

Activists still have a compelling case for increasing federal funding to reduce homelessness. San Francisco and other cities have reduced homelessness through a combination of housing and on-site services known as "supportive housing." This successful model shows that ending homelessness is entirely a question of spending priorities. Reviving campaigns to invest in ending homelessness won't be easy, but continuing to accept widespread visible homelessness in the United States is unacceptable. Ending homelessness remains a winnable national fight, but only if activists frame the debate around the millions of ill-housed eager to have a home.

CRIME FIGHTING: DEFENSIVENESS AT ITS WORST

Activists have paid the biggest price for responding defensively on the issue of crime. Unlike homeless activists, whose strategic errors never involved abandoning principles, some "progressives" zealously embraced law-and-order solutions to crime out of calculation and expedience. Other residents of low-income communities embraced longer sentences and prison expansion as part of a broader anti-crime strategy whose other key components, such as job training, housing, and education, were never implemented. Fearing being labeled soft on crime, many progressive politicians have backed the conservative framing of crime as requiring a "war on drugs" and the multibillion-dollar creation of a "prison industrial complex." From the 1980s, when Republicans first saw the political benefits of promoting and maintaining a "war on crime," through at least 2010, increased spending on prisons has diverted desperately needed money from schools, housing, and health care without making low-income communities safer. In fact, while states spend billions housing inmates guilty of nonviolent crimes, local police departments struggle for money to reduce crime at the street level.[20]

Defensive Crime Fighting in the Tenderloin

I became aware of the inherent strategic shortcomings of progressive-led anti-crime efforts from my own experience in San Francisco's Tenderloin district. The Tenderloin has long been considered a high-crime neighborhood. After the rezoning battles of the early 1980s, the focus shifted to crime. Although most of the neighborhood's crime involved property break-ins and disputes between drug dealers, enough seniors had been mugged or rolled to motivate people to organize an anti-crime campaign.

Because of these residents' concerns, I became involved in the development of neighborhood anti-crime efforts. The Tenderloin Housing Clinic's street-level office had relocated to a high-crime corner, so I needed only to look out our window to see why residents felt threatened. The primarily elderly residents of the Cadillac Hotel, located right across the street from our office, were particularly upset about drug dealing close to their building; some had been robbed right outside the gates. The hotel's nonprofit owner, Reality House West, was headed by Leroy Looper, a charismatic leader and savvy tactician who had risen from a life on the streets and in prison to transform the Cadillac from an eyesore to a neighborhood jewel. Looper responded to his tenants' complaints about crime by forming the Tenderloin Crime Abatement Committee (CAC). The CAC met monthly at the Cadillac Hotel. When Looper asked me to participate, I readily agreed. At the time, I was almost alone among progressive social change activists in getting involved in anti-crime efforts. Gradually, however, Looper brought in representatives of religious groups, refugee organizations, and other social service agencies.

In addition to my admiration for Looper and desire to support residents' concerns, what attracted me to the campaign was the high percentage of African Americans participating in the CAC. The Tenderloin's African American residents had participated little in the long-running land use battles, and I thought their involvement in anti-crime efforts might encourage community participation in other issues. The fact that Looper and key Cadillac Hotel management staff were African American contributed to the CAC's high level of ethnic diversity.

During 1984 and 1985, I regularly attended CAC meetings and ended up presiding over many of the meetings, which were festive occasions. A Cadillac Hotel resident would prepare a buffet lunch. Everyone in the audience had the opportunity to comment on the issues being discussed, and the district police captain and beat officers would provide updates on crime statistics and respond to concerns raised at the meeting. The CAC reflected the type of ethnically diverse, broad-based community empowerment effort that social change activists in all fields aspire to create. The committee stressed the need for employment, training, and substance abuse programs and for other strategies that would address the underlying causes of crime.

There was a consensus, however, that until such systemic programs were in place, a stronger police presence was necessary. Many of us naively believed that the Tenderloin residents' opposition to crime in their community would bring increased government funding for programs to ameliorate the preconditions causing high levels of crime. Looper, the community's most revered leader, always saw economic development and increased local employment as key to reducing neighborhood crime. The CAC was not demanding more police simply as a tactic for obtaining economic development assistance; rather, we believed that expressing serious concern about crime would stimulate a broader influx of resources into the Tenderloin.

The committee decided to publicize the community's resolve with a "March Against Crime." Marches are now commonplace in low-income neighborhoods, but such events were somewhat rare in 1985, and we expected—and received—tremendous media coverage. One goal of the march was to demonstrate that the Tenderloin was a residential neighborhood whose residents and businesses deserved the same level of police services as inhabitants of other communities received. We also sought to show that the Tenderloin housed *victims* of crime, not simply perpetrators. As long as the public believed that Tenderloin residents were themselves to blame for crime, and thus tolerated thefts, drug deals, and muggings, there would be less support for anti-crime measures and other programs designed to help the neighborhood. The march was the perfect tactic for a community trying to reverse long-held but erroneous public attitudes about it.

CAC activists were thrilled by the success of the event. We felt the march had not only accomplished its goals but also galvanized community activism around fighting crime. Attendance at CAC meetings increased steadily, and it seemed as if police visibility rose in the area. Crime appeared to be the new issue necessary to maintain resident activism after the historic rezoning victory. The North of Market Planning Coalition began increasing its emphasis on crime, which soon became its chief focus and organizing vehicle. A Safe Streets Committee was formed. Although it was unclear whether the neighborhood's anti-crime efforts were actually reducing crime, many residents felt empowered because top police brass appeared to take their concerns seriously.

By 1987 we still had not received the hoped-for assistance for attacking crime's economic underpinnings, but most of us attributed this lack to the pro-downtown policies of the reigning Feinstein administration. We believed that a new, progressive mayor would deliver neighborhood-oriented economic assistance to the Tenderloin, and when Art Agnos succeeded Feinstein in January 1988, we all thought the Tenderloin was poised for a major turnaround. I shifted away from the crime issue after 1986 and returned to focusing on housing and homelessness, but I continued to support the neighborhood's campaign against crime and won a formal commendation in 1986 from the San Francisco Board of Supervisors for my crime-fighting efforts.

On March 1, 1990, Mayor Agnos announced that a police station would open in the Tenderloin. I was initially excited by the announcement, as the community had finally received something tangible after years of anti-crime advocacy. I saw the police station as a building block that would be followed by additional government efforts to improve the neighborhood's social and economic climate. But I soon learned that the police station was all the Tenderloin would ever get.

The problem was that the Agnos administration did not look beyond the portion of the neighborhood's agenda demanding more police. The other anti-crime strategies on the table—such as employment, job training, economic development, and assistance in attracting new business— were essentially viewed as throw-ins garnishing the primary demand for a more visible police presence. Our failure to develop an achievable action plan for attaining goals other than "more police" allowed outsiders to think such goals were not central to our overall agenda. I know from talking to Agnos soon after the station opened that he truly believed he had given the Tenderloin what it wanted most. He seemed surprised to learn that we had never claimed the crime problem could be solved solely or even largely by police, and that the community considered the rest of the anti-crime agenda even more important. He did not have to tell me that for elected officials striving to make an immediate, visible anti-crime impact, providing additional police officers or a police station is a comparatively inexpensive strategy that always takes precedence over more systemic, nonpunitive anti-crime initiatives. Responding to the demand for more police frees politicians from committing the resources necessary for a more comprehensive anti-crime program.

The announcement of the new police station (which opened in a temporary location before moving to its current space in 2000) marked the high (or low) point of the Tenderloin 1980s anti-crime efforts. Leroy Looper, as shrewd a tactical activist as ever walked the streets of a major city, saw his own expectations for a government-assisted economic revival of the Tenderloin fall victim to the "more police, more arrests" approach. Looper's Reality House West had opened a Sizzler restaurant in the Cadillac Hotel's commercial space in the mid-1980s in an attempt to jump-start the Tenderloin's economic revitalization. Looper always assumed that city government would appreciate this investment in the neighborhood and would assist similar businesses seeking success in the economically depressed community. This government assistance never materialized, leaving the Sizzler on its own to survive in a difficult business environment.

Looper's vision of new employment opportunities and job training for Tenderloin residents was central to his crime-prevention strategy, and the Sizzler fulfilled both objectives. Unfortunately, Looper and the rest of us learned that even self-identified progressive politicians have come to address crime solely in punitive terms. The Sizzler closed down around the same time the neighborhood police station opened—a sad but fitting parallel that perfectly captures how even the best-intentioned progressive-led anti-crime campaigns inevitably fall prey to officials' preference for law-and-order solutions.

Where did we go wrong? The answer lies in our failure to follow the fundamental tenet of tactical activism: we responded to the crime problem without ensuring that crime reduction remained part of a larger campaign for neighborhood revitalization. By putting an economic development and social action agenda under the rubric of crime prevention without making specific demands for these positive goals, we allowed law-and-order-minded residents, law-enforcement personnel, and politicians with repressive agendas to narrow our demands to "more police, more arrests." Such an agenda is insufficient for a community desperately needing government-aided and private economic revitalization.

Simply put, the Tenderloin's grassroots anti-crime campaign failed to frame the crime problem in a way that would lead to concrete improvements in the lives of residents. Although the number of arrests and police officers both rose in the Tenderloin, there was no focused advocacy to force government to address the *preconditions causing crime.* When I speak of preconditions, I am not referring simply to pervasive inner-city problems such as poverty, unemployment, and racial discrimination, which progressives frequently stress as the underlying causes of crime. I mean preconditions that realistically could have been addressed to increase neighborhood safety. For example, the city could have installed more street and sidewalk lighting, passed laws mandating outside lights on all buildings, and reduced vacant storefronts by providing tax breaks or subsidies, or both, to encourage new businesses to move to the Tenderloin.

We could have eliminated bus shelters and telephone booths used by drug dealers, and taken civil legal action against property owners who allowed nuisance activities in and around their premises. Increased funding to expand neighborhood cultural facilities would have increased the presence of the legitimate nighttime activities necessary to crowd out problem behavior. We also could have figured out ways for property owners to contribute more money to clean streets and sidewalks, making the neighborhood more pedestrian friendly.

Sadly, most if not all of these changes could have been achieved during the late 1980s. Our failure to achieve them resulted from tactical and strategic errors, not political weakness. Neighborhood plans included many of these ideas, yet residents rarely transcended the push for more police.

Signs of Progress

Tenderloin activists learned from the strategic errors of the 1980s, and in the past decade did initiate many of the non-law-and-order strategies noted above to reduce neighborhood crime. Crime remains unacceptably high, but there is recognition that reducing this problem must be part of a broader action plan for the neighborhood.

The Tenderloin's learning curve is part of a broader trend. Democratic Party politicians are finally recognizing that they cannot deliver for their constituents while diverting massive numbers of dollars toward imprisoning nonviolent drug users and small-time sellers. In 2004 Oakland mayor Jerry Brown appeared in television ads opposing a November ballot measure to modify the state's costly three-strikes law. This law was designed to stop violent predators from leaving prison after their third offense, but the "third strike" also included nonviolent property crimes such as stealing a loaf of bread. Brown's opposition helped narrowly defeat the measure.

But after Brown returned to the governor's office in 2011, he took aim at budget-busting prison costs. He transferred nonviolent offenders from state prison to county jails, and backed Prop 36, a revision to three strikes on the November 2012 ballot. The measure passed by nearly 70 percent of the vote, indicating that voters are revisiting costly criminal justice strategies they once handily approved. Prop 36's passage, the legalization of marijuana by Colorado voters in the same election (Amendment 64), and high-profile efforts in New York City to end police "stop and frisk" procedures used on 700,000 primarily African American and Latino men each year show that activists can reshape the debate on crime through proactive strategies. And when you see 47 percent of California voters vote to end the death penalty in the same November 2012 election—after support for such a policy was long considered politically essential for statewide candidates—using proactive strategies to roll back decades of crime-dominated politics is an opportunity to be seized.

Elected Officials

Inspiring Fear and Loathing

Ernesto Cortes, Jr., organizer of the Industrial Areas Foundation net-work in Texas and the San Antonio–based Communities Organized for Public Service (COPS), has plainly described activists' necessary relation-ship to elected officials: "It's unfortunate that fear is the only way to get some politicians to respect your power. They refuse to give you respect. They don't recognize your dignity. So we have to act in ways to get their attention. In some areas, what we have going is the amount of fear we can generate. We got where we are because people fear and loathe us."[1]

This assessment by one of the United States' premier community activists and tacticians is harsh but accurate. Today's activists all too often work tirelessly to elect "progressive" politicians who then require strong prodding before trying to implement their progressive campaign goals. Without such pressure, self-identified progressive elected officials frequently prefer to "broaden their base" rather than deliver for those responsible for their election.

The backgrounds typical of "progressive" officeholders explain much of the problem. Their career path no longer begins with years of grassroots activism; instead, one becomes an aide to a legislator, a job that provides access to funders and puts the aspirant in the position to be tapped for electoral openings. Today's "progressive" official rarely achieves power through a grassroots or democratic nominating process, and views politics as a career vehicle rather than a means for redressing social and economic injustice. He or she is not ideologically driven, takes pride in "pragmatic" problem solving, values personal loyalty over ideological consistency, and views social change activists as threatening because they place their constituency's interests ahead of the official's political needs.

When candidates from a neighborhood or other grassroots base do get elected, they often soon become like other politicians. Their drive for reelection or to attain higher office leads them to make new or stronger connections with a whole range of financial interests. After all, even grassroots field campaigns cost money, and progressive candidates require significant funding if they are to prevail in all but the smallest local races. The ever-growing power of money in politics has led most politicians to put their funders' interests above those of their volunteer base. Raising money nationally through small online donations has helped restore some of the connection between politicians and their funders, but statewide or national races still require large donors. Even before *Citizens United* opened the floodgates to corporate donations, the best-intentioned, most progressive candidates still had to seek out potential funders who were more conservative than the candidate's core supporters.

Once in office, grassroots politicians are contacted by representatives of financial interests who opposed their candidacy. These representatives soon ingratiate themselves by offering to help retire the inevitable campaign debt. Many local elected officials receive low salaries, making them receptive to offers of the luxurious fund-raising events that are a regular part of political business. Like most other people, elected officials are awed by power and wealth. They don't go home and report, "I met with some poor people from the Tenderloin, and it was exciting"; rather, they boast, "I met with the president of Wells Fargo!" The trappings of power and the social component of their new status easily excite them. The election-night celebration is often the last opportunity for meaningful personal contact between the candidate and the volunteers who sacrificed their personal lives to walk precincts, staff phone banks, and get out the vote on his or her behalf.

Although some progressive politicians help bring social change, far too many suppress activists' agendas as effectively as clearly labeled enemies do. This occurs because progressive constituencies feel loyalty toward the politicians they help elect. This loyalty leads progressives to avoid holding politician "allies" accountable for their campaign commitments and to refrain from criticizing them for acts they would strongly oppose if undertaken by conservatives. Concerns over maintaining access, appearing "reasonable," and fulfilling the personal ambitions of organizational leaders contribute to this pattern of nonaccountability. Progressive constituencies' failure to demand accountability of the officials their votes and volunteer labor put into office is a major obstacle to achieving social change. In fact, it might be the biggest obstacle, since it means that progressives do not produce the sweeping results from election victories that conservatives secure from their wins. Activists must understand that people feel betrayed when politicians fail to deliver on their campaign promises to support progressive change, and they respond with cynicism to subsequent social change efforts. Some join the ranks of nonvoters, impairing the election prospects of authentic progressive candidates. Without political accountability, working to elect candidates to office becomes a fool's errand.

It seems obvious that activists would focus on results rather than promises when it comes to elected officials. After all, this is how we evaluate performance in our workplaces, investments, and consumer choices. But in my experience, activists often view elected officials as allies without their having done anything to earn the moniker. Politicians need only agree to take certain positions in the future to earn the support of many progressive organizations. This makes strategic sense for politicians but not for advocates of social change. Given the ease with which they can achieve progressive credentials, politicians have no incentive to actually *do* anything to serve progressive constituencies. As a result, few officials feel it politically necessary to wage a major fight against the status quo on behalf of progressive reform. As a former leader of San Antonio's COPS (Communities Organized for Public Services) puts it, "When politicians deliver, we applaud them. Not until then. . . . Politicians' work is to do your work. When you've got somebody working for you, you don't bow and scrape."[2]

Adopting a "fear and loathing" approach toward elected officials, particularly self-identified progressives, is essential for achieving social change. Activists must focus on results, not promises; they must pursue their agenda, not the politician's. The Obama administration's first term showed that many activists allow great speeches to substitute for concrete actions; only the latter bring progressive change. Political accountability is even more difficult when organizational leaders form close ties with politicians that subtly (or not so subtly) affect how the group deals with constituent issues. Progressive politicians understand the value of forming these relationships. They know that a union leader or progressive activist repeatedly invited to the White House or governor's mansion is prone to become more protective of the politician that grants such access. Even when an organization wants to hold a supposedly friendly politician accountable, the politician has many tactics to delay, damage, or deny fulfillment of the organization's agenda. Politicians employ highly paid consultants to develop strategies for achieving their goals; social change activists must employ their own strategies for using politicians to fulfill their agendas.

"WE'RE WITH YOU WHEN YOU'RE WITH US, AND AGAINST YOU WHEN YOU'RE NOT"

After Jerry Brown's reelection as California governor in 1978, an unusual alliance developed between Brown and antiwar activists Tom Hayden and Jane Fonda. Hayden had formed a statewide citizens' organization in the mid-1970s called the Campaign for Economic Democracy (CED) and had run a high-profile, though unsuccessful, challenge to California's incumbent Democratic senator, John Tunney, in the 1976 primary.

When Hayden was challenged over his organization's apparent alliance with the then–very fiscally conservative Brown, he claimed that CED would support the governor when he supported the group's stand on issues and oppose him when he opposed its position. While some saw Hayden's assessment of the ideal relationship between social activist organizations and elected officials as simply designed to bring CED more power, this ideal is the best model for tactical activists in dealing with elected officials.

The ideal of supporting candidates only when they support your positions may seem obvious; the difficulty lies in the implementation. Elected officials value personal loyalty above all else; because tactical activists must place their constituency's agenda over the politician's, the potential for conflict always exists. The strains of this tension are most severe when a self-styled neighborhood activist or progressive is elected to office. These officials, feeling entitled to the unwavering loyalty of neighborhood and progressive organizations, argue that any criticism from the political left lends comfort to their conservative enemies. Adopting a "tough love" stance toward such officials thus makes many activists feel disloyal or, even worse in the current political world, "unreasonable" or "too idealistic." Nevertheless, for tactical activists striving to accomplish social change, an independent stance brings both power and respect; to succeed, they must accept the credo that, in regard to elected officials, it is better to be feared than loved.

Let us recall what Texas organizer Ernesto Cortes, Jr., said: "We got where we are because [politicians] fear and loathe us." Cortes arrived at this conclusion not after years of battling exclusively with conservatives who refused to deal fairly with his Latino constituency, but rather after dealing with his many political allies. Among COPS's closest allies was then–San Antonio mayor Henry Cisneros, later Clinton's secretary of housing and urban development. Rather than revel in Cisneros's historic victory as the city's first Latino mayor and then sit meekly by as promises were broken and commitments left unfulfilled, COPS demanded performance. When Cisneros failed to perform, COPS publicly attacked him for ignoring his constituency's concerns. Unlike far too many progressive groups, Cortes says, COPS does not endeavor to be liked by politicians: "When we start worrying whether or not politicians like us . . . then we'll be just like everybody else."[3]

I wish I could say that Cortes is wrong and that fear need not be used to motivate elected officials. It would be so much easier if progressive constituencies were treated with the same respect as large financial donors. It would also be great if activists could relate on some basis other than intimidation to politicians they have supported. Cortes's comments, however, mirror my own experiences with many politicians. Far too many take the low-income constituencies whose votes help elect them for granted. Activists who put their constituencies' needs ahead of the politician's agenda must be willing to sacrifice friendship with the official in order to achieve their goals.

Tactical activists must let officials know when they are right and when they are wrong. Politicians deserve public credit when they fight hard for fairness and social justice. The favorable publicity they receive will prompt similar conduct in the future. But there is virtually never an excuse for silently allowing a supposed ally to act against your constituency. Particular members of an organization or constituency may have personal reasons not to protest, publicly or privately, a wayward vote, but tactical activism requires that some element of the constituency take such action. Organizations that engage in the necessary strategic and tactical discussions in formulating a proactive agenda will have determined in advance when and how to respond to betrayal by a supposed political friend.

This chapter offers both local and national case studies of political accountability. I begin with my personal experience dealing with San Francisco mayors, and go on to discuss how the lessons that national environmental groups learned about "fear and loathing" early in the

Clinton administration helped the movement strengthen the Clean Air Act in his second term and delay and potentially defeat construction of the Keystone XL oil pipeline during the Obama administration. I then describe how immigrant rights' and gay rights' groups initially took contrasting approaches toward holding President Obama's feet to the fire on key campaign commitments. A less experienced immigrant rights movement failed to hold Obama accountable for inaction on comprehensive immigration reform, and was quiet too long as the administration increased the number of deportations. It was not until young DREAM Activists applied a fear-and-loathing approach to the president that progress was made on immigrant rights. In contrast, gay rights activists took a fear-and-loathing approach from the outset toward Obama's failure to promptly repeal "Don't Ask, Don't Tell" (DADT) and to take legal action against the Defense of Marriage Act (DOMA). Their success not only advanced the movement but greatly helped President Obama politically.

FOCUS ON RESULTS, NOT PROMISES

I witnessed firsthand the damaging consequences of going easy on progressive officials during Art Agnos's tenure as mayor of San Francisco. Agnos ran for mayor in 1987 as a self-identified progressive. His eagerness to wear this label, coupled with his excellent record as a state legislator, brought him broad support among social change constituencies. Activists saw the race as their big chance to win City Hall after enduring nearly ten years under Dianne Feinstein, a centrist who had failed to identify herself with any of the powerful movements—gay liberation, anti-development/neighborhood preservation, or rent control—sweeping San Francisco during the 1980s. There was a general feeling that the city had undergone great changes but the person in charge hadn't grown with it. By 1987 the gay community had built its own political organization and wanted a mayor who would support "domestic partners" legislation and appoint more gays and lesbians to city commissions. Anti-development forces, which had won a critical battle to restrict high-rise development through a 1986 ballot measure, wanted a mayor who would appoint a Planning Commission favoring the preservation and development of affordable housing. Rent-control activists particularly felt the need for a new mayor. The key issue on their agenda—the imposition of rent control on vacant units—had twice passed the Board of Supervisors, only to be vetoed by Mayor Feinstein.

Rent-control advocates felt it essential to elect a mayor committed to signing a vacancy control law; Agnos's promise to do just that gave him the nearly unanimous support of tenant groups.

Agnos and his tacticians created a grassroots campaign organization unprecedented in the city's history. The campaign included more than five hundred precinct leaders, many of them motivated primarily by the candidate's support for stronger rent control. I was extremely enthusiastic about Agnos; my wife and I spent most of our nonworking time contacting voters for the campaign. My own interest centered on Agnos's commitment to enact a new homeless policy, his personal interest in improving the Tenderloin, and his support of various measures to preserve and expand low-cost housing. I never had great expectations that Agnos would back strong vacancy control legislation, but I believed political factors would force him to sign whatever measure his tenant supporters passed through the Board of Supervisors.

Agnos was elected with a staggering 70 percent of the vote. Rent-control activists should have had no problem quickly cashing in. However, they violated the fundamental rule of dealing with elected officials: demand results.

Soon after taking office, Agnos met with rent-control activists to discuss a strategy for enacting vacancy control. After establishing a clear tone of friendship, Agnos explained that he had promised real estate industry representatives that he would at least "sit down with them" prior to moving forward with vacancy control. He requested that tenants meet with landlords in his presence to see if a "win-win" compromise on vacancy control could be reached. Agnos emphasized his continued support for rent control but felt he must first attempt to mediate a settlement.

Rent-control activists expressed virtually no protest against Agnos's plan. A few pointed out that dialogue with landlords on the issue had already been tried and had failed, and others argued against wasting time on such a charade. Nobody asked Agnos why he never expressed a desire to mediate between landlords and tenants during a campaign in which he consistently identified tenants as his allies. Neither did anyone question his sudden concern for a constituency that had actively worked against his election and funded his chief opponent.

Why did rent-control activists meekly accept Agnos's waffling on the chief issue on their political agenda? Because Agnos's carefully crafted campaign identity as a friend of tenant interests overshadowed post-election reality. This led tenant activists to accept as good-faith action a clear betrayal of their constituency. Agnos had done nothing as mayor to demonstrate his pro-tenant stance; he had merely created personal relationships with leading rent-control activists during the campaign, which became "proof" of his support for tenant interests. The consensus among rent-control activists was that Agnos was "our" mayor, whom "we" had elected. Denying Agnos the political space he claimed to need, it was argued, would be the height of arrogance and eventually could turn him against tenants. Having felt left out for more than a decade, rent-control activists did not want to jeopardize their new access to power by fighting over what seemed nothing more than a procedural delay. A course was thus established whereby Agnos would have no reason to fear the tenant constituency. As a result, for the balance of his term he afforded tenants and their chief agenda item no respect.

Agnos's "procedural delay" was only the first of many clever strategies he used to brush aside vacancy control while steadfastly proclaiming his commitment to it. After several months spent in pointless meetings with landlords, Agnos was forced to admit the failure of the "mediation process." He then announced a new justification for his failure to enact vacancy control: lack of votes on the Board of Supervisors. This excuse had superficial validity during Agnos's first year in office, but by 1989 the newly elected Board of Supervisors could have passed vacancy control if Agnos had made it a priority. But the reputedly pro-tenant Mayor Agnos did not.

Agnos's lack of commitment to passing vacancy control became clearer in 1989 when he showed the kind of fight he could put up for a goal he really wanted. This involved his all-out effort to pass a November ballot initiative for a new stadium for the San Francisco Giants baseball team. To achieve a goal that he had never backed in his mayoral campaign and that his core neighborhood supporters opposed, Agnos used every political chit at his disposal. He had gay and lesbian leaders announce that the stadium would (somehow) increase funding for AIDS services; he got the Sierra Club to support the proposed stadium as good for the environment; and he made political deals with various supervisors in exchange for their backing. Despite all this, the stadium initiative failed.

Meanwhile, Agnos still had not lifted a finger to help the passage of vacancy control. I was not alone among tenant activists in recognizing the discrepancy between Agnos's vigorous work on the stadium initiative and his lack of effort on vacancy control. Despite their recognition of Agnos's inaction, however, leading rent-control activists continued to view him as committed to their cause. Had these activists evaluated the mayor's actual accomplishments in the same way they would evaluate the performance, say, of any consumer product, they would have concluded that Agnos was, on his own, never going to produce on vacancy control. Nevertheless, as long as the mayor remained publicly committed to the proposal, rent-control leaders continued to identify him as tenants' friend.

The November 1990 election offered a prime opportunity for vacancy control advocates. With a governor's race, high-profile state-wide environmental and consumer initiatives, and strong local candidates from the gay and lesbian community, the election promised to attract an unusually high progressive-voter turnout. But Agnos, and hence rent-control advocates, ignored this special opportunity to submit vacancy control to the voters, instead working to elect a clear pro–vacancy control majority on the Board of Supervisors. When this majority was achieved, vacancy control was finally enacted in 1991 (with Agnos's approval). Almost immediately, however, the measure became subject—as advocates had always predicted it would—to a landlord-sponsored referendum on the November 1991 ballot. After the landlords qualified the referendum for the ballot, Agnos held a meeting with rent-control activists. He observed that, fortunately, the referendum would appear on the same ballot on which he sought reelection; therefore, his campaign could also fund the pro–vacancy control effort. I was not alone in recognizing the true import of the mayor's statement: he had intentionally delayed vacancy control so as to assure a high tenant turnout for his reelection bid.

Ironically, Agnos's secret strategy resulted in both his and vacancy control's defeat. The real estate interests Agnos had tried so hard to placate in 1988 poured more than $1 million into defeating vacancy control. When other mayoral candidates who supported vacancy control unexpectedly entered the race, Agnos compounded his betrayal of tenants by playing down the issue and failing to provide the funding he had promised. The result: lacking both money and any grassroots campaign, vacancy control lost in a landslide. The candidate Agnos finished second to in November, former police chief Frank Jordan, drew strong support from elderly tenants who, having reaped no benefit from Agnos on rent-control issues, went instead with the law-and-order candidate.

Jordan failed to muster a majority, however, necessitating a December runoff between him and Agnos. That election crystallized the deep hostility that rent-control activists felt toward the mayor. Agnos and tenant activists met soon after the runoff campaign began, and, for the first time since Agnos took office, tenants spoke bitterly of his betrayal of their interests. I began the meeting by confronting the mayor with my belief—shared by many others—that he had sabotaged vacancy control by waiting until November 1991 and then breaking his promise to fund the campaign. Agnos agreed he had broken his promise, claiming his "political survival" was at stake. The meeting continued in this vein, with tenant activists torn between their anger at Agnos and their fear of aiding Jordan.

Agnos lost in the runoff—glaring proof of his personal unpopularity. Although I ignored his campaign in the general election, I believed his reelection was preferable to four years under his anti-poor, pro-landlord opponent. I contacted dozens of tenant activists about working for Agnos in the runoff but made no effort to change their minds when they declined to participate. They had good reason to shun Agnos, and I was not about to jeopardize my credibility by defending him. Some savvy political activists refused to endorse Agnos in the runoff, and though I took a different approach, their position was understandable.

Rent-control activists made a major tactical error at the beginning of Agnos's term in establishing a relationship with him based on friendship rather than fear and in allowing him to substitute promises for action. When, right after taking office, the mayor sought to mediate between landlords and tenants, rent-control activists should have refused. Tactical activism required tenants to make it clear at the outset that, having helped elect Agnos, they were now entitled to results. Silence in the face of a politician's initial betrayal sends a clear message that your constituency feels itself too weak, too confused, or too afraid to merit respect.

Suppose Agnos had employed the tactics of most politicians and expressed hurt and dismay at rent-control activists' refusal to meet with landlords. Suppose he had also claimed that the activists were being "unreasonable," were only "shooting themselves in the foot." What should have been the response? Tactical activism would have had the rent-control activists give the mayor an ultimatum: either be our ally or be widely publicized as our betrayer. The activists should have declared that the campaign was over and that the time had come for results, not promises. By thus demonstrating their willingness to stand up for their agenda, rent-control activists would have conveyed a sense that they believed in the power of their constituency and were not afraid to take on the mayor. Had they done so, one of three possible results would have followed. First, and most likely, Agnos would have backed down. He was not seeking a political fight with tenants, but merely trying to manipulate them in furtherance of his own agenda. Second, Agnos might have sought to divide the activists by offering to meet with who-ever was willing to attend. This strategy probably would have failed, because rent-control activists unified enough to give the new mayor an ultimatum would not be so easily divided. Third, Agnos could have announced his refusal to work further with rent-control activists. This would have been the most unlikely scenario of all, because a new mayor hardly wants to break with a main campaign constituency early in his term.

Had rent-control activists carefully analyzed the tactical and strate-gic avenues available both to them and to the mayor, they would have recognized that they would gain more credibility with the mayor by refusing his delaying tactic than by agreeing to it. Because they caved in at the outset, Agnos came to count on their subservience to his political agenda in the years ahead. The result four years later was a landslide defeat on rent-control activists' chief issue, the temporary decline of San Francisco's once-powerful tenant movement, and the election of a new mayor openly beholden to real estate interests. The bright hope of the Agnos years ended in tragedy for progressive interests.

The model of the relationship between rent-control activists and Art Agnos has been repeated many times with other constituencies and other elected officials throughout the country. San Francisco's rent-control activists are certainly not alone in erroneously identifying elected officials by their promises rather than their actual performance. And to their credit, when Willie Brown was elected as a "pro-tenant" mayor in 1995 and began breaking commitments after taking office, San Francisco tenant activists responded differently. Tenants became the first group to hold a protest event against Brown, encircling his car in a direct action that brought multiple arrests. Unlike Agnos, Brown saw tenants as a constituency that would cause him trouble if he failed to deliver on his commitments. The most sweeping pro-tenant legisla-tion in the city's history would pass during Brown's first term.

Today's self-styled progressive politicians are uniquely adept at using their power and winning public personalities to distract social change activists from their agendas. These politicians are experts at the psy-chology of "win-win"—they know how to make their campaign sup-porters feel bad for demanding action instead of promises. Moreover, their patronage power enables them to make strategic allies of social change leaders. By appointing such leaders to prestigious boards, commissions, or task forces, the politician can display loyalty to social change constituencies without implementing their agendas. The elected official can also use these leaders to suppress dissatisfaction with official policies at the grassroots level and to provide press quotes disputing charges that the officeholder has betrayed her or his base. Neighborhood activists who have toiled for years in obscurity are understandably flattered at being invited to meet with the mayor, the governor, or a legislator. It is not easy to attend such a meeting and then strongly oppose the official's reasonable-sounding plans.

Political leaders have such an array of tactics to divert social change that tactical activists must demand results and the fulfillment of campaign promises. Once activists understand and accept this fundamental relationship between social change groups and elected officials, they will avoid the principal pitfalls preventing change. Elected officials spend millions of dollars on campaign consultants to develop tactics and strategies to woo voters; social change activists must engage in their own, less costly but equally productive tactical sessions to create the relationships with politicians necessary to achieve progressive aims.

PURSUE YOUR AGENDA, NOT THE POLITICIAN'S

Self-styled grassroots officials are also effective at subordinating activists' agendas to their own. This commonly occurs when politicians and activist groups start out on the same page but then find their agendas diverging. In one typical scenario, a politician commits to an issue and then learns that certain other constituency groups oppose it. The politician does not want a big political fight with the opposition group, but he or she also does not wish to be seen as having betrayed the social change organization. The solution? Reframe and repackage the activists' agenda so that the politician can claim "victory" and convince the activists of the same.

Politicians commonly accomplish this by vowing action to address a problem but then forming a task force to find the "best" solution. The creation of a task force is an ideal strategy for new-style "win-win" politicians to subsume activists' agendas into their own. They subtly switch the agenda from "We demand action now" to "We created a task force to address this critical problem." As the politician gives victory pats on the back, the activists' goal of getting something concrete done disappears.

Task forces sponsored by government officials are usually boondoggles. Approach them with caution. Elected officials seeking to avoid real change often use them as appeasement measures. How many times have you seen the announcement, amid great fanfare, of a new task force, one that will take twelve months to produce a report on an "urgent" problem? Task forces are excellent weapons for slowing activist momentum. They can divert activists from their real goal, and nearly always eat up a lot of time that could be better spent. Yet serving on a task force can be an attractive proposition for a grassroots organizer, who may get no other sign of recognition from the powers that be. However, such official flattery can undermine activist goals. Similarly, serving on a task force may appeal to politically ambitious activists whose real agenda is personal advancement. Those personal goals often end up conflicting with the goals of social change. Activist organizations should determine the function of any member assigned to serve on a government task force and hold him or her rigorously accountable for promoting the organization's views.

Progressive social activists who enthusiastically participate on task forces usually argue, "If we don't participate on a task force, it will come out with horrible recommendations." I say, so what? If that happens, discredit the recommendations. Discrediting task force reports is a fairly simple exercise. One can point to the group's biased composition, question individual member's agendas, point to the heavy political pressures placed on the task force, or note its failure to consider vital information. In any case, after an initial splash, most reports from task forces, commissions, and the like are widely ignored. The task force tactic has become so transparent that it is a wonder that anybody outside the official's staff accepts its legitimacy.

Besides creating task forces, politicians also supplant activist groups' agendas with their own by holding a public hearing to address an activist organization's concerns. Public hearings may be more effective even than task forces in funneling activist energy into the politician's agenda. Typically, the social change organization seeks a government response to a problem. A politician, seeking to play the white knight, announces a hearing to investigate the issue. Social change groups agree to the hearing because it gives them both a chance to mobilize their members and the expectation of tangible results. The organizers pack the hearing room, and the crowd cheers as speaker after speaker rails against the injustice in question. The official who called the hearing plays to the crowd and shows that he or she is squarely in its corner. The media are out in force, and excitement is in the air.

There is only one problem. All too often, such hearings are held by officials with no legal authority to address the targeted problem. Or the hearings occur prior to the drafting of legislation on the subject, whereas the real work for accomplishing change—through either legislation or public-pressure campaigns—occurs afterward. The politician accomplishes his or her goal through the hearing itself, gaining the audience's loyalty and the general public's approval for promptly responding to an injustice. After the hearing, the politician moves on to other issues, leaving the activist organization on its own. Social change organizations rarely achieve their goals through public hearings. Tactical activists can avoid this pitfall by making their agenda clear at the outset to the politician seeking involvement. If a politician is not committed to fighting beyond the hearing, do not allow said official to reap the publicity benefits of the event.

Hearings can energize a constituency base, but this benefit will backfire if people see that nothing concrete has come from their trip to City Hall. Tactical activism requires that groups work only with officials committed to fulfilling the social change agenda. The smart politician understands that working for the group's agenda is also the best strategy for achieving his or her own political aims.

FEAR AND LOATHING ON THE ENVIRONMENTAL TRAIL

Since Earth Day 1970, the United States environmental movement has made tremendous gains. The nation's air is cleaner, its waterways are less polluted, its communities are healthier, and a mass environmental consciousness has prompted mandatory recycling laws in cities large and small. But most environmentalists remain frustrated by the failure to accomplish more. Climate change threatens the future of species and the planet's long-term survival, industry and business groups work overtime to subvert environmental health measures, and we are still engaged in the false choice between jobs and the environment that should long ago have been resolved.

Many grassroots activists blame the environmental movement's failures on the strategic shortcomings of national environmental organizations. These groups are said to be so concerned with appearing "reasonable" to the Washington, D.C., establishment that they unnecessarily compromise on key environmental goals. They are also criticized for failing to hold politicians accountable. We saw a textbook example of both problems in the first year of the Clinton-Gore administration.

As Goes East Liverpool, So Goes the Nation

The battle waged by Greenpeace and residents of East Liverpool, Ohio, to force the Clinton-Gore administration to keep a well-publicized campaign promise to prevent the opening of a dangerous incinerator should not have been necessary. Rejecting a permit for the proposed Waste Technologies Industry (WTI) hazardous waste incinerator was easily justified: the proposed site was close to houses, churches, and schools, and the incinerator would emit such toxics as lead, mercury, and dioxin into a low-income neighborhood. During the 1992 Clinton campaign bus tour, Democratic vice presidential candidate Al Gore described the WTI incinerator as an unbelievable idea that highlighted the concrete differences between the parties on environmental issues. Speaking of the incinerator in Weirton, West Virginia, in July 1992, Gore said, "I'll tell you this, a Clinton-Gore administration is going to give you an environmental presidency to deal with these problems. We'll be on your side for a change, instead of the side of the garbage generators, the way [previous presidents] have been."[4]

Because Gore's environmental treatise *Earth in the Balance* attacked solid-waste incinerators and praised their grassroots opponents, environmentalists saw the election of Clinton-Gore as the death knell for the WTI facility. This expectation was heightened when the vice president issued a press release on December 7, 1992, stating that "serious questions concerning the safety of an East Liverpool, Ohio, hazardous waste incinerator must be answered before the plant may begin operation. The new Clinton-Gore administration will not issue the plant a test burn permit until these questions are answered." Attached to Gore's release was a letter to the comptroller general raising several questions about the impact of the incinerator and how it had been approved. Gore and six U.S. senators signed the letter. The *New York Times* interpreted Gore's statement as "sending a clear signal" that the "new administration plans an aggressive approach to enforcing environmental laws." Incinerator opponents had even greater reason to cheer when the new administration appointed Carol Browner to head the Environmental Protection Agency. In the early 1980s, Browner had worked on anti-toxic issues for Clean Water Action and Citizen Action.[5]

But the Clinton administration broke its pledge to environmental supporters by issuing a temporary permit in March 1993 that allowed the incinerator to begin commercial operation. It did so despite the Ohio attorney general's assertion that the facility violated state law and the EPA's own assessment that it could pose health risks 130 times above the agency's acceptable level.[6]

The Clinton-Gore-Browner flip-flop on the WTI facility was an early test of environmentalists' willingness to hold the new Democratic administration accountable. It was no different from San Francisco mayor Agnos's asking his core rent-control supporters to meet with their opponents as a condition of fulfilling his promises to their constituency. Just as the tenants' surrender early in Agnos's term paved the way for four years of broken promises and political inaction, Clinton's betrayal on the WTI project, if unchallenged, would set a precedent for future betrayals on other issues. Every major environmental group, along with grassroots activists, should have recognized Clinton's agenda and demanded accountability. Clinton, Gore, and Browner should have been heckled and protested at every public appearance. This confrontational approach was essential because the response to the WTI flip-flop would determine environmentalists' power during the balance of Clinton's term.

But Greenpeace was the only major national environmental organization to join the East Liverpool struggle. Greenpeace recognized that "if Clinton-Gore can break their promise on WTI—their first environmental commitment after the election, their first promise to an individual community—they can break them all." Rick Hind, legislative director of Greenpeace's toxics campaign, has learned from experience that politicians "only give you attention when you blast them, and in some cases activists must use the equivalent of a two-by-four."[7]

Greenpeace and East Liverpool activists used a number of confrontational tactics to pressure the Clinton administration. In March 1993, anti-incinerator leader Terri Swearingen and seven other East Liverpool residents took the public tour of the White House. Once inside, they refused to leave until they could speak to Clinton. The eight activists were then arrested. Following this action, Swearingen and her fellow residents joined with Greenpeace for a "Put People First, Not Polluters" national bus tour. The motto perfectly captured the contradiction between Clinton's campaign bus theme of "putting people first for a change" and his sacrifice of the people of East Liverpool to benefit garbage interests.

The bus tour began in April 1993 and traveled across the nation to twenty-five communities with hazardous waste incinerators. It won publicity for the East Liverpool campaign in local papers wherever it went. The tour arrived in Washington, D.C., on May 17, 1993, and more than two hundred people protested in front of the White House, chanting for Al Gore to "read his book" and singing "We Shall Not Be Moved." Seventy-five people were arrested, including actor Martin Sheen and Greenpeace executive director Barbara Dudley. The *Washington Post* noted that the demonstrators seemed to be Clinton voters who never expected to march against him; one East Liverpool mother of three said of Clinton, "We have got to make him more afraid of us." Terri Swearingen observed, "Clinton talks about change and about giving us an environmental presidency. And so far, where is the change? There is no difference between Clinton and Bush."[8]

Regrettably, other national groups and grassroots activists throughout the country failed to mobilize around this litmus-test issue. As Greenpeace's Hind put it in April 1993, "The dirty secret is that we have been soft-pedaling this administration because we hoped that they would live up to their commitment. But it's clear that they are either totally incompetent or are on the other side."[9]

Predictably, the failure of national organizations to attack Clinton-Gore over the issuance of a permanent permit for the WTI incinerator wreaked further damage to the environmental cause. After twelve years of anti-environment Republican presidents, the first two years of the Democratic Clinton administration brought only one significant piece of national environmental legislation. This measure, the California Desert Protection Act, was passed at the last minute of the 1994 congressional session solely to assist California Democratic senator Dianne Feinstein in her tough reelection battle. Even worse, national environmental issues receded to the deep background of the public agenda; public opinion polls in 1994 regularly found that fewer than 5 percent of Americans viewed such issues as among the country's most pressing problems.[10]

Strengthening the Clean Air Act

Some national environmental groups learned from Clinton's first term that this was a president and an administration that responded only to the fear-and-loathing approach. Al Gore had declared in his popular book *Earth in the Balance,* "The people in a democratic society need to be prepared to hold their elected officials accountable." Yet national groups in the East Liverpool struggle passed up the opportunity to target Gore, who should have been held accountable for his broken promise on the WTI facility and for the Clinton administration's entire record of environmental failure.

In 1997, environmental groups got a chance to revisit this issue. On November 27, 1996, EPA chief Browner announced long-awaited new standards for protecting the public from breathing smog and soot. Supposed to have been issued within five years after amendments were made to the Clean Air Act in 1990, these standards were finally released after the American Lung Association sued the EPA and the court ordered the agency to act. Browner's proposed standards were far stricter than anticipated, and her announcement set in motion a public hearing process that would culminate in President Clinton's decision to accept, reject, or modify the new standards.

In other words, the future of the Clean Air Act regulations would be decided through the political process. And rather than trusting Bill Clinton and Al Gore to do the right thing, national groups led by the Sierra Club and the national network of state and local Public Interest Research Groups (PIRGs) built a national campaign to pressure the Clinton administration to do the right thing. In contrast to the WTI struggle, this battle made Al Gore a public target. Gore had long claimed to be an environmentalist (this was a decade before he won the Nobel Peace Prize for his work on climate change), and his personal relationships with environmental leaders had protected the Clinton administration from attacks despite repeated betrayals during much of its first term. The willingness of national environmental leaders to sacrifice green interests in exchange for continuing invitations to the monthly Al Gore power breakfast symbolized the inside-the-Beltway approach to national politics that grassroots activists condemned.

When Gore was silent about the new standards, some suspected that the leading contender for the 2000 Democratic presidential nomination feared alienating organized labor and Democratic mayors and governors in the Midwest, who did not want the new clean air regulations adopted. These suspicions were heightened when a May 30, 1997, unbylined news brief in the *Wall Street Journal* claimed that pressure was mounting on the EPA to "ease proposed antipollutant rules." Reporting that the White House had "privately ordered EPA head Browner not to sign the tough regulations until weaker measures got another look," the brief added that "environmental groups complain Browner hasn't gotten support from

Gore, her former boss." Would environmental groups adopt the fear-and-loathing route of grassroots activists and make Gore publicly responsible for the regulations, or would they follow the "Don't blame Al, he's our friend" approach that had brought failure in the past?[11]

The answer was soon revealed. On June 3, 1997, Kathryn Hohmann, the Sierra Club's director of environmental quality, launched the organization's "Where's Al?" Northeast tour. Speaking from New Hampshire, the site of the first primary for Gore's expected presidential bid, Hohmann told Reuters News Service: "We're here to say 'come out, come out wherever you are.' Our goal is not to bash someone, but there are some very large shoes he needs to fill in leading environmental causes." Hohmann's "Where's Al?" tour sent a message to the presidential aspirant that his environmental credentials were on the line in the clean air campaign. It also used the Club's Northeast chapters to build local media pressure on the region's politicians to formally endorse the new standards.[12]

The strategy of focusing on Gore soon paid off. The lead story in the Sunday, June 1, issue of the New York Times, "Top EPA Official Not Backing Down on Air Standards," had the subtitle "Gore's Voice Could Be Pivotal in Contentious Baffle over Tighter Pollution Rules." Noting that Gore would play a "major role—probably the decisive one—in deciding whether to back up Ms. Browner," the article reaffirmed Hohmann's argument that the clean air outcome would affect "how enthusiastically environmentalists support his presidential effort in 2000."

U.S. PIRG's Gene Karpinski was given the front page of the most widely read edition of the nation's most influential newspaper to state: "Since this is the top priority issue for the national environmental community at this time, any weakening of public health protection by the White House would certainly be a huge negative for Vice President Gore that would not be forgotten." A June 5 USA Today story on clean air noted that Gore "has been particularly conspicuous in his low-key role," and quoted Paul Billings of the American Lung Association, who said that "the silence from the White House has been deafening. There's a Gore watch out. We can't find Al."[13]

The pressure on Gore intensified. On Sunday, June 22, a front-page, unbylined story in the New York Times, "Environmental Groups Say Gore Has Not Measured Up to the Job," further explored the issue. "Organizations that have sided with the vice president throughout his public career," the article stated, "are now using extraordinarily blunt language to warn that 'green' voters might abandon him in the

Democratic primaries in 2000 unless he delivers now." Deborah Callahan of the League of Conservation Voters found it "perplexing" that the vice president would "step back from providing the leadership" that she and her colleagues expected. Phillip Clapp of the National Environmental Trust told the *Times* that "the failure of the White House to provide any leadership on the clean air standards raises real questions about what real environmental progress Vice President Gore can point to in claiming the mantle of the environmental candidate in the year 2000."

But the article also noted that complaints about "Al Gore's silent spring" had begun to bring results. It stated that Gore had recently moved to act "behind the scenes" to ensure that the clean air decision would satisfy environmentalists. Environmental groups' adoption of the fear-and-loathing approach would soon bring victory.

"I Think Kids Ought to Be Healthy"

On June 25, 1997, President Clinton announced his approval of virtually every aspect of Browner's original Clean Air Act proposal. Ironically, while the president was making his announcement at a fundraising dinner, three members of the PIRG's Nashville canvass were outside wearing gorilla suits and holding signs saying "See the smog," "Hear the EPA," and "Speak up for Clean Air." When the organizers learned that Clinton had used the Nashville event to announce support for the standards, they changed their messages and were shown on television with a sign reading "Thank you, Mr. President." Calling Clinton's action "one of the most important environmental decisions of the decade," the *New York Times* reported that the administration credited the intervention of Al Gore, "after lobbying by environmental groups," for resolving the "fierce behind-the-scenes battle" over the standards. Environmentalists' aggressive targeting of the vice president had clearly paid off, and it was no coincidence that Gore was present for the president's announcement and that it occurred in the presidential aspirant's home state.[14]

OBAMA AND THE KEYSTONE XL PIPELINE

The Clean Air Act campaign's grassroots mobilizing strategy provided a road map for the movement's future. After eight years of the anti-environmentalist presidency of George W. Bush, environmentalists' next chance to hold a president they politically supported accountable occurred when Barack Obama took office in 2009.

Unlike Bill Clinton, Obama got off to a good start with environmentalists. During 2009–10, when Obama enjoyed large Democratic majorities in Congress, he increased fuel efficiency standards twice and made significant investments in clean energy. His EPA took hundreds of administrative actions that got little media attention but made a big difference to the environment. Some criticized Obama for failing to enact a broad climate change bill during these years, but getting such sweeping new regulations through the Senate during a recession was likely beyond even the most aggressive president's ability. It was not until 2011 that environmentalists saw Obama as clearly backtracking on his green agenda, and it would be the Keystone XL pipeline that would test their ability to challenge the president with a fear-and-loathing approach.

Little known to most Americans prior to 2011, TransCanada's proposed seventeen-hundred-mile Keystone Pipeline XL extensions would transport synthetic crude oil and diluted bitumen from the Athabasca Oil Sands in northeastern Alberta, Canada, to multiple destinations in the United States, including Montana, South Dakota, Nebraska, Kansas, Oklahoma, and Texas. A report by the Natural Resources Defense Council in March 2011 concluded that it would bring "dirty fuel at high cost, lock the United States into a dependence on hard-to-extract oil and generate a massive expansion of the destructive tar sands oil operations in Canada." The extension also "threatens to pollute freshwater supplies in America's agricultural heartland and increase emissions in already-polluted communities of the Gulf Coast." Bill McKibben, a longtime environmental activist who founded 350.org to focus on climate change, spearheaded what became a worldwide campaign to pressure Obama to deny the Keystone XL pipeline permit. McKibben and the entire environmental community saw the Keystone project as undermining the positive impact of nearly all of the Obama administration's new environmental protections.[15]

To call public attention to Keystone, McKibben and 350.org began civil disobedience in front of the White House on August 26, 2011. McKibben drew publicity by being among the first to be arrested. The crowd of protesters grew from 300 in the first week to well over 1,000, with 1,254 people committed enough get arrested. By the following week hundreds of thousands of people had sent in petitions opposing Keystone to the White House and the State Department. Participants in the protests included such "unusual suspects" as ranchers, members of indigenous groups, and even many representatives of labor unions. Wisely making sure that everyone knew that it was the president who should be targeted over Keystone, McKibben announced, "President Obama can stop this climate killing disaster with the stroke of a pen," and vowed: "We will be outside the White House hoping we can inspire the president to live up to the promises that so inspired us in his 2008 campaign. And without Congress in the way, this is the clearest test he'll ever have."[16]

As pressure on Obama over Keystone was building, the president made the shocking and unexpected announcement on September 2, 2011, that he was reversing the EPA's proposed new restrictions on smog. As seen in the account of the 1997 Clean Air Act struggle, reducing smog is a top priority for many national and local environmental groups. All were outraged by Obama's action. In March the EPA's independent panel of scientific advisers had unanimously recommended strengthening the smog standards. The panel had concluded that the evidence was "sufficiently certain" that the range proposed in January 2010 under Obama's EPA would benefit public health. Now Obama was citing the regulation's alleged negative impact on jobs to justify ignoring the scientific experts whose assessments he had long pledged to follow.

"The Obama administration is caving to big polluters at the expense of protecting the air we breathe," said Kate Geller, press spokesperson of the League of Conservation Voters. "This is a huge win for corporate polluters and huge loss for public health." Even Al Gore, who had rarely publicly criticized the president up to that time, wrote on his blog, "Instead of relying on science, President Obama appears to have bowed to pressure from polluters who did not want to bear the cost of implementing new restrictions on their harmful pollution—even though economists have shown that the US economy would benefit from the job creating investments associated with implementing the new technology. The result of the White House's action will be increased medical bills for seniors with lung disease, more children developing asthma, and the continued degradation of our air quality." The green reaction was echoed by broader progressive organizations like MoveOn.org, whose executive director, Justin Ruben, said, "Many MoveOn members are wondering today how they can ever work for President Obama's re-election, or make the case for him to their neighbors, when he does something like this."[17]

Among those quoted in the *New York Times* story on Obama's reversal was Bill McKibben, who found the president's move "flabbergasting," adding, "Somehow we need to get back the president we thought we elected in 2008." McKibben's words were clearly aimed at influencing Obama's decision on Keystone. National environmental groups did not mobilize against Obama's reversal on the smog regulations, because his action was entirely unexpected. But after the president disregarded the scientific experts on smog, the environmental movement went into high gear to prevent him from backing a project that would bring 3 million barrels of tar sand oil into the United States each year; this hardly comported with Obama's promoting a national shift from oil to renewable resources.

Jobs versus the Environment

Keystone backers portrayed the pipeline as a jobs creator. But estimates of how many permanent jobs would actually be created varied widely. An expert on Fox Business News estimated the project could create "one million high paying jobs." And conservative radio host Rush Limbaugh told listeners that the pipeline would create 200,000 jobs when completed. But an independent study by Cornell University researchers found that only 2,000 to 3,000 jobs would be created, and that they would be temporary construction jobs. When asked by CNN about the contrasting job estimates, TransCanada vice president Robert Jones denied that thousands of permanent jobs would be created and instead placed the number in the hundreds. Despite the inflated job claims, the endless repetition of false jobs projections created a stiff challenge for environmentalists in persuading a president running for reelection on a jobs platform to deny the pipeline permit. Obama had used the jobs issue to justify reversing smog regulations, and many feared he would apply the same reasoning to back Keystone.[18]

McKibben recognized organized labor's need for jobs, but told labor leaders in early September 2011 that, for environmentalists, the Keystone pipeline was "our Wisconsin." He was referring to labor's recent occupation of the Wisconsin Statehouse to prevent legislation ending collective bargaining for public employees; just as unions saw the Wisconsin fight as a life-or-death struggle, they should understand the depth of green feeling about the pipeline. The AFL-CIO ultimately stayed neutral on the pipeline, as opposition from the nation's two largest public transit unions balanced strong support from the Building Trades Council. On November 6, more than 12,000 people encircled the White House to demand that President Obama stop the pipeline. As the crowd linked hands to surround the executive mansion, demonstrators chanted, "Yes, we can / stop the pipeline," evoking the 2008 campaign rallying cry that Obama borrowed from Cesar Chavez and the United Farm Workers', "Sí, Se Puede."[19]

On November 10, 2011, President Obama announced that he was delaying a decision for twelve to eighteen months, pending further State Department review. Pressure from environmental groups had clearly paid off. As McKibben described the development in his email announcing the victory, "Six months ago, almost no one outside the pipeline route even knew about Keystone XL. One month ago, a secret poll of 'energy insiders' by the *National Journal* found that 'virtually all' expected easy approval of the pipeline by year's end. As late as last week the CBC [Canadian Broadcasting Corporation] reported that TransCanada was moving huge quantities of pipe across the border and seizing land by eminent domain, certain that its permit would be granted. A done deal has come spectacularly undone." Sierra Club executive director Michael Brune attributed Obama's decision to "people power," noting that "the earth moved in Washington, D.C., today" and that "without such a strong, organized, and righteous movement, we never would have prevailed."[20]

McKibben, Brune, and other environmental leaders recognized that Obama might simply delay Keystone's final approval until after the election. He could use the temporary denial to secure environmentalist support for his reelection campaign, then uphold the pipeline during his new administration. But they also believed that a State Department review would almost certainly find the pipeline impact report deficient, making the project as proposed unlikely to ever be built.

GOP Plan Backfires

But there would be yet another twist to the story. As part of a December 2011 deal on extending popular payroll tax cuts, Republican pipeline supporters demanded that Obama make a decision on Keystone within two months of the budget agreement. Although initially opposed to such a rider to a debt ceiling measure, Obama angered environmentalists by reversing course and agreeing to the two-month deadline. Sierra Club president Michael Brune described the inclusion of Keystone in the tax deal as "bullshit." McKibben made sure that anger over the reversal targeted Obama: "People literally put their bodies on the lines and they thanked the president when they took him seriously. And the president said he was acting on principle and that it was important and if that resolve lasts five weeks and that's it, if all it takes is Newt Gingrich getting up and expostulating San Francisco and environmental extremists for him to turn around, that's really sad." Betsy Taylor, a philanthropic adviser to climate donors and foundations, helped organize more than eighty-five donors and volunteers for the 2008 campaign to send a letter to Obama urging him to reject Keystone. Taylor echoed McKibben's theme: "If the president waffles on this or fails to act decisively, it will send a huge chill through the community. Will people vote for him? Yes. Will they work for him, raise money for him and activate their networks for him? Not likely."[21]

To maintain pressure, 350.org scheduled a mass rally at the White House on January 24, 2012, only days before Obama's expected decision on the permit. But on January 18 the president preempted this event by denying the permit. "The rushed and arbitrary deadline insisted on by Congressional Republicans," Obama announced, "prevented a full assessment of the pipeline's impact, especially the health and safety of the American people, as well as our environment." McKibben, astutely using the positive side of the fear-and-loathing strategy, responded to Obama's denial by saying, "The knock on Barack Obama from many quarters has been that he's too conciliatory. But here, in the face of a naked political threat from Big Oil to exact 'huge political consequences,' he's stood up strong." Obama's decision allowed TransCanada to make another application for the pipeline, but McKibben noted that even a "re-route will do nothing to address the climate impacts of burning tar sands, the economic downside of continuing our addiction to oil, the risks the pipeline poses to other states along the route, or the political influence Big Oil continues to use to override the interests of the American people. If this pipeline comes back, so will we."[22]

The Keystone XL campaign illustrates how far the environmental movement's strategic savvy has come since Bill Clinton's first term. Environmental groups that did not want to burn bridges with the Clinton-Gore administration over the East Liverpool incinerator chose a different course here. Part of this shift was due to the framing of Keystone as a national and even international climate change issue that demanded an all-out fight. But equally important was that environmental groups had learned that giving politicians a pass on breaking environmental commitments to one constituency leads to further betrayals. As a result of environmentalists adopting a clear fear-and-loathing approach, a "done deal" for Big Oil unraveled and green political clout grew.

On February 17, 2013, an estimated 50,000 anti-Keystone activists convened at the Washington Monument and marched past the White House in the largest climate change rally in U.S. history. Primarily organized by the Sierra Club, 350.org, and the Hip Hop Caucus, the event urged President Obama to move "ForwardOnClimate," cleverly using the president's 2012 campaign theme of "Forward" to hold him accountable on climate change. Four days earlier, on the day after Obama vowed to combat climate change in his 2013 State of the Union address, the Sierra Club engaged in civil disobedience for the first time in its 120-year history when its executive director, Michael Brune, was among dozens of activists arrested at a White House anti-Keystone protest. Keystone had become the key environmental litmus test for the president, and a case study for how green activists should hold politicians accountable.

NO SE PUEDE ON IMMIGRANT RIGHTS

Like environmentalists, immigrant rights activists began the Obama presidency with high hopes. Their chief goal was comprehensive immigration reform that would create a path to citizenship for 8 to 12 million primarily Latino undocumented immigrants. Momentum appeared to be on the activists' side. The movement had brought millions into the streets in support of comprehensive reform in the spring of 2006. In 2008, a higher Latino voter turnout helped Obama win four states that had gone Republican four years earlier (Nevada, Colorado, New Mexico, and Florida). Many believed that the Republican Party could not afford to sacrifice Latino votes in future elections by opposing immigration reform, and President Obama was publicly committed to its enactment. Immigrant rights advocates regarded Obama as an ally; his administration would provide the movement its first real test of its ability to hold a Democratic president accountable.

Unfortunately, as too often happens after a long-disenfranchised constituency gains additional power and helps elect a political ally, immigrant rights leaders failed to confront Obama with the fear-and-loathing approach necessary for success. Like San Francisco tenant leaders after helping elect Art Agnos as mayor, immigrant rights activists continued to trust Obama well after it became clear that he would not honor his commitments. The president had close relations with many of the key immigrant rights movement stakeholders, including the president of the Service Employees International Union (SEIU), Andy

Stern, who often talked about his many invitations to the White House. These relationships and other factors allowed Obama to entirely ignore comprehensive immigration reform during his critical first year in office, and, even worse, to set new records for deportations.

Danger signs about Obama's commitment to enacting comprehensive immigration reform emerged even before he took office when he selected Arizona governor Janet Napolitano to be secretary of homeland security. Napolitano had maintained popularity by allowing anti-immigrant attitudes to fester in her state, which was becoming notorious for the racist outrages of Maricopa County sheriff Joe Arpaio. Obama's appointment of Napolitano reflected a defensive strategy that sought to reduce opposition to comprehensive reform by addressing opponents' demands for strengthened border control and increased deportations. Napolitano's replacement as Arizona governor was a Republican, so Obama's appointment of her also increased the power of the state's anti-Latino forces.

Immigrant rights activists understood that getting an economic stimulus bill through Congress was President Obama's first priority. They also recognized that his next priority was health care, but were told that this would not sidetrack work on immigration reform. Here's where activists made their first mistake. As the above examples from San Francisco and the Clinton administration show, politicians use their first months in office to test activists to see what they can get away with. And what Obama learned during this period was that he could maintain good relations with key immigration reform leaders without providing a specific timetable for action on their top legislative goal.

Obama announced in early April 2009 that he would begin looking for a path for illegal immigrants to become legal in that year. A senior administration official announced that President Obama "plans to speak publicly about the issue in May, and over the summer will convene working groups, including lawmakers from both parties and a range of immigration groups, to begin discussing possible legislation for as early as this fall." This timetable, the official said, was consistent with pledges Obama had made to Hispanic groups in the previous year's campaign, including the promise that comprehensive reform would be a priority of his first year in office. Immigrant rights leader and Congress member Luis Gutierrez discussed Obama's approach to comprehensive reform at the 2009 UNITE HERE convention in Chicago in late June. Gutierrez, a Chicago representative who went way back with Obama, described a serious meeting he and others had had with the president in which they had expressed concern about his lack of action on immigration reform. Assuring his audience that Obama remained committed to the issue, the congressman said he expected a comprehensive measure to pass by Christmas. While echoing activists' disappointment over the slow pace of progress, he and the larger movement still believed the president would come through.[23]

Gutierrez expressed this measured optimism before Obama turned health care reform over to "moderate" Republicans, and before Tea Party activists disrupted town hall meetings in August as part of a concerted strategy to derail health care. When Congress returned to the Capitol in September 2009, health care was the talk of the town, and immigration reform was completely off the political radar. This undermined faith in the Obama administration's early assurances that health care would not crowd out other priorities. Activists responded by having Gutierrez introduce a comprehensive immigration reform bill on October 13. The introduction was accompanied by large rallies in Washington, D.C., and twenty other cities, but the effort appeared to be more of a strategy by immigrant rights groups to placate an increasingly anxious base than a serious step toward enacting comprehensive reform.

As early as fall 2009, the once-high hopes for comprehensive immigration reform were on life support. Obama's election had moved the Republican Party even further to the right, so that one-time immigration reform supporters like Arizona's John McCain—who had once sponsored a reform bill with Ted Kennedy—would no longer touch the issue. After House moderates cast a tough vote to narrowly pass a climate change bill that never went anywhere in the Senate, Speaker Nancy Pelosi realized that she could not ask her caucus to repeat this pattern and agreed with Senate leader Harry Reid that action on immigration reform had to begin there. In light of the Republicans' strategy of filibustering everything they opposed, this meant that all sixty Democrats might be needed to pass immigration reform. This was a highly unlikely event, as some conservative Democrats always opposed reform and success had long depended on at least some Republican support. (Even the modest reforms President George W. Bush had supported would have been impossible in the fall 2009 political climate.)

Meanwhile, President Obama was missing in action. And immigrant rights groups allowed him to stay missing. They engaged in no public protest over his failure to follow through on immigrant rights. After losing political momentum by subsuming their political timetable to the president's, activists had a golden opportunity with the October 13 nationwide rallies to force Obama to at least explain why his administration was increasing enforcement and deportations without doing anything to mitigate the harm such actions did to undocumented immigrants. Instead, the rallies created a misleading impression of progress toward reform, reducing rather than increasing pressure on the president.

In addition to giving Obama a pass on comprehensive reform, leading immigrant rights groups also failed to publicly demand that Obama take administrative actions that did not require congressional approval. For example, he could have used his executive power to protect students who would qualify under the DREAM Act bill. First introduced in 2001, this measure offered a path to citizenship to undocumented young people who graduate from U.S. high schools and then complete two years in the military or two years at a four-year institution of higher learning. Obama could also have declared a moratorium on deportations that break up families or do not involve serious criminal conduct (he did the latter in 2011).

President Obama could have taken any number of actions in 2009 to help undocumented immigrants short of comprehensive reform, but he did nothing. He felt so politically comfortable with his inaction that his administration was deporting more people each year than the preceding Bush administration had, a remarkable betrayal of a constituency whose votes had helped put him in office and that he claimed to want to help.

Giving Obama a Pass

Many immigrant rights leaders were longtime activists who had to know that failing to approach President Obama with a fear-and-loathing strategy was a mistake. Rich Stolz, the campaign manager for Reform Immigration FOR America, a national campaign to pass comprehensive reform, wrote in 2011 that among the lessons learned from the failed effort was that "you have to be hard on your friends." Stolz noted that although Obama had often told activists he wanted to pass immigration reform during his first term, "we would have to make him do it. I do not think we realized what it would take to keep the President and his advisors on task."[24]

Candidate Obama often talked about how constituencies would have to "make him" do things once he was in office. Recalling Franklin Delano Roosevelt's similar challenges to his base, this admonition appeared to demonstrate Obama's encouragement of grassroots activism. But it turned out that Obama and his administration did not want to be held accountable for campaign promises, particularly by progressive groups. In January 2010, Obama chief of staff Rahm Emanuel told activists pressuring conservative Democrats to support health care reform that they were "fucking retarded." On August 10, 2010, Press Secretary Robert Gibbs denounced the "Professional Left," which he claimed "would never regard anything the president did as good enough." The White House was said to be "simmering with anger at criticism from liberals who say President Obama is more concerned with deal-making than ideological purity." If Emanuel's January comment had not already made it obvious to activists, Gibbs's statements confirmed that Barack Obama did not appreciate being pushed by his base. He would need to be made to fear and loathe activists in order to implement their agendas.[25]

After 2009 ended with no action on immigration reform, Obama continued ignoring the issue. In his January 2010 State of the Union speech, Obama declared, "We should continue the work of fixing our broken immigration system—to secure our borders, enforce our laws, and ensure that everyone who plays by the rules can contribute to our economy and enrich our nation." Anti-legalization activists could have made Obama's first two points for him. His third was a thinly veiled endorsement of a path to legalization for undocumented immigrants likely understood only by those in the field. Despite his failure to deliver anything to the immigrant rights movement in his first year in office, the president felt no pressure even to use the term *legalization* in the speech laying out his priorities for the year.

Obama's inaction also sent the message that the federal government was not addressing the immigration issue. In April 2010, Arizona took advantage of this policy vacuum by enacting the nation's most restrictive anti-immigrant law. Alabama and several other states then passed their own draconian laws, showing that Obama's strategy of increasing deportations and strengthening border enforcement had done nothing to reduce anti-immigrant hostility. Activists increasingly grumbled that Obama was using the "stick" against undocumented immigrants without offering any "carrot"; life for such immigrants was now worse than under President Bush.

In May 2010, Congressman Gutierrez, who had only a year earlier expressed such faith in Obama's commitment, was arrested in front of the White House in a protest demanding action on comprehensive reform. By that time it was clear that such a measure was politically dead for the foreseeable future and that focus had shifted to enacting the DREAM Act. Obama made an effort to secure Senate passage of the bill (it easily passed the House), but by December 2010 it was clear that the measure lacked the necessary Senate votes. Activist attention then became entirely focused on the president's administrative powers. In July 2011, Gutierrez, joined by Deepak Bhargava (from the Center for Community Change) and other activists, sat down in front of the White House below a banner reading, "One million deported under President Obama." This protest action followed Obama's letter to Gutierrez rejecting his proposal to suspend deportations of undocumented college students having no criminal record. The immigrant rights leader replied that Obama's stance "didn't disappoint me as much as I was saddened." After intense protests continued, the Obama administration announced on August 18, 2011, that it would no longer actively seek to deport illegal immigrants who have no criminal record and would review existing deportation cases involving noncriminal immigrants on a case-by-case basis.[26]

Could Comprehensive Reform Have Passed in 2009?

Establishing a fear-and-loathing relationship with politician "allies" does not guarantee success, but it gives activists the best chance to prevail. In the case of comprehensive immigration reform, Obama's election to the presidency provided activists with some major advantages. First, Latino voters had played a critical role in Obama's victory and so had the right to expect immigration reform in return. Second, Obama appeared to personally care about remedying the injustices faced by undocumented immigrants. Third, SEIU and other labor unions that strongly backed Obama with both money and campaign staff saw comprehensive reform as a top priority. Fourth, a nationwide network of immigrant rights groups, many connected through the Center for Community Change, was ready for an all-out mobilization to pass reform legislation. Many immigrant rights organizers were as highly skilled and motivated as any organizers in the country. Finally, many of the most powerful proponents of immigration reform, including SEIU's Andy Stern and Representative Gutierrez, believed their close personal relationships with Obama meant that he would not let them down.

But these advantages came up against two factors, only one of which a fear-and-loathing strategy could overcome. That factor—Obama's failure to demonstrate leadership and build political support for comprehensive reform—should have been met as early as 2009 when it became clear that the president was not moving forward on the issue. Obama was the only politician who could unify advocates behind a consensus proposal. But he never took on this role, and activists did not publicly pressure him to do so. As a result, no specific comprehensive reform bill that activists could mobilize around was even introduced, and there was no up-or-down vote on any legislation addressing the issue (or even a vote to cut off debate). In retrospect, it is remarkable that, following a massive Latino voter turnout in the 2008 elections, no comprehensive reform bill supported at least by a Democratic majority ever emerged.

Because he was not held accountable, Obama completely abandoned an issue that his base saw as a top priority. And by not pushing the issue and demanding that Obama show leadership, immigrant rights activists paved the way for future betrayals. The combination of increased deportations, workplace raids, and the mistakenly named "Secure Communities" program reflected an Obama administration immigration policy that activists would have gone publicly ballistic over if adopted by a President John McCain. Obama's inaction empowered anti-immigrant forces while disillusioning grassroots activists, forcing the latter to fight defensive state struggles. Activists did not really start attacking Obama's lack of action on immigrant rights until 2011, and it is no coincidence that only then did the president finally take his first meaningful actions to reduce the number of deportations.

To be clear, the Republican Party's sharp anti-reform shift after the 2008 elections made passing comprehensive immigration reform more difficult than expected. Obama's best efforts might not have succeeded in passage of such a measure. But the lack of a specific bill and an actual vote was the worst possible option. It created the sense of federal inaction that prompted anti-immigrant state measures, leaving the grass roots mystified about who and what were to blame for the lack of progress.

Had Obama ensured an up-or-down vote on a definite immigration reform measure, even losing would have rallied the base and shown the grass roots that Obama and most Democrats were on their side. This is what occurred when activists pushed Senate leader Harry Reid (re-elected in Nevada in 2010 thanks to huge Latino voting) to hold a vote on the DREAM Act at the end of 2010. Young DREAM Activists marched, protested, and took to the streets across the nation (see chapter 9). They took justifiable pride in winning fifty-five Senate votes, just five short of the sixty necessary to end a filibuster (the measure had passed the House earlier). Comprehensive reform should have followed a similar legislative course.

The immigrant rights movement did not become a powerful political force until 2006. Barack Obama was the first president it helped elect. Just as environmental activists learned from their experiences during the Clinton years, immigrant rights activists learned from their setbacks in 2009 and 2010 that, like any politician, Obama is best motivated to act on their behalf out of political fear, not friendship. As discussed in chapter 9, in 2012 the movement used fear and loathing on Obama to win temporary legalization for those eligible under the DREAM Act. In the wake of large Latino majorities having voted for Democrats in the November 2012 election, the movement proceeded in 2013 with the same strategy of pressuring the president and Congress to enact comprehensive reform. And, unlike prior efforts, the 2013 campaign for comprehensive reform will likely result in victory.

GAY RIGHTS ACTIVISTS HOLD OBAMA ACCOUNTABLE

As with immigrant rights, the gay rights movement greatly expanded during the hostile presidency of George W. Bush. By the time Barack Obama took office, gay rights supporters believed that changes in federal policies were long overdue. Two measures opposed by the gay community had been enacted during the Clinton years—the military policy known as "Don't Ask, Don't Tell" (DADT) in 1993 and the Defense of Marriage Act (DOMA) in 1996—and during his 2008 campaign Obama pledged to repeal both. But as activists have seen time and time again, such pledges can mean little absent constituency pressure.

Of the two measures, repealing a policy that required gays and lesbians in the military to keep silent about their sexual orientation—hence the phrase "don't ask, don't tell"—was seen as far easier politically. In committing to repeal, Obama stated during his campaign, "We're spending large sums of money to kick highly qualified gays or lesbians out of our military, some of whom possess specialties like Arab-language capabilities that we desperately need. That doesn't make us more safe."[27]

But even before Obama took office, his administration appeared to back off from what activists thought was his ironclad commitment. On January 14, Press Secretary Robert Gibbs addressed questions about Obama's plan regarding DADT. "There are many challenges facing our nation now," he said, "and the president-elect is focused first and foremost on jump-starting this economy . . . so not everything will get done in the beginning, but he's committed to following through." Activists did not expect repeal to take precedence over the stimulus package, but Gibbs hardly sounded as if repeal were a front-burner issue. In late March, Defense Secretary Robert Gates expressed his desire to push DADT "down the road a little bit," and in late April the White House "altered language on its Web site in a way that appeared to soften the administration's commitment to changing the policy."[28]

Amidst these warning signs about the president's commitment, Sandy Tsao, a U.S. Army officer dishonorably discharged in January for coming out to her superiors as gay, received a handwritten letter from Obama on May 5, 2009, reaffirming that the president was "committed to changing our current policy." Yet Obama's "commitment" did not extend to preventing Tsao and others from being discharged under DADT. This disconnect became even more obvious two days after Obama's letter to Tsao, when Dan Choi, a National Guard officer fluent in Arabic, learned that he would be dismissed from the military for being too openly gay. Choi became a leading figure in the struggle to repeal DADT. Later in May, a study from the University of California, Santa Barbara, concluded that the president had the legal authority to suspend dismissals for sexual orientation without legislative action. While the report confirmed that a permanent repeal required congressional approval, it allowed activists to pressure Obama to take action in the meantime.[29]

On May 20, Pentagon statistics were released showing that dismissals under DADT had remained steady despite Obama's stated opposition to the policy. "The numbers continue to make the case for the repeal of the statute," said Aubrey Sarvis, executive director of the Servicemembers Legal Defense Network. "This will help make the case to the president and Congress that they need to proceed with urgency." In noting that Obama's delay in moving for repeal was empowering opponents, Sarvis and others cited "a recent letter sent to the president by 1,000 retired admirals and generals organized by the conservative Center for Military Readiness that urged him to maintain the ban or risk severely damaging troop morale." Delays in enacting comprehensive immigration reform had similarly empowered anti-immigrant forces, and gay activists were not going to fall into this trap. Richard Socarides, a lawyer who had advised Bill Clinton on gay issues, spoke for many when he told the *Boston Globe*: "It is the one area where the federal government is blatantly engaging in discriminatory conduct. For [Obama] to now be completely silent on this at best—and at worst have Gates equivocating—is very troubling to a lot of people."[30]

In June, the United States Supreme Court declined to review the petition of a gay soldier dismissed under DADT who had filed a legal challenge to the law. The Obama administration had filed a brief backing the lower court's decision to uphold the ban. James Pietrangelo II, the former army soldier who filed the lawsuit, said of President Obama, "He's a coward, a bigot and a pathological liar. This is a guy who spent more time picking out his dog, Bo, and playing with him on the White House lawn than he has working for equality for gay people." While Pietrangelo had no leadership role in the gay community, his words reflected gay activists' growing sense of betrayal by a president who had publicly committed to repealing DADT.[31]

In July, the Human Rights Campaign (HRC) and Servicemembers United kicked off a nationwide "Voices of Honor" campaign featuring military veterans telling their stories of the hardships and unfairness of DADT. The tour reached more than fifty cities and connected national advocacy groups with local organizations capable of applying pressure at the grass roots. Obama acknowledged this pressure when he appeared in October at the Human Rights Campaign's annual dinner. After his statement that he would repeal DADT evoked a standing ovation from the crowd of three thousand, he noted: "I appreciate that many of you don't believe progress has come fast enough. Do not doubt the direction we are heading and the destination we will reach." Longtime gay activist Cleve Jones noted that Obama delivered a brilliant speech, but "it lacked the answer to our most pressing question, which is when. He repeated his promises that he's made to us before, but he did not indicate when he would accomplish these goals and we've been waiting for a while now." Aubrey Sarvis of the SLDN echoed Jones, saying "an opportunity was missed tonight." He said his group "was disappointed the president did not lay out a timeline and specifics for repeal."[32]

Some saw Obama's speech as a clear betrayal. Activists carrying signs attacking the president's inaction on repeal marched outside the HRC dinner, and gay blogger John Aravosis sounded a lot like Ernesto Cortes, Jr., on the need for a fear-and-loathing approach to politicians. In a blog post responding to Obama's HRC speech titled "Where's the Beef?" Aravosis argued.

> What did President Obama say new tonight? Absolutely nothing. What did the Human Rights Campaign get in exchange for once again giving our president cover for all of his broken promises to our community? Absolutely nothing. All in all, the evening was a disappointment, but not unexpected. President Obama doesn't do controversy, and we, my friends, are controversy. So,

the bad blood between this administration and the gay community will remain, and continue to worsen. It's unfortunate, but at some point you have to have enough dignity to say enough is enough. The Obama administration doesn't respect our community, and doesn't respect the seriousness of our cause. It's our job to hold them accountable. And we will.[33]

Keeping Up the Pressure

As 2010 began, anti-DADT activists understood it was now or never. Their strategy now was to include repeal in the annual defense authorization bill, a strategy backed by House Speaker Nancy Pelosi. To push the Obama administration in this direction, on March 18, 2010, the SLDN took out an advertisement in the newspaper *Roll Call* for an open letter to Obama:

> [I]f you do not include repeal in your defense budget, it will be tough to win repeal this year. You have yet to say to Congress, Let's finally end this embarrassing and archaic law and here's how we do it.
> The time is now. Not next year or the second term. To delay another year is to stand aside and okay the daily firing of service members merely because they are gay. Patriotic gays and lesbians are fighting and dying for our country in two wars, just like their straight comrades-in-arms.

SLDN's Sarvis said the ad "was just the first salvo in a longer, broader, campaign to push the administration's hand. A number of other organizations feel the same way and I will anticipate that you will be seeing more of a united and direct message."[34]

Not taking anything for granted, the Human Rights Campaign launched its "Repeal DADT Now Campaign" in February, modeled on the "Voices of Honor" campaign of 2009. The renewed effort focused on key swing senators in Florida, Indiana, Virginia, West Virginia, Nebraska, and Massachusetts (where Republican Scott Brown had won an upset special election victory in January), reaffirming the movement's political savvy. The grassroots pressure worked. On May 27, the Senate Armed Services Committee approved an amendment to the Senate defense authorization bill that repealed DADT. The full House passed a defense bill the following day that included the repeal amendment, and the Senate was to consider final passage after the November midterm elections.

On December 22, 2010, Obama signed the repeal of DADT. The new law ending the ban on gays serving in the military would not take effect until September 2011, but gay activists' two-year pressure campaign to force Obama to keep his campaign pledge achieved its goal. Given his inaction absent pressure, activists' willingness to hold Obama politically accountable was essential. While politicians often complain that activists are too impatient for results, had DADT activists accepted Obama's much slower timetable, they would have lost the chance for repeal after Republicans took control of the House in the 2010 elections. By using a fear-and-loathing approach, DADT activists raised the political price of continued inaction too high for Obama to ignore, and they won a historic victory.

Four critical lessons emerge from the DADT repeal campaign.

First, activists must require politicians to set a timetable for fulfilling campaign commitments. The SLDN's Kevin Dix noted that Obama "said on health care if you want to get anything done in Washington, set a timeline. We're just following what he laid out." Obama understood that timelines would limit his political options, and he refused to commit to one on either comprehensive immigration reform or DADT. But whereas immigrant rights activists did not publicly protest Obama's refusal to set a timeline, DADT activists used it to show Obama in a negative light. Activists do not benefit from giving a politician they are targeting more political options, and a refusal to even set a timeline is pretty good evidence that a political "ally" is backtracking if not abandoning a commitment altogether. That's why activists must demand timelines and then hold politicians accountable for meeting them.[35]

Second, the DADT repeal campaign included both influential insider and influential outsider groups; the latter engaged in the more confrontational accountability strategies focused on the president that are often necessary for success. An absence of strong outsider groups enabled San Francisco mayor Art Agnos to betray tenant activists on vacancy control, and clearly facilitated Obama's inaction on comprehensive immigration reform. Key immigrant rights leaders were too vested in organizational and even personal relationships with Obama in 2009 to publicly criticize his lack of positive action on this priority.

Third, instead of waiting for Obama, DADT activists took the initiative by arranging to include the repeal in the defense appropriations bill. Activists made it clear that they were going to move the process forward and that the president would either get on the bus or become a public obstacle; given this choice, Obama could do little else but back the plan. In contrast, immigrant rights activists developed a strategy that required Obama to demonstrate a type of arm-twisting leadership he was unwilling or unable to do; and then they did not publicly criticize him when he did not perform this role. And once it became objectively clear in mid-2009 that Obama was no Lyndon Johnson when it came to getting Congress to do things his way, activists failed to effectively pressure the Democratic Senate leadership to spend political capital on a potentially winning legislative strategy.

Finally, DADT activists never stopped organizing and successfully expanded their base from the moment Obama took office. In contrast, immigrant rights activists appeared to be waiting for a signal from the president to put their mobilizing in high gear—a signal that never came. While immigrant rights activists understood the importance of building a broader political base for comprehensive reform, they put more faith in President Obama's willingness to deliver on their movement's behalf than did DADT activists.

The Struggle against DOMA

In addition to pledging to repeal DADT, candidate Obama supported overturning the Defense of Marriage Act (DOMA), a federal law that allowed states to refuse recognition of same-sex marriages performed elsewhere and that also barred federal benefits for same-sex couples (in the form of, e.g., income taxes, Social Security, and immigration rights) even if they lived in states that allowed gay marriage or civil unions. Bill Clinton signed DOMA in 1996 in order to prevent Republicans from using the gay marriage issue against him in his reelection campaign. At the time, no state had legalized gay marriage, and most of its proponents saw the prospect as decades away. But after San Francisco galvanized the movement for marriage equality by approving gay marriage in early 2004, activists targeted a number of states to legalize same-sex marriage. Gay marriage was legal in California during Obama's 2008 campaign, and has subsequently become so in New York and other states. This has made DOMA's repeal an activist priority.

Unlike "Don't Ask, Don't Tell," activists recognized that the votes were likely not there for DOMA's repeal even during 2009–10, when Democrats had large House and Senate majorities. While not expecting immediate action on DOMA, activists were surprised to see Obama's Justice Department file a brief in early June 2009 defending a constitutional challenge to DOMA that read like something from the Bush administration. The brief did not merely refute the lawsuit on technical grounds, but advanced legal arguments that if backed by the courts could greatly damage gay and lesbian rights.

A gay couple that had legally married before California's Prop 8 (discussed further in chapter 7) repealed the state's authorization of gay marriage in the November 2008 election sued to repeal DOMA on constitutional grounds. The Justice Department brief in *Smelt v. United States* raised a number of procedural arguments, but also argued that the Full Faith and Credit Clause of the U.S. Constitution does not bar states from denying out-of-state gay marriages. The brief cited prior cases of out-of-state marriages between (a) an uncle and his niece, (b) a sixteen-year-old minor and an adult, and (c) first cousins. Gay activists were outraged that a president who said he wanted to repeal DOMA would have his Justice Department equate same-sex marriage with incest and pedophilia.

The brief also defended DOMA as "related to legitimate government interests," though the only clear interest was the revenue the federal government would receive by denying gay couples the income tax benefits associated with marriage. In other words, anti-gay bias is "legitimate" if it saves the government money. Yet the Justice Department also argued elsewhere that DOMA "does not discriminate against gays for federal benefits." Opponents of DOMA questioned why the Obama administration would make such a claim when DOMA expressly says the federal government *will not recognize* gay married couples, even if a state chooses to do so.

Following the pattern used to hold Obama accountable for repealing DADT, gay and lesbian organizations publicly blamed the president for the Justice Department position. On June 12, 2009, the American Civil Liberties Union joined the National Gay and Lesbian Task Force, the Human Rights Campaign, Lambda Legal, the National Center for Lesbian Rights, and Gay and Lesbian Advocates and Defenders (GLAD) in expressing deep disappointment in the Obama administration's brief. The groups noted that the "administration is using many of the same flawed legal arguments that the Bush administration used," and declared they were also "extremely disturbed by a new and nonsensical argument the administration has advanced suggesting that the federal government needs to be 'neutral' with regard to its treatment of married same-sex couples in order to ensure that federal tax money collected from across the country not be used to assist same-sex couples duly married by their home states." The legal groups concluded: "When President Obama was courting lesbian, gay, bisexual and transgender voters, he said that he believed that DOMA should be repealed. We ask him to live up to his emphatic campaign promises, to stop making false and damaging legal arguments, and immediately to introduce a bill to repeal DOMA and ensure that every married couple in America has the same access to federal protections."[36]

Obama Shifts His Stance

Obama soon faced a more pressing test of his commitment to repeal DOMA. On July 8, 2010, a federal district court in Boston ruled that portions of DOMA were unconstitutional on the grounds that it compelled Massachusetts (which had legalized gay marriage) to discriminate against its own citizens in order to receive federal money for certain programs. In a separate suit filed by GLAD on behalf of another married gay couple, the same court ruled that DOMA violated the Equal Protection Clause of the Constitution by denying benefits to one class of married couples—gay men and lesbians—but not others. Neither suit challenged DOMA's granting states the right not to recognize marriages in other states, but the combined rulings again put the Obama administration in the increasingly politically untenable position of having to legally defend a law the president believed should be repealed.[37]

As pressure for action on both DADT and DOMA increased, Obama was reassessing his view concerning marriage equality. During an interview with bloggers on October 27, 2010, the president responded to a question about the issue by saying, "I also think you're right that attitudes evolve, including mine. And I think that it is an issue that I wrestle with and think about because I have a whole host of friends who are in gay partnerships. I have staff members who are in committed, monogamous relationships, who are raising children, who are wonderful parents. And I care about them deeply. And so while I'm not prepared to reverse myself here, sitting in the Roosevelt Room at 3:30 in the afternoon, I think it's fair to say that it's something that I think a lot about."[38]

A little more than a week after Obama's comments, two new lawsuits against DOMA were filed by plaintiffs from New York, Connecticut, Vermont, and New Hampshire. These suits raised new facts and legal theories challenging the 1,138 federal laws and regulations that DOMA potentially impacts. The new suits posed a new challenge for the Obama administration in that they were filed in districts covered by the federal appeals court in New York—which had no modern precedent on laws discriminating against gay people. This meant that the president could not defend legal briefs backing DOMA on the grounds that he was simply enforcing legal precedent; rather, his Justice Department would have to file papers setting forth its position on whether federal laws can discriminate against gay people.[39]

On December 22, 2010, Obama was asked by *The Advocate* about defending DOMA in the courts now that the Republicans, who had won a majority of House seats in the November elections, could effectively bar legislative repeal. Obama replied, "I have a whole bunch of really smart lawyers who are looking at a whole range of options. I'm always looking for a way to get it [ending DOMA] done, if possible, through our elected representatives. That may not be possible."[40]

On February 23, 2011, Attorney General Eric Holder sent a letter to Congress stating that the administration was changing its policy of the past two years and would now refuse to defend DOMA. "The president and I have concluded that classifications based on sexual orientation should be subjected to a strict legal test intended to block unfair discrimination. As a result, a crucial provision of the Defense of Marriage Act is unconstitutional."[41]

"A Watershed Moment"

On July 1, 2011, the Justice Department filed a brief in the case of *Golinski v. U.S. Office of Personnel Management* arguing that DOMA's prohibition of federal recognition of same-sex marriage is unconstitutional. Joe Solmonese, president of the Human Rights Campaign, described the Justice Department's brief as "a watershed moment" in the LGBT rights movement. Even John Aravosis, whose America.blog had long criticized Obama on both DADT and DOMA, felt the Justice Department's new court filing "looked pretty amazing." Still, Aravosis panned the administration for filing it late on a Friday night before a holiday weekend. "The brief appears to be quite historic, so why attempt to hide it? It's hard not to conclude that this brief was intentionally buried by the administration in order to minimize mainstream media coverage."[42]

Hard-to-please activists like Aravosis irritate less confrontational allies, but they are vital to social movements often unwilling to hold political allies accountable. And "amazing" is a good description of how effectively gay rights advocates moved Obama on both of their top priorities at a time when the president was disappointing other progressive constituencies. The U.S. Supreme Court will decide DOMA's constitutionality, and the Obama administration's stance increased the chances that the High Court would defer to the federal government's view of its constitutionality. Obama gave the gay community little choice but to use fear-and-loathing tactics against him. As is typically the case, when gay-marriage activists adopted this approach, its success boosted their target's political popularity and advanced progressive change. While Obama deserves credit for publicly endorsing marriage equality in 2012 and for promoting it during his 2013 inaugural address, it is unlikely that either would have occurred without the gay community's commitment to demanding political accountability.

3

Coalition Activism

Rounding Up the Unusual Suspects

I am a great believer in coalition politics. The sight of social change organizations accomplishing goals by working with other organizations and
constituencies is wonderful to behold. Unfortunately, building and
maintaining activist coalitions is not easy. And when funding shortfalls
cause many organizations to aggressively compete with one another for
scarce foundation dollars, coalition building can become even harder.
The absence of effective coalition building has often deprived social
change activists of what often represents *the* strategic key to success. It is
therefore critical for tactical activists to understand how, when, and why
coalitions should be used, and to draw important lessons from successful
activist coalitions forged among even the most disparate constituencies.

Although the term *coalition* can mean many different things, activist
coalitions typically combine two or more organizations in pursuit of at
least one mutual objective. Some coalitions involve organizations whose
members are actively involved in an issue; others comprise a paper list
of groups whose participation may not extend beyond the endorsement
of a particular cause. Historically, progressive activists have identified
strongly with coalition building. From the worldwide coalition of anti-
fascist activists fighting for a free Spain in the 1930s to the broad antiwar coalitions of the 1960s and 1970s, social change organizations
have allied in common struggles. The signature chant—"The people,
united, will never be defeated"—reflects the left's almost spiritual faith
in coalition politics.

The question thus emerges: If activists preach and practice unity, why are progressive causes so often defeated? Are "the people" not united, or are they not united with the right combination of other people to prevail? The simple answer to both questions is yes. Progressive social change activists often fail to unify; more important, when they do unify, they often fail to create a broad- or powerful-enough coalition to win.

THE PROBLEM OF UNITY

Many social change organizations do not believe in working in coalitions. Perhaps the most prominent example is the highly regarded Industrial Areas Foundation–Texas. IAF-Texas is a spinoff of Saul Alinsky's original Chicago-based Industrial Areas Foundation. Like Alinsky's "back of the yards" organization in Chicago, IAF-Texas was largely created through parish-based organizing efforts. The hundreds of families that comprise IAF-Texas are overwhelmingly Latino, Catholic, and working class. The organization's success at empowering and mobilizing its members has improved the quality of life for its constituency and brought national acclaim.

In praising the group in *Who Will Tell the People? The Betrayal of American Democracy,* William Greider makes a point about coalitions that I have heard repeated time and time again: "IAF leaders see . . . hollowness in many [coalitions]: Real people are absent from the ranks. The IAF leaders are also wary of using their people as fodder in someone else's crusade." This view reflects legitimate concerns about coalitions widely held by organizers of membership-based social change organizations. These concerns raise four important issues. First, participation in coalitions may enable groups without a political base to use yours to pursue their own agenda. Second, coalitions may allow other organizations to claim credit for your work. Third, coalitions may hamper organization building. Groups seeking foundation support need to show a track record of accomplishments; press clippings crediting a coalition rather than specific groups could impair fund-raising efforts and ultimately threaten an organization's survival. Finally, coalitions require individual groups to cede control of strategy and tactics. The need to compromise on tactics, as well as on style and substance, makes some groups wary of joining coalitions.[1]

If leaders of groups such as IAF express doubts about coalitions, it's easy to understand why many organizations view unity suspiciously.

However, IAF-Texas members also acknowledge that forming coalitions with non-Latino working people in Texas is essential for the accomplishment of significant political, economic, and social goals. Greider, citing IAF-Texas leader Ernesto Cortes, Jr., writes, "Cortes does not think the IAF-Texas network will achieve full status as a major power in the state until it succeeds at creating a presence among the white blue-collar workers in Eastern Texas and elsewhere—people who have common economic interests but are in social conflict with blacks and Hispanics."[2]

The lesson from IAF and similar groups regarding coalitions is clear. Social change organizations that can fulfill their agendas on their own do not need coalitions. When the agenda broadens, however, success requires expansion of the political base through coalition building.

With Whom Should "the People" Unite?

After social change organizations recognize that they can best achieve their goal by working in coalition with other groups, the question arises: With whom should they unify? Claude Rains's line in *Casablanca* about "rounding up the usual suspects" often seems to apply. The usual suspects (i.e., national progressive organizations) are regularly rounded up into coalitions for or against a particular cause. In many cases, the coalition's existence does not extend beyond the listing of organizations in a *New York Times* advertisement or a sign-on to an email message on the issue. Many of the groups frequently included on these lists lack a viable political base, which may explain why they are so eager to join coalitions, whereas groups like IAF-Texas that do have such a base are wary of such involvements. A similar smoke-and-mirrors approach occurs at the state and local levels, as coalitions rapidly come and go without regard to the ideological uniformity (or lack thereof) among the diverse organizations and individuals named.

A coalition of groups identified solely with the political left is fine so long as the campaign's target is potentially swayed by exclusively progressive constituencies. Unfortunately, in today's United States this is rarely the case. A coalition of groups with similar constituencies often brings no greater results than the actions of a single group would likely achieve, which further explains why tactically sophisticated organizations like IAF-Texas disdain such involvements.

The great value of coalitions lies in their ability to propel groups to success that could not prevail on their own. To gain this advantage, an activist often must find a basis for partnership with organizations whose culture, politics, and overall agenda differ greatly from his or her own group's, but whose interests on a particular issue coincide. Forming coalitions with groups one may oppose on other issues requires the highest level of tactical expertise. The process involves defining the essential point of mutual interest and creating a structure for decision making and accountability. An astonishing example of tactical coalition building at the grassroots level took place when Hasidic Jews and Catholic families joined forces to fight construction of a waste incinerator plant in the Brooklyn Navy Yard. The ability of these two constituencies, long at each other's throats over distribution of public resources, to unify for a common goal shows what can be accomplished through coalition politics.

An Alliance for the Ages

The Williamsburg neighborhood of Brooklyn, New York, is known today for newly built condominiums, trendy restaurants, late-night dancing in former warehouses, and rapidly escalating housing prices. But blocks away from the heart of Bedford Avenue's hipster scene is a very different part of Williamsburg. This lesser-known area is a working-class community primarily inhabited by two ethnic groups: the Satmar sect of Hasidic Jews, a deeply religious group whose customs, practices, and appearance harken back to earlier centuries; and Latinos, primarily Puerto Rican and Dominican Catholics. The fittingly named Division Avenue separates largely Hasidic northern Williamsburg from the primarily Latino south side. These disparate groups share one of the most environmentally dangerous neighborhoods in all of New York. Williamsburg is part of the city's "lead belt," and the Latino section is home to the Radiac Corporation, a multimillion-dollar business that serves as a storage and transfer facility for toxic, flammable, and radioactive waste. Radiac sits adjacent to homes and businesses, less than a block away from a public school serving more than one thousand local children. The facility could not meet current minimum buffer-zone requirements, and its federal permit has long expired. No environmental impact study has ever been done on Radiac.[3]

The Brooklyn Navy Yard incinerator project was conceived in 1979 after state environmental officials started pressuring New York City to stop using the world's largest landfill, Fresh Kills on Staten Island, as its exclusive repository for trash. The unlined and unlicensed Fresh Kills had become a threat to local waterways, and Mayor Ed Koch had proposed building at least five massive incinerators, one in each borough, to replace it. Koch's response to landfill problems reflected a national trend. Incinerators seemed an easy way to get rid of trash and create energy at the same time. The Brooklyn Navy Yard incinerator was supposed to generate 465 million kilowatt-hours of electricity a year. The flaw in the logic of incinerators, however, is that almost everything that is safe to burn is better off recycled. Burning toxic and nonrecyclable materials reduces them to an ash that endangers people's health. Moreover, incinerators emit hazardous chemicals into the atmosphere, including lead, mercury, and dioxin.[4]

Although the incinerator was discussed throughout the 1980s, widespread opposition to the project did not galvanize until Mayor David Dinkins announced in September 1991 that the city was going forward with its plan to build a fifty-five-story incinerator at the Brooklyn Navy Yard. The incinerator would burn three thousand tons of trash daily, emit half a ton of lead each year, and be Brooklyn's largest stationary source of nitrogen oxide (a component of smog), according to a New York Public Interest Research Group (NYPIRG) analysis. The Environmental Protection Agency has determined that lead is a "probable human carcinogen." The particular impact of lead poisoning on children is well recognized, and the U.S. Public Health Service estimates that one out of six children nationwide is at risk because of lead exposure. With studies of the Williamsburg lead belt already having found high concentrations, the proposed new source of lead sent alarm throughout the community.

In addition to sharing environmental problems, the Hasidim and Latinos of Williamsburg compete for what few public resources flow to the community. These resources fund various services, including schools, police, and, most important, housing. Historically, community activists from each group have felt that the other got more than its proportionate share of subsidized housing units in the neighborhood. In an area with high housing costs and limited incomes, access to government housing subsidies is highly prized. Both groups have rapidly growing populations. Because they do not use cars or public transit on the Sabbath, the Hasidim must live within walking distance of their synagogues. Latinos' resentment toward the Hasidim over the housing issue has led to violence between members of the two groups and would seem to make partnership on any issue unimaginable.

Concern about children, however, has a way of making anything possible. The culture and traditions of both groups focus on children and family, and both groups have a long-term commitment to the community. Because the proposed waste incinerator would add another environmental risk to children in a community already beset with such problems, the Hasidic community strongly opposed the project. The Latinos also recognized the environmental risks for their community. A Latino organization called El Puente (The Bridge) runs a community development center that includes a clinic, a high school, and various programs, many for youth. As part of its program to improve community health and inspire youth service and leadership, El Puente started a "Toxic Avengers" project designed to close down or limit the scope of activity at Radiac. The Toxic Avengers had discovered that, in the event of a fire at Radiac, a poisonous cloud of smoke and gas could travel as far as four miles in only thirty minutes. The deadly fumes could do severe harm to eyes and skin, inflict neurological damage, and cause birth defects in the children of victims.

In 1991, the Toxic Avengers obtained a state hearing on Radiac. In planning outreach for the event, the group decided to ask the Hasidim to participate. Rabbi David Niederman, who had recently become executive director of the United Jewish Organizations (UJO) of Williamsburg, agreed to come to a planning meeting after receiving assurances that he would be welcomed. Thus, in May 1991 Niederman walked through a Roman Catholic church into the offices of El Puente and offered to help lead a march through Latino streets to publicize the Radiac hearing. The young people from the Toxic Avengers wanted to work with the Hasidim on environmental issues and were deeply impressed by the rabbi's offer. So astounding was Niederman's gesture that El Puente founder Luis Garden Acosta compared Niederman's visit to Nixon's first trip to China; thus was the necessary contact made for the two often-warring groups to work in coalition against the incinerator plant.[5]

Upon becoming UJO's director, Niederman had tried a new approach for addressing Hasidic-Latino relations in Williamsburg. For most of his career, he had been involved primarily in international Jewish refugee work and only recently had become significantly involved in local community affairs. His background of negotiating with often-hostile world leaders to achieve freedom for Jews in areas such as the Middle East gave him a perspective on international and ethnic cooperation that helped him in his work at the UJO.

In 1985 the Satmars had turned out 15,000 people for a march across the Brooklyn Bridge in an attempt to prevent the city from signing a contract for the incinerator. That effort failed to kill the project, however, and it seemed clear now that they would need additional political allies to prevail. Nearly ten years into the fight, Niederman and his Hasidic constituency sought to broaden the anti-incinerator campaign from primarily the Satmars and NYPIRG to include Williamsburg's dominant population group, the Latinos.

Luis Garden Acosta, the founder and leader of El Puente, spear-headed Latino efforts to build a coalition with the Hasidim. Garden Acosta, a health administrator, had helped develop "environmental racism," an idea that emphasizes the government's policy of disproportionately imposing environmental hazards on minority communities. He frequently expressed the view that the Williamsburg Latinos' culture included an appreciation for nature and a connection to the land. Moreover, the community struggles El Puente had led against the Hasidim over education and police gave the group the credibility necessary to work on the incinerator issue with a constituency many Latinos distrusted. Like Rabbi Niederman, Garden Acosta brought an international worldview to his local activities. His perspective on global unity led him to reach out to the Poles, Italians, and other white ethnics of Williamsburg so as to make the anti-incinerator coalition as inclusive as possible. El Puente's creation of the Toxic Avengers to fight for environmental justice brought the group widespread publicity even before Garden Acosta entered into a coalition with Niederman and the UJO. Despite Garden Acosta's awareness of environmental issues, however, NYPIRG and the UJO had limited contact with the Latino community around the waste incinerator proposal prior to 1991. Niederman clearly recognized that in a community whose majority-Latino population resented the Hasidim's allocation of resources, the UJO would have to make the initial public overture to begin the coalition process.

In opposing the incinerator, Williamsburg's low-income residents found themselves up against powerful moneyed interests. Wall Street was eager for the business it would get when the city issued the bonds necessary to pay for the facility's construction. Among Wall Street investment firms with a stake in the incinerator was Lazzard Frères, whose managing director, Felix Rohatyn, was New York City's most powerful and influential investment banker. Rohatyn's power over municipal credit and city budgets made ambitious elected officials extremely reluctant to oppose him. Wall Street firms were major sources of campaign funding for local and state politicians, who could then support projects like the incinerator without having received funds from the project sponsor. Business groups strongly supported the incinerator, as did unions eager to benefit from the project's construction jobs. The *New York Times* took a vehemently pro-incinerator editorial stance, joining various other power brokers in the city. The law firm retained by Wheelabrator Environmental Systems, the company hoping to build the incinerator, made major contributions to local and state legislative campaigns, including $45,000 for Rudy Giuliani's 1993 mayoral race.

The politically savvy Satmars, however, had the other kind of capital politicians can't live without: votes. They had delivered a large vote for David Dinkins in a close mayoral race in 1989 because of his stated opposition to the incinerator. Candidate Dinkins had promised to delay a decision on the incinerator project until 1993 and had won strong support among Brooklyn voters for this stand. His reversal on the issue in the fall of 1991 brought the mayor public condemnation from the Satmars, Latinos, and other incinerator opponents. Niederman told the *New York Times* on September 8, 1991, that "this plan repudiates everything that had been told to us by mayoral candidate Dinkins and suggests that cynical politics as usual is the engine driving this decision." Environmental groups expressed similar feelings of betrayal and were alarmed that the mayor's new, pro-incinerator stance appeared to be coupled with abandonment of the city's commitment to step up recycling. In November 1990 the Dinkins administration had frozen citywide recycling efforts, and now it appeared that trash incineration had replaced recycling as the centerpiece of the city's solid-waste management program. Further fueling suspicion over the decision was the fact that Dinkins's top deputy mayor, Norman Steisel, was widely viewed as Wall Street's representative in the administration. Steisel had been Koch's city sanitation commissioner when the incinerator project was first proposed.

In a show of political arrogance and foolishness, Dinkins did not inform the Williamsburg activists about his decision in advance. Instead, the UJO, NYPIRG, and El Puente learned of the city's action through a front-page story in the *New York Times*. The Dinkins bombshell was announced only two weeks prior to a New York state legislative joint hearing regarding the environmental impact on racial-minority and low-income communities.[6] The Brooklyn Navy Yard trash incinerator fit perfectly into the proceedings. When the Koch administration and its corporate allies had sought an incinerator site in the 1970s, the Brooklyn Navy Yard had seemed ideal. The city owned the land, and the site was not slated for gentrification or office development. Finally, and perhaps most important, the Navy Yard was located in the type of economically depressed minority community regularly subjected to environmental hazards.[7]

In response to Dinkins's announcement, Garden Acosta and Nieder-man held a joint press conference attacking the city's attempt to impose an environmental hazard on yet another minority, low-income commu-nity. Ludovic Blain III, chairman of the board of NYPIRG, placed the incinerator proposal in the context of the 1967 Kerner Commission report detailing the nation's movement toward a society of separate and unequal racial groups. The three groups' joint participation in a high-profile event solidified their unity in opposing the incinerator.

The press conference spurred a rush of grassroots activity against the project. In January 1992 a standing-room-only crowd of more than five hundred residents from the nearby Clinton Hill and Fort Greene neigh-borhoods attended a rally to support recycling and oppose the Navy Yard incinerator. Over the next several months, similar meetings were held around the city, including one in the heart of the predominantly African American Farragut housing projects, across the Navy Yard from Williamsburg. Religious leaders turned out in force, including an impassioned Reverend Mark Taylor of the Church of the Open Door. Taylor didn't mince his words: "These are issues of death. The issue cannot be separated from the gunshots in Farragut and Fort Greene Houses. It's like the issue of Rodney King's beating, and the issue of wanton violence. . . . I, too, am of the mind that if you elect someone who looks like you and talks like you, but doesn't vote like you—you need to think twice." Taylor's and many others' dedication to the issue would parallel and combine with the Williamsburg activists' efforts.[8]

As anti-incinerator pressure mounted from elected officials, environ-mental groups, community organizations, and residents of neighbor-hoods adjacent to the Brooklyn Navy Yard, city officials claimed they would take no position on the project until the city's comprehensive solid-waste management plan was presented. To ensure that the plan would exclude all proposed burn plants, the anti-incinerator coalition successfully pushed for legislation requiring prior approval of the solid-waste management plan by the city council. Such an approval process would not only transfer some decision-making authority away from the now pro-incinerator Dinkins administration but also create an opportu-nity to kill the project at last through city council rejection.

On March 23, 1992, a day prior to the city council's scheduled vote on the incinerator, Emily Lloyd, the mayor's sanitation commissioner, pledged to delay construction of the facility until 1996. Because the city had previously planned to begin building in 1994, Dinkins's decision to "cool it" on trash burning, as a headline in the *New York Daily News* put it, appeared to mark the beginning of the end of the incinerator proposal. The press focused on the political value of Dinkins's decision, noting that the mayor had removed an "explosive issue" from his 1993 reelection campaign.[9]

The anti-incinerator coalition did not stop the pressure, however. An April 1992 meeting brought more than one thousand residents to a neighborhood school to show unified opposition to the incinerator. Attendance was drawn equally from the Satmar and Latino communities. The particular school that hosted the event, PS 16, had been the subject of a bitter fight between El Puente and the Satmars in 1986. In that dispute, which focused on a wall erected to create an exclusive entrance for Hasidic girls in an overwhelmingly minority school, El Puente led a nearly monthlong school boycott and protested in front of the home of the Satmars' chief rabbi (not Niederman). The anti-incinerator event, as Garden Acosta noted, transformed PS 16 from a "symbol of segregation into a symbol of unity."[10]

Yet Dinkins failed to accept the prevailing assessment that killing the Brooklyn incinerator was to his political advantage. Instead, as part of a citywide deal to obtain the necessary approval of his solid-waste plan from the city council, Dinkins agreed to close down two smaller incinerators in other communities, upgrade a third, and increase citywide recycling in exchange for council votes to include the Williamsburg project in the plan.

The anti-incinerator coalition blasted the mayor's decision. On the eve of the city council vote on the waste management plan, activists brought nearly eight hundred children—Hasidic, Latino, and African American—to City Hall to urge the council to reject the mayor's plan. Rabbi Niederman told the crowd that "just because we are poor does not mean our children must breathe air made poisonous by garbage-burning incinerators." Luis Garden Acosta of El Puente focused on the pathbreaking coalition that had been formed between the often-warring groups, noting that "in our common air we have found our common ground. Emboldened by this special unity, we urge the council to reject the solid waste plan." The UJO, El Puente, and other groups had joined NYPIRG to create a "no burn" and "recycle first" alternative to the mayor's plan. Despite the coalition's effort, in August the council approved a solid-waste plan that included the incinerator project. The battle then shifted to the New York State Department of Environmental

Conservation (DEC), long criticized by environmentalists for simply rubber-stamping incinerator permit applications.

The Williamsburg coalition redirected its energies toward convincing Governor Mario Cuomo's administration to deny the necessary permits. Of central concern was the need to delay state issuance of the building permit until after November 15, 1992. That date was critical because the 1990 amendments to the federal Clean Air Act applied to projects whose permits were issued after this deadline. The amendments prohibited new sources of pollution in smog-plagued cities until pollution from other sources was reduced. New York City did not want construction of the Navy Yard incinerator conditioned on reduction of pollution elsewhere and was pressuring the Cuomo administration to act promptly to exempt the project from the amended Clean Air Act.

The anti-incinerator campaign thus needed to marshal all of its resources to defeat what *New York Newsday* aptly described as the city's "Race to Pollute."[11] The UJO, NYPIRG, and El Puente sought to increase their strength by creating a formal coalition called the Community Alliance for the Environment (CAFE). CAFE also included representatives of the nearby African American community of Fort Greene, among them the charismatic Reverend Taylor of the Church of the Open Door and Mildred Trudy of the community organization Crispus Attucks. Also joining were local environmental groups such as the Fort Greene/Clinton Hill Coalition for Clean Air and Williamsburg, Waterfront, the World (WWW).[12]

On October 2, 1992, CAFE learned that the state was planning to skip its normal bureaucratic procedures in order to ensure a ruling on the Williamsburg incinerator prior to November 15. The Department of Environmental Conservation made no secret of its plans, stating in a letter that it was concerned about meeting the Clean Air Act deadline. A DEC spokesperson further tipped the agency's hand, telling *Newsday,* "This thing has been going on for a long time. It's time to bring it to an end." The anti-incinerator coalition immediately seized on the agency's willingness to sidestep standard procedures for the benefit of the toxin-spewing project. Larry Shapiro of NYPIRG set the tone, calling the state's plan an "outrageous abuse of power." Rabbi Niederman described the state's fast-track timetable as "a conspiracy between the state and the city to rush a health hazard into the community."[13]

As anybody who has tried to gain support for controversial projects knows, it is a terrible mistake to allow process questions to emerge. People who may feel uncomfortable opposing a project on the merits can seize on procedural irregularities to justify opposition. The DEC thus opened up an entirely new front of controversy, and CAFE exploited it to the hilt. On October 29, 1992, CAFE and NYPIRG filed suit in U.S. District Court in Brooklyn to enjoin the state DEC from issuing the incinerator permits before the Clean Air Act amendments took effect on November 15. The suit condemned the state's aiding and abetting the city's "mad rush" to obtain the trash incinerator permit. Although the DEC spokesperson correctly pointed out that the permitting process for the incinerator had been in progress for nearly a decade, this fact was lost amidst the clamor created by the agency's effort to sneak in under the old Clean Air Act. Opponents described the fast-track process as a "railroad job," and the lawsuit specifically denounced DEC commissioner Thomas Jorling for "devastating the administrative review process for the purpose of adding more pollution to the environment."

The Latino-Hasidic-NYPIRG alliance thus succeeded in using a procedural irregularity to turn the history of the incinerator project on its head. A project commenced in the 1970s, whose permit process began in 1985 and whose original timetable called for completion by 1986, was understood in 1992 to have been "railroaded" through the process. Opponents hammered the state's chief environmental officer for making a mockery of his own administrative procedures and circumventing state and federal law in order to turn "the lungs of New Yorkers into toxic waste dumps."[14]

The pressure on Jorling was coupled with a campaign to persuade Governor Cuomo to intervene. Though wary of statewide environmental leaders, Cuomo knew how to count votes. Members of his administration also recognized that missing the November 15 deadline would not kill the incinerator project outright. In late October a DEC regional director, appropriately named Carol Ash, told the *Staten Island Advance* that the city's agreement to close two existing incinerators and reduce emissions at a third would readily satisfy the Clean Air Act requirement. The Cuomo administration could thus eliminate the stench of state procedural improprieties, keep New York City happy, and keep the Brooklyn incinerator alive by ignoring the November 15 deadline. And that is precisely what happened. On November 3, 1992, only days after the filing of CAFE's lawsuit, Jorling issued a two-sentence memo that effectively ensured that he would not issue his ruling before the more stringent federal rules went into effect. On December 23, 1992, however, the DEC's administrative law judge gave New York City what it sought by ruling that the more stringent Clean Air Act requirements did not apply to the Williamsburg incinerator.

The ruling catalyzed incinerator opposition. Continuing to implement a proactive strategy and keep incinerator supporters on the defensive, CAFE launched a new, multipronged attack. On December 26, only three days after the judge's ruling, the UJO's attorney announced that CAFE would file an administrative appeal and that one basis of the appeal would be newly discovered evidence that showed the proposed incinerator site sat atop the graves of Revolutionary War prisoners. The existence of the burial site had been documented in a Revolutionary War–era map of Brooklyn located in the New York Public Library. The map labeled the incinerator site "Prisoners Graves"; the dead were fighters for independence who died in British captivity.[15]

The need to protect the burial site as a piece of history raised yet another issue for incinerator backers to overcome. Although the Williamsburg activists used other tactics and strategies, the burial site issue demonstrated their boundless ingenuity and creativity. In May 1993 veterans and community residents marched to the Navy Yard and held a memorial for the Revolutionary War dead to raise public awareness of the city's plan to construct an incinerator over veterans' graves. Such groups as the Society of Old Brooklynites, the Wallabout Landmarks Preservation Committee, and the George P. Davis American Legion Post No. 116 sponsored the march. None had previously been publicly involved in anti-incinerator efforts. CAFE was also a sponsor but wisely made sure the other groups were the center of attention.[16]

While the alleged existence of the burial site never posed a major threat to the project, the issue expanded the anti-incinerator coalition. CAFE was constantly looking to include new and diverse constituencies. Although coalition politics would seem to reward ongoing openness to new allies, concerns over turf, control, and credit often forestall a coalition from broadening after its initial creation. Coalition expansion also requires an understanding of how to attract a potentially valuable new participant. Had CAFE used the discovery of the burial site as part of its own campaign, the issue would not have been more than a one-day news curiosity. By allowing control of the issue to remain with the groups most concerned about veterans and landmarks, CAFE both expanded the anti-incinerator base and made the burial site seem a serious obstacle to the project.

CAFE was also willing to work in concert with local and state elected officials. Although this may seem an obvious tactic in a campaign that included legislative strategies, many coalitions reject such alliances for fear of being either sold out or accused of selling out. The anti-incinerator coalition had nothing to fear on either front, because it represented what every politician respects most: a real electoral base. Officials such as Mayor Dinkins who betrayed the coalition lost future electoral support. The coalition's ability to obtain strong support from Republicans and Democrats, reformers and machine politicians, and urban and suburban legislators (even though the latter's constituents may never have visited Williamsburg) became critical to its success. The same tactical activism that led to the formation of the diverse anti-incinerator coalition created a broad legislative alliance that brought politicians of radically different styles and ideologies to the cause.

CAFE's chief strategic response to the administrative law judge's December 23 ruling was at last to hold the long march from Brooklyn to Manhattan that had been delayed by the Latino housing activists. More than a thousand people participated in the march across the Williamsburg Bridge. The marchers included Hasidim, Latinos, and African Americans, many of them carrying candles. Brooklyn-bound traffic on the bridge was snarled for forty minutes. The march, like the 1991 state hearing on environmental racism and the July 1992 rally prior to the city council vote on the solid-waste plan, highlighted the unity among the coalition's diverse groups. CAFE used its public comments at the pre-march rally to accentuate the community's united front. Niederman of the UJO declared, "We are proud to have all of our communities together to demonstrate a health hazard in our community. We are here united and we will march united." Alexei Torres, a CAFE spokesman from the Latino community, noted that the march was occurring "on the eve of Martin Luther King's birthday. We are marching for unity and in light of the racial tension that has a hold of the city, we will demonstrate, different ethnic groups together, in a show of outrage." The *New York Times*'s photo of the march was captioned "Environmental Concerns Unite a Neighborhood."[17]

Less creative activists would have used the march to focus solely on the environmental hazard of building a fifty-five-story incinerator adjacent to a residential neighborhood, and the media coverage would have interested only those New Yorkers concerned about environmental issues. CAFE, however, used the march for a larger purpose: what was really on display was a show of racial unity. Martin Luther King's dream has not been realized in most of the United States, but it was being transformed into reality in Williamsburg. A community striving to realize King's dream, the marchers seemed to say, must not be torn asunder by a $550 million trash incinerator. CAFE's message had particular resonance in New York City, a once-famed melting pot now being unpleasantly transformed by racial segregation and ethnic warfare. All New Yorkers, even those totally uninterested in the incinerator issue, could find in the march a sense of hope and a model for the future of the city and perhaps even the nation. The coalition put Governor Cuomo, a son of poor Italian immigrants, in a difficult position: building the incinerator would mean wrecking a multiracial, multiethnic, unified community. It is no wonder that the Cuomo administration continued to take its time before making a decision.

Following CAFE's January appeal of the administrative law judge's ruling, several months passed without a final decision from DEC chief Jorling on the Navy Yard permits. CAFE used this period to press publicly for a state hearing in Williamsburg prior to the permit decision. Although the DEC judge found no need for a new hearing, Luis Garden Acosta noted that "no other community in New York State has had a permit process for a facility like this without a public hearing." The last hearing on the incinerator had been held in 1987, but it had not taken place in Williamsburg. CAFE wanted Jorling to hold and attend a meeting in the affected community. This new demand had two strategic advantages. First, it brought to the forefront another process defect surrounding the incinerator: public officials and individual citizens could rightfully question why the state's top environmental officer would refuse to come to Williamsburg to hear residents' concerns firsthand. Second, although Jorling sought to eliminate this controversy by actually holding and attending a Williamsburg meeting, the event certainly would receive statewide media attention. There is nothing the media like more than footage of a state official trying to justify his or her conduct before a hostile and disbelieving local audience. Jorling would have greater difficulty ruling for the incinerator if Williamsburg's fierce opposition received great statewide publicity.[18]

In addition to targeting Jorling's refusal to hear the community's concerns, CAFE used the period prior to his ruling to press for state legislation mandating that the 1990 Clean Air Act amendments apply to the Williamsburg incinerator. After complex negotiations between Cuomo and legislative leaders, a compromise agreement was reached on July 7, 1993, that only partially exempted the Williamsburg incinerator from the new federal rules. The agreement also required the city to study the possible health effects of the project on the surrounding neighborhoods. The legislative compromise meant that a state decision on the permit was no longer an imminent possibility. The November 1993 mayoral election was approaching, giving CAFE a new political opening. Dinkins had drawn broad support from Williamsburg and surrounding neighborhoods in 1989 for his pledge to halt progress on the project until 1993. His 1989 opponent, Rudy Giuliani, had strongly supported the incinerator. When asked in 1989 what he thought would happen if the project were not built, Giuliani had replied, "The dirtiest city in America would become dirtier."[19]

By 1993 Dinkins had already positioned himself as pro-incinerator. The UJO remained bitter over Dinkins's betrayal on the issue, and the mayor's mishandling of a conflict between African Americans and Hasidim in Crown Heights left the Williamsburg Satmars aligned with Giuliani. The Latino and African American residents surrounding the Navy Yard also were angered by Dinkins's incinerator switch—and they were a constituency the mayor had to have in order to win reelection. Partly in an effort to weaken the mayor's pro-incinerator stance, a Fort Greene community organization invited Dinkins to a meeting scheduled for September 21. After he agreed to attend, the mayor's staff learned that most of those likely to be present wanted to discuss the incinerator. On the 21st, as more than two hundred people awaited the mayor's arrival, a call to his campaign office revealed that Dinkins would not be appearing. His absence angered the crowd. Dinkins thus sacrificed his political allies for the construction of a burn plant. It did not speak well for the mayor's reelection hopes that he was afraid to appear in front of his natural base.[20]

Giuliani had lost in a very close election in 1989, and a change in his stance on the incinerator could enable him to make inroads into the mayor's base. He therefore switched from ardent supporter of the incinerator to skeptic; his favorite phrase was that the city should retain incineration as a "last option" in case recycling and other alternatives failed to cope adequately with the city's waste. Two weeks before the election, Giuliani moved even further toward an anti-incinerator stance, telling a Brooklyn community newspaper that as mayor he would launch "a massive recycling program so there isn't a need to build a new incinerator."[21]

Giuliani prevailed in the 1993 mayor's race by only 55,000 votes. Although Dinkins's switch on the incinerator was not central to his defeat, the Hasidim's move to Giuliani, similar defections by Latinos and even African Americans, and a lower African American voter turnout affected the outcome. All of these constituencies had opposed Dinkins on the incinerator issue.

After taking office in January 1994, Giuliani seemed willing to reconsider the need for the entire project. He asked his sanitation department to study which would be more cost-effective: to haul garbage to out-of-state landfills or to build the $550 million incinerator. Only a month after his request for a study, however, Giuliani appeared to reverse himself. He proposed major cuts in city recycling programs and asked the city council to scale back its recycling goals. Giuliani also decided to continue to seek a state permit for the Navy Yard incinerator. A mayor who had begun his term viewing incineration as a "last hope" and "an insurance policy" if all else failed now appeared to have adopted the agenda of his predecessor.[22]

Rosie Baerga, a CAFE leader, accused the mayor of having pulled a "snow job" to mask his pro-incinerator position. Other factors were also at work. *New York Newsday* reported on March 8, 1994, that Wheelabrator, the incinerator developer, had assembled an all-star team of lobbyists to obtain state and city go-aheads on the project. Wheelabrator's lobbying team included a former state assembly Speaker, a law firm with close ties to the Giuliani administration, and a political consultant to the top Republican on the state legislative solid-waste commission. While the hiring of this team represented a new, aggressive approach on the part of incinerator proponents, CAFE was finding it easier to win enthusiastic backing from liberals and African Americans who had hedged on their anti-incinerator position while Dinkins was mayor.[23]

While Giuliani equivocated, CAFE maintained its focus on the DEC's pending decision on the permit. CAFE got a boost when a hot new issue surfaced: samples taken from the Navy Yard revealed high levels of toxic chemicals in soil and groundwater. The presence of such toxic waste had apparently gone undetected for the almost fifteen years since planning had begun for the incinerator. CAFE and its allies reacted to this discovery with renewed attacks on both the permitting process and the incinerator plan itself. Luis Garden Acosta described the Navy Yard as "Williamsburg's Love Canal." He also attacked incinerator proponents as people unconcerned about the interests of children and families and "locked into a plan without the courage to say 'Enough!'" Rabbi Niederman echoed Garden Acosta when he observed, "There are so many unknowns in the process and at the site that it requires us to dig in and not leave even one stone unturned." Reverend Mark Taylor led a highly effective news conference that included Niederman, Delia

Montalvo of El Puente, NYPIRG delegates, and a host of other community leaders. Taylor called for an end to environmental racism at the Navy Yard, declaring, "Community residents are being shut out and ignored by the process."[24]

Garden Acosta's and Niederman's responses to the toxic discovery illustrate coalitions' capacity to use the one-two punch. NYPIRG also responded publicly, demonstrating that three separate constituencies reflecting broad and diverse support could share a unified position. By contrast, when organizations not working in coalition are asked to comment on an event, each organization is likely to address its own discrete issues, advancing no unified strategic position. Readers of an article containing these widely varying responses could well conclude that the groups are out of sync or perhaps even in conflict. Groups not working in coalition frequently leave such an impression; coordinating a press response requires the type of mutual discussion and analysis that typified CAFE.

The discovery of toxic waste required the state DEC to investigate whether the Navy Yard should be assigned to the EPA's Superfund program. Such a designation would delay the project for at least a decade and likely kill it. The discovery also started a debate over why the toxic chemicals had not previously been discovered, even though the historic use of the Navy Yard for shipping made the presence of toxic chemicals likely. In April 1994, CAFE found out that the New York City sanitation department had learned of the toxic contamination of the incinerator site in 1988, but had failed to inform the state agency considering approval of the project. Charges of a cover-up by incinerator advocates thus emerged. Mayor Giuliani ordered an investigation to determine why the report was not forwarded to the state, and the attorney general looked at whether any laws had been broken. Although the DEC now insisted that no construction permit would be issued until an investigation and cleanup at the site was completed, it continued its permitting process and, amid all of these new concerns, preliminarily approved the city's pollution trade-off application. Perhaps Wheelabrator was actually getting something from its high-priced lobbyists. However, the preliminary approval became clouded by the discovery in late April that the DEC's regional counsel had reviewed the city's application while seeking employment with the city. Questions were raised over possible bias, as the counsel knew his prospective employer desperately wanted DEC approval of the application under his authority.

As the incinerator plan entered its second decade, it confronted a dizzying array of social, political, and economic obstacles. On June 13, 1995, CAFE, New York City public advocate Mark Green, and more than one hundred health care professionals launched a drive to force the city to prepare a new environmental impact statement on the incinerator. Although Mayor Giuliani rejected the request, it was only a matter of time before the burial ground at the Navy Yard symbolically included the incinerator.

Victory and the Navy Yard's Revival

The coalition of "unusual suspects" led by Williamsburg's once-warring Latino and Hasidim communities ultimately defeated the incinerator project. To understand the magnitude of this achievement, consider the massive gentrification and development boom that swept New York City through most of the 1980s. The Koch administration was accustomed to getting what it wanted, particularly when its opponents were predominantly low-income, minority people. Wall Street also expected to obtain what it desired (in this case, the lucrative bond contracts that were part of the incinerator project); Felix Rohatyn and his colleagues were not accustomed to being stymied by the likes of Williamsburg's Latinos and Hasidim.

In addition to surmounting Wall Street, the anti-incinerator coalition had to overcome nearly fanatical pro-incinerator editorializing from the vaunted *New York Times*. It is often remarked that the *Times'* editorial policy becomes more progressive the further the issue lies from the paper's New York City headquarters. Readers of its daily national edition often miss its pro–Wall Street, pro-development, anti-rent-control local editorial slant. Support for the incinerator became a litmus test for political candidates seeking the coveted *New York Times* endorsement. The perceived objectivity of the *Times*—despite its inflammatory anti-incinerator comments—gave politicians the ability to claim they supported the incinerator "on the merits" rather than because of the campaign funds donated by pro-incinerator forces.

The *Times*'s emphasis on politicians' position on the incinerator became apparent when Elizabeth Holtzman sought the Democratic nomination for the U.S. Senate in 1992. Holtzman, a vocal incinerator opponent, had spent four years in Congress before serving as Brooklyn district attorney and then New York City comptroller. With her Senate bid, however, she became a victim of the *Times*'s pro-incinerator zealotry. In a September 13, 1992, editorial evaluating candidates for the Senate primary, the *Times,* after briefly noting Holtzman's expertise and proven track record, stated:

> Still, legislative effectiveness also depends on a capacity for conciliation, not a strong point for Ms. Holtzman, who sometimes seems to prize the image of a brave, lonely figure standing up for principle even when she has to sacrifice principle to make her stand. A notable example is her position on the decision to build a new incinerator in Brooklyn.
>
> There is no choice: even if the city takes all the other steps needed to manage its waste, the incinerator must be built. Every responsible observer accepts that—yet even now Ms. Holtzman opposes it with distortions that play to the exaggerated fears of New Yorkers who need facts, not demagogy.

The coalition was thus opposed by Wall Street, the Koch and Dinkins administrations, and New York's most prestigious media outlet. Governor Cuomo, himself allied with Wall Street and the *Times,* was more an opponent than a friend of the coalition. Cuomo's environmental appointees strongly supported the incinerator and kept the project alive well after its existence could be rationally justified. New York State's self-proclaimed liberal fighter for the common person could have killed the project at any time; yet his administration would have promptly approved the plan if not for the fear of political reprisals from incinerator opponents.

With the influential business, legal, government, media, and construction union interests all behind it, the Brooklyn Navy Yard incinerator project must have seemed a walkover. The idea of Williamsburg's Spanish-speaking Latinos allying with their neighborhood enemy, the Satmars, initially appeared unimaginable, and the project sponsors likely gave little thought to the possibility that Williamsburg's residents could defeat their plan.

Many people played critical roles in the anti-incinerator campaign, but the entire effort would not have happened without the tactical activism of the unlikely duo of Rabbi David Niederman and Luis Garden Acosta. Both men risked their standing in their respective communities by working together for a common goal. Each leader had the courage and wisdom to recognize the benefits to his community of forging a coalition.

Niederman viewed the alliance with Latinos against the incinerator as the beginning of "a new era for the community." Garden Acosta in 1991 saw El Puente as a vehicle for bridge building with the Satmars and was willing to make a leap of faith to create a new, positive relationship with his community's longtime adversaries. Neither the Latinos nor the Hasidim were planning on leaving Williamsburg, and both recognized community war as a very real and mutually destructive possibility. This danger motivated leaders of both communities to improve their relations. Moreover, both communities faced the same threat from the incinerator: failure to block it would leave future generations of Hasidim and Latinos alike forever menaced by a pollution-spewing furnace. As Garden Acosta observed, "We all breathe the same air." This long-term commitment to a particular piece of land made possible a partnership that otherwise may not have occurred.[25]

The Williamsburg partnership illustrates how progressive groups can overcome their suspicions of coalitions, as voiced by IAF-Texas and others. First, because El Puente and the UJO each had a true constituency base, neither group could be accused of using the other's base for its own ends. Second, the coalition was able to forestall each group's concerns that it would not get its fair share of credit for the coalition's success. This was no simple task, because CAFE included many organizations and individuals in addition to the three central participants. But a mutual interest was at work: defeat of the incinerator would redound to the individual credit of all participating organizations. Rabbi Niederman and Garden Acosta made sure that their constituencies came to view the coalition as a partnership whose members shared responsibility for every gain or loss. All participants displayed a willingness to subordinate individual glory to the broader goal.

The makeup of the Williamsburg coalition rendered moot the issue of who would win credit for the successful campaign. CAFE was a temporary entity, created as a vehicle through which UJO, El Puente, NYPIRG, and other groups could oppose the incinerator. For the same reason, the success of CAFE never had the potential to negatively impact any of the organizations' funding streams. The credibility of each group was only enhanced by participation in the coalition.

If we assume that even those organizations most suspicious of coalition participation would agree to the benefits of the Williamsburg alliance, we must wonder why similar efforts are so rarely pursued. The greatest factor is the tendency among social change activists and organizations to wear ideological blinders when it comes to coalition building. Organizations become so committed to working with their cultural and political allies that they fail to recognize opportunities to make common cause with groups that have conflicting agendas. In retrospect, David Niederman's overture to El Puente and Garden Acosta's positive response seem obvious tactical moves. Experienced activists in either community could readily foresee that public interest in the incinerator issue would jump dramatically through formation of such an alliance; Niederman's decision to attend the Radiac meeting was such a slam dunk that if he had not initiated the contact, it would have happened anyway . . . right?

Wrong. Before Niederman's overture to El Puente, his UJO constituency often viewed Latino neighbors as violent, anti-Semitic, and fervent in their desire to drive the Hasidim out of Williamsburg. The very idea of trusting Latinos was absurd to many Hasidim. Niederman's simplest and easiest decision would have been not even to consider working with Luis Garden Acosta and the Latino community. He could have echoed the many committed activists who view an opponent on one issue as the enemy on *all* issues. But Niederman placed his constituency's true interests over a desire for ideological conformity. He told Garden Acosta during their first meeting that he saw the incinerator fight as "a beginning, a bridge to bring the two communities together." Working together on a common issue could serve to dispel distrust and improve chances for defeating the project. Although Garden Acosta considered this a "clear act of courage," Niederman saw it simply as a necessary step for groups facing the same environmental hazards. The UJO never conditioned its alliance on either group's relinquishing its demands on housing, jobs, or school issues, so Niederman understood that his overture might be only a limited proposition. It is a tribute to Niederman's tactical activism that a decision that seemed shocking at the time appears logical, obvious, and even inevitable in retrospect.[26]

Luis Garden Acosta faced even greater risks in choosing to work with the UJO. His constituency seethed over the Hasidim's ability to use their political skills, bloc voting, and mass mobilizations to extract what the Latinos considered (with some justification) a disproportionately high share of public resources. They were not about to work in partnership with their enemy. After Garden Acosta and Rabbi Niederman shared leadership of the May 1991 march through the streets of the Latino community, many concluded that El Puente had capitulated to the Hasidim. People passing Garden Acosta in the street asked him to explain his rationale for working with the Satmars. In response, a lesser leader or strategist might have sought to elevate his or her community status by publicly snubbing the UJO. Alternatively, Garden Acosta might have offered to work only with NYPIRG on the incinerator issue. Instead, he stood firm behind his belief that an alliance with the Hasidim was in the best interests of both communities. After years of feeling that his community spent too much time acting defensively, Garden Acosta saw the alliance with the Satmars as a proactive strategy to move Latinos into a more positive relationship with their longtime adversaries.[27]

Thanks to the defeat of the incinerator, the Brooklyn Navy Yard is now a remarkable success. In 2007 it became a three-hundred-acre industrial park, and now has over forty buildings, 4 million square feet of leasable space, over 240 tenants, and more than five thousand workers. It is home to such diverse businesses as movie studios, furniture manufacturers, ship repairers, architectural designers, electronics distributors, and jewelers. One of its buildings houses an exhibition space on the Navy Yard's illustrious nearly 400-year history.

FORGING COALITIONS WITH IDEOLOGICAL OPPONENTS

The Williamsburg alliance shows how two groups with valid reasons for distrusting each other can unite to stop a harmful project. But activists can also move proactively to unite with traditional adversaries to achieve a common goal. I tried this approach to coalition politics when I was seeking support for a charter amendment on San Francisco's November 1994 ballot. The initiative sought to improve housing-code enforcement by removing this responsibility from a bureaucracy hostile to tenants and transferring it to a citizens' commission. Low-income tenant advocates supported the measure because they were angry about the city's lax approach to substandard housing, whereas landlords and builders were persuaded to join us on fiscal grounds—they had to pay fees to fund the city housing- and building-code administration. All three groups had an incentive to support a measure that would impose citizen budget oversight and were angry that fees were being spent on new, highly paid administrators while staff serving the public was cut. Landlords, the Tenderloin Housing Clinic's longtime adversaries, had no problem agreeing with our position that eliminating substandard housing should be the city's top priority; their objection was to the city's costly and misplaced focus on inspecting housing that was not substandard. The builders had their own list of bureaucratic grievances, but they agreed that slumlords must be the prime target of city action. The resulting coalition was widely perceived as the most unusual and unexpected in recent city history.

Some people were amazed that landlords would agree to work with me on any issue, particularly something as major as a charter amendment affecting control of a department with a $19 million annual budget. A few tenant activists argued that if landlords supported our measure, it must not be as progressive as we claimed; others thought there must be a pro-landlord loophole in the initiative, though they knew I was the sole author. These attitudes reflected a common misunderstanding of the strategy necessary for achieving significant social change. Activists should not pursue an agenda based on what one's adversary will oppose; the goal is to achieve what one's own constituency needs. The first approach not only is actively defensive and reactive but also prevents the accomplishment of goals that may be obtainable only through a coalition with longtime adversaries.

The tenants' most active partner in the initiative campaign was a group of Irish American residential builders. Though not adversaries of low-income tenant advocates, they were perceived at the time as being among the city's more conservative constituencies. The Tenderloin Housing Clinic was accused of making a deal with the devil; some people felt it was better for low-income children to continue to live in heatless, rodent-infested apartments than for a reputable progressive activist like me to give credibility to the builders. It was presumed that our alliance with builders was based on political considerations other than our constituencies' mutual self-interest. Advocates for low-income tenants, the homeless, and other victims of lax code enforcement understood the need to make strategic alliances and strongly supported our broad, coalitional approach. The charter amendment passed in the election of November 1994, ending years of hostile bureaucratic control of city housing-code enforcement. Since 1995, San Francisco housing-code enforcement has gone from an unworkable process to a model that Los Angeles and other cities across the nation have sought to replicate. Despite such success, tactical activists willing to work with traditional adversaries to achieve their constituencies' goals should expect to be criticized, regardless of the results, by some of their usual allies.

THE LIMITS OF COALITION POLITICS

Coalition activism has its risks. The most obvious scenario is an irreconcilable dispute over strategy. I was involved in a coalition in 2002 to stop my alma mater Hastings Law School from building an eight-story, 885-spot parking garage on the border of the Tenderloin neighborhood. My organization and its close allies saw this as demanding a "by all means necessary" approach to stop the project; so we organized a plan to shut down the Hastings school board meeting prior to its scheduled vote to approve the project. I gave the signal during my testimony before the board for the disruption of the meeting to begin, and a number of us, including our district member of the Board of Supervisors, were arrested. The board later reconvened and approved the project.

That afternoon I called our state senator, the legendary John L. Burton, and told him what had happened at the board meeting. He immediately sent a letter to Hastings telling the board to either reverse its vote or lose all of the school's state funding (which he had the political clout to do). Before the contents of his letter were made public, some of our more moderate coalition allies attacked me personally for engaging in such disruptive conduct. They even got a *San Francisco Chronicle* columnist to write that we had sacrificed our moral high ground with our tactics and that they had backfired (which made no sense since the board was going to approve the project absent the disruption). Once Burton's letter went public, Hastings reversed its vote, and it became clear to our coalition critics that the tactics they denounced had worked. The garage ultimately was built at half the size originally planned, spurred 172 new low-cost housing units nearby and became a neighborhood asset rather than a liability.

Coalitions also can fail when the participating organizations have different standards for success. Given that coalitions among ideological opposites are often alliances of convenience, the coalition's opponents often can undermine unity by neutralizing one or more members. Such members are often chided for having been "bought off," though it may simply be a case of groups honestly disagreeing about what constitutes victory. For example, a San Francisco coalition of activists and social service groups seeking additional city money to address homelessness in the early 1980s fell apart when certain of the more traditional social service providers became satisfied with the mayor's response to their demands. Some of this satisfaction no doubt was caused by the mayor's decision to fund homeless programs operated by coalition members; other groups simply had different expectations of what constituted a reasonable response to the crisis.

An equally common scenario concerns diverse coalitions whose groups have wide-ranging demands. If a group seeking traffic mitigations for a new development wins this commitment, is it required to devote resources to pressing for the coalition's nontransit goals? Or to spend political chits on nontransit issues in the name of coalition solidarity? While it may strike some as selfish for a coalition member to withdraw resources once its specific priorities are met, the question can get cloudier when that particular coalition member may have far greater clout with political decision makers; some will question whether it should use this clout to pressure political allies over some other group's priority.

As with any effective tactic, coalition politics can become more hindrance than help if improperly used. For example, social change activists regularly attend meetings of diverse groups to discuss pressing issues. Invariably, someone at the meeting suggests that "we" need to "bring in" other groups before deciding how to respond to a particular issue. The development of a strategy for the problem immediately ceases as people go around the room suggesting who should be invited to the next meeting. Someone may suggest that further discussion or decision be deferred until the subsequent meeting, leaving activists frustrated at having wasted their time. Some of these activists may skip the next meeting, preferring to move forward in solving the problem rather than make a resolution subject to the approval and timetable of other groups.

Regrettably, coalitions provide a perfect forum for activists and organizations that prefer talking about problems to initiating a prompt and effective response. Action-oriented groups often find themselves penned in by the coalition approach and quickly realize that some, if not most, of the groups involved do not bring anything of political value to the table. In such instances, activists would be foolish to continue working through the coalition format, because the process frustrates rather than advances social change. Tactical activists should accept the risk of being attacked for refusing to work in coalitions rather than sacrifice their constituencies' agendas. It may be in a group's interest to defer substantive discussions until a key constituency can be brought into the process. Too often, however, delay occurs in order to round up the *usual* suspects rather than to round up groups whose diversity may change the political calculus and help ensure victory.

Coalitions also become problematic when the decision-making process grows unnecessarily cumbersome. For example, if a board of directors must approve all of the organization's positions on coalition issues, this effectively prevents the coalition from making the immediate response to events that is often necessary. Activists can respond to the approval problem either by avoiding coalitions with groups that have impractical decision-making procedures or by moving forward in their own name rather than the coalition's.

Even when all groups accept the tactical benefit of forming a coalition, agree on a set of demands, and resolve issues of decision making, there remains the problem that many nonprofit social change groups believe they can secure foundation funding only by winning victories on their own. This belief not only leads organizations to choose smaller, more winnable fights, but makes groups reluctant to engage in coalitions in which others can also take credit for success. Fortunately, the UJO and El Puente in Williamsburg were not concerned about who got credit for defeating the incinerator. Both Niederman and Garden Acosta understood, as the coalition's Reverend Mark Taylor put it, that "you can't pursue real social justice by only picking small and winnable fights." As progressive support alone is usually inadequate for winning major campaigns, creating diverse coalitions is increasingly essential to success.[28]

4

Ballot Initiatives

The Rules of the Game

On December 5, 2011, California Democratic Party chair John L. Burton appeared on Jon Stewart's *The Daily Show* to denounce the state's initiative process as "a tool of the special interests to screw the people." Many agreed. California's public services have never recovered from Prop 13's passage in 1978, and voters have approved measures promoting race discrimination (Prop 14, 1964), barring affirmative action (Prop 209, 1996), and voiding California's marriage equality law (Prop 8, 2008). Burton's progressive leadership of the state legislature ended in 2004 when a 1990 voter-approved term limit initiative forced him to leave office; passage of the measure greatly boosted lobbyists' power in state politics.

Because the side spending the most money on initiatives usually wins, the initiative process has clearly strayed far from its roots. Along with the referendum and the recall, social reformers enacted the initiative process at the turn of the twentieth century to curtail wealthy interests' growing control of political institutions. All three measures were designed to regain public control over government by allowing "the people" to legislate directly (the initiative), overturn laws they did not like (the referendum), and remove officeholders who were betraying the public good (the recall). The West Coast led this populist approach. Oregon adopted the initiative process in 1902, and California followed in 1911 as part of the campaign platform of its Progressive Party governor, Hiram Johnson. Nearly half of the states now allow ballot initiatives.

California has been the national trendsetter for statewide initiatives. The nationwide "taxpayer revolt" began with California's Proposition 13 in 1978 and spread as far east as Massachusetts, which passed the less drastic Proposition 2 1/2. California's approval of a term-limits initiative in 1990 made the concept a staple of state ballots throughout the country. California even set the pace with anti-gay ballot measures when it voted, as early as 1978, on the Briggs initiative, which would have barred gays and lesbians from teaching in public schools. "A populist stick has become a business sledgehammer," one observer wrote; another said that Hiram Johnson "would turn over in his grave if he saw how special interests have taken over the initiative process."[1]

But so long as initiatives are an available political strategy, activists must understand how to use them to achieve their goals. Activists also must do a better job in opposing hostile ballot measures, avoiding the consequences that have harmed California and other states. Ballot measures are another strategy in the activist's proactive toolbox; if effectively used, they can put conservatives on the defensive, forcing them to divert resources from pursuing their own goals.

THE FIVE RULES OF PROGRESSIVE INITIATIVES

Rule 1: There Is No Other Way

The first rule for progressive ballot initiatives is to examine alternative approaches to achieving the measure's goal. Progressive ballot measures are typically difficult to pass. Initiative campaigns are costly and time consuming, often requiring activists and organizations to put other issues on hold during the several months leading up to Election Day. It simply makes no sense to try to pass an initiative if its objective can be accomplished through the legislative process, direct action, or other less daunting means. Most progressive ballot measures have satisfied this test; in fact, progressives are more likely to err on the other side, investing too much time in noninitiative strategies unlikely to achieve their goal.

For example, San Francisco children's advocates spent three years creating annual "children's budgets" that showed how city funds could be redirected to more effectively serve kids. Despite large public turnouts at budget meetings and support from city department heads, the mayor continually failed to include the children's budget in the city's final overall budget. Children's advocates finally took the measure to the ballot in 1991, and San Francisco became the nation's first city to guarantee annual increases in funding for children's services in its annual budget. After three years of frustrating attempts to work "through the system," one children's leader concluded that going straight for the ballot might be the movement's best strategy.[2]

Delay in going to the ballot can have more severe consequences. After California governor Gray Davis was recalled from office in 2003 over the state's massive budget deficit, incoming Republican governor Arnold Schwarzenegger refused to put a tax increase measure on the ballot. Instead of seizing the initiative and putting their own revenue measure before voters, progressives in this very blue state also failed to act. They did not put a tax initiative on the ballot even when huge Democratic turnouts were projected for both the 2008 and the 2010 November elections. Democrats finally put a tax increase (Prop 30) on the November 2012 ballot, after nearly a decade of draconian cuts to public services and steep college tuition hikes. Given the chance to raise taxes, voters passed a $6 billion annual tax increase by a 54 to 46 percent margin.

Rule 2: Appeal to Voters' Self-Interest

Successful initiatives also require that a significant portion of the electorate view its passage as in its own self-interest. As much as social change activists may decry American society's emphasis on individualism and self-interest, most Americans espouse these values. Noted organizer Saul Alinsky made this point when he said, "Political realists see the world as it is: an arena of power politics moved primarily by perceived immediate self-interest, where morality is rhetorical rationale for expedient action and self-interest."[3]

By contrast, social change organizations disproportionately include people *not* motivated by economic or personal self-interest. As a result, their ballot measures, legislative campaigns, and direct action struggles often ask the public to act not out of self-interest but rather out of concern for "good government" or "fairness." Although many issues cannot be framed as in the self-interest of a major segment of the public, those lacking a personal stake in the outcome of an initiative are more likely to be swayed by misleading opposition commercials and mailers. As a result, initiatives lacking the requisite self-interest component typically fail, increasing progressive cynicism about the initiative process.

The infamous Proposition 13 of 1978, which launched a nationwide anti-tax revolt that has yet to subside, won because it offered a majority of the electorate a reduction in property taxes. The campaign against Proposition 13 focused on how lost tax revenue would negatively impact schools, social services, and the public infrastructure. This noteworthy and altruistic "Do what is good for society" theme could not overcome individuals' desire for lower property taxes. More than thirty years later, all the fears raised by opponents of Proposition 13 have proven correct. California's spending on its schools, social services, and once-top-notch infrastructure has now dipped close to the notoriously low levels of Mississippi. Nevertheless, the self-interest motivation remains so strong that polls show continued support for Proposition 13, and no ballot initiative to overturn its core provisions has arisen.

Many social change activists responded to Proposition 13 by crafting progressive initiatives appealing to the same philosophical motivation. Proposition 13's passage in 1978 immediately prompted action from tenants, who had been promised during the campaign that their landlords' property-tax savings would be passed on to them in the form of lower rents. When tenants failed to receive the promised benefits, they used local ballot initiatives to enact rent controls in Berkeley, Santa Monica, and West Hollywood. Other cities, such as San Francisco, enacted weak forms of rent control to preempt stronger ballot measures planned by tenant organizations. Although real estate interests consistently spent millions in local races to defeat rent control, the ad campaigns such expenditures bought failed to convince tenants to vote against their direct financial self-interest.

The self-interest motivation explains why measures raising the state's minimum wage have easily passed even in politically moderate states like Florida (71% approved a 2004 measure) and Missouri (76% in 2006). Initiatives raising local minimum wages also prevail. Of course, the self-interest motivation has a downside. Proponents of tax-slashing measures win approval by promising to "give money back to taxpayers." Savvy opposition campaigns turn the self-interest theme against such measures by highlighting how returning tax money to taxpayers actually *takes* it from schools, public transportation, police and fire protection, and other public services that offer a better deal for taxpayers. And California governor Jerry Brown showed with Prop 30 in 2012 that appealing to voters' self-interest in receiving such services can also be used affirmatively to pass tax increase measures.

Rule 3: Keep It Simple

Lack of simplicity is the fatal flaw in many progressive ballot initiatives. Activists often create "Christmas tree" measures designed to achieve wide-ranging goals. But measures that try to solve too many problems at once run into problems. They cannot be explained to voters in one sentence, and opponents can defeat them by spreading confusion without even addressing the merits. Attempts to remedy multiple social problems with one measure resemble a football team that, having fallen three touchdowns behind, tries to catch up by throwing long passes into the end zone on every play. This tactic doesn't work in sports, and it doesn't work in achieving social change.

Many progressives were surprised when Proposition 128, the Big Green initiative, on California's November 1990 ballot failed by a large margin. Environmentalists assumed that huge public support for the twentieth anniversary of Earth Day earlier that year would guarantee victory for any environmental measure. The initiative's authors, who included the state's leading environmental groups and longtime activist and state legislator Tom Hayden, must have believed likewise, because the Big Green initiative was a multifaceted measure seeking valuable but entirely diverse environmental goals. Big Green included provisions to regulate pesticide use to protect food and agricultural workers; phase out chemicals that potentially depleted the ozone layer; reduce emissions of gases contributing to global warming; limit oil and gas drilling in ocean waters; require oil-spill prevention plans; establish water-quality criteria; create an elective office of environmental advocate with the power to enforce all state environmental and public health laws; and issue $300 million in bonds to fund the acquisition of ancient redwood forests and another $40 million for environmental research.

The initiative was intended to address the self-interest of environmentalists in diverse fields, but Big Green's Christmas tree approach allowed opponents to argue that the thirty-nine-page, 16,000-word measure tried to do too much. Opponents argued that each of its provisions should be debated and voted on separately, and that voters could oppose the measure on these grounds without conflicting with their self-image as pro-environment.[4]

The need to keep things simple does not mean that an initiative's language cannot be complex. As long as the measure can be explained in one sentence, most voters will not need to review the text carefully. In 1986 Tom Hayden sponsored an environmental initiative, the Safe

Drinking Water and Toxic Enforcement Act (Proposition 165), that was as textually complicated as could be. Yet its message was simple: vote yes for protections against toxics. Had Proposition 165 also included provisions to create a state toxics commissioner or issue environmental bonds, à la Big Green, it would likely have gone down to defeat. California's historic and successful Coastal Protection Act of 1972 was another textually complex, big-picture initiative whose message—protect our coast—could easily be explained in a sentence.

Keeping it simple has another advantage: forestalling opposition attacks. The easiest way to defeat an initiative is to focus on its most controversial point. My favorite example comes from the opposition to a school voucher initiative on California's November 1993 ballot. Sponsored by conservative interests, the complex measure included a provision allowing public financing for schools operated by religious sects, including witches. With the assistance of cooperative members of the Wicca cult, opponents of the voucher initiative pointed out that it allowed practicing witches to open schools with taxpayer money. Few people knew how many witches operated private schools in California, but voters had to oppose the voucher initiative to ensure that public funds were not spent on such schools. Voucher proponents included many controversial features in their measure, ensuring that even voters unhappy with public schools would reject the initiative.

Rule 4: Create the Initiative through Due Process

Successful progressive initiatives must also be developed through due process. Is the initiative the project of a single wealthy donor? Has it been developed by only a small portion of an impacted constituency? If the answer to either is yes, the initiative faces an uphill battle unless other key constituencies decide to strongly back it. Consider two examples.

Hollywood producer Stephen L. Bing spent $49.5 million of the nearly $62 million total campaign budget to support Prop 87, a 2006 California initiative to impose a severance tax on California oil production. The measure would raise $4 billion for alternative energy programs. California needed the revenue from an oil severance tax, and Bing deserves credit for pursuing a popular progressive goal. But passing an oil severance tax would have required years of grassroots organizing prior to placing an initiative on the ballot, because the measure was guaranteed to provoke a massive oil company–funded opposition campaign. Such organizing did not precede Bing's measure, and

Prop 87 never developed the ground campaign necessary to win. Oil companies and their allies predictably spent an estimated $100 million in defeating Prop 87 by a nearly 10 percent margin.

Rob McKay, a progressive philanthropist from San Francisco and heir to the Taco Bell chain, spent at least $5.4 million on Prop 52, a 2002 ballot initiative to allow same-day voter registration. I recall activists wondering why McKay put so much of his own money in a cause that few thought was a top priority, particularly as California had recently moved the registration deadline from thirty to fifteen days before the election. Many thought the money would have been better spent funding electoral outreach to low-income, infrequent voters. Absent the excited grassroots base necessary to win a campaign expanding voter rights, Prop 52 lost by a 60 to 40 percent margin.

To be clear, there is nothing wrong with individuals spending significant sums to pass progressive initiatives. In 2003, San Francisco enacted a local minimum wage that qualified for the ballot because of a signature drive almost entirely paid for by Barry Hermanson, a local activist. But a broad coalition including San Francisco ACORN (Association for Community Organizations for Reform) conceived and developed the proposal, so the due process necessary for success was fulfilled. Similarly, hedge fund manager Thomas Steyer put over $32 million into Prop 39 on California's November 2012 ballot, a measure that eliminated $1 billion annually in corporate loopholes and redirected the money to green technology and jobs. Because Steyer's measure was done in concert with, and was backed by, labor and environmental groups, it had the due process necessary to win easily.

Rule 5: Evaluate the Political Context

The process of determining whether to take the initiative route must not occur in a political vacuum. This seems obvious, but people active on a particular issue can become unmindful of broader political events. When this happens, progressive initiatives such as tax rebates for renters, or park acquisition bond issues requiring a large voter turnout, may be placed before voters in projected-low-turnout elections where they cannot win.

Poor timing was a problem with both the Rob McKay and Stephen Bing initiatives described above. Turnout for McKay's same-day voter registration measure in November 2002 was projected to be low due to lack of interest in the governor's race. While turnout was even worse than anticipated, it was foreseeable that McKay's measure would have had a much better chance if he had put it on the 2000 ballot or waited until 2004. Similarly, Bing's Prop 87 appeared on a November 2006 ballot that foreseeably lacked a strong Democratic challenger to incumbent Republican governor Schwarzenegger; this meant that Prop 87's battle against oil companies would not attract the large Democratic turnout it needed to win.

Evaluating the political context also means progressives should not promote hot-button measures that boost conservative turnout. A small California group's ill-advised decision to place a weak gun-control measure on the November 1982 ballot caused a higher-than-projected turnout among gun-owning conservative rural voters. Having come to the polls to vote against gun control, these traditional nonvoters also voted overwhelmingly for George Deukmejian, the Republican candidate for governor. Deukmejian was expected to lose narrowly to Democrat Tom Bradley, the African American former mayor of Los Angeles, but turnout spawned by the gun-control measure gave him a narrow victory. (The initiative was also put on the ballot without due process, could not be simply explained, appealed more strongly to opponents' self-interests than to supporters', and ignored the November 1982 political context.)

Progressives have tried to boost progressive turnout through initiative measures requiring police to make the enforcement of marijuana laws a low priority; this often increases the student vote in local elections in university towns. Ballot measures seeking to raise the minimum wage or to reduce fares or improve service for public transit also have the potential to bring lower-income, infrequently voting progressives to the polls.

Understanding the broader political context can result in ballot measures that achieve important organizational goals even if defeated at the polls. For example, once the signature drive for California's 1990 Forests Forever initiative began, the lumber industry on the north coast began reducing the all-out clear-cutting that had spurred the measure. Initiative proponents estimated that nearly a million old-growth redwoods were temporarily spared between the launching of the initiative and Election Day. Presumably, the lumber industry's political consultants advised their clients to avoid massive clear-cutting that would outrage voters prior to the election. Launching an initiative thus proved an effective tactic because, even in defeat, the measure slowed the elimination of old-growth forests.

Similarly, urban slow-growth initiatives almost always have an immediate impact on unbridled development. The narrow defeat of anti-high-rise measures in San Francisco in 1979 and 1983 led even the ardently pro-development Feinstein administration to impose development and transit impact fees on office developers. These regulations came in response to voter support of the 1983 initiative's demand that downtown pay its fair share of the cost of city services. Although the initiative failed, it played a key role in achieving new development restrictions. Further, the two initiatives helped make clear that even supporters of downtown office development wanted approvals conditioned on payments for affected public services, including child care, housing, and public transit.

In 2011, California labor unions showed their understanding of the importance of political context when they helped enact legislation prohibiting state measures from appearing on ballots for lower-turnout primaries rather than those for general elections. The shift prevented a ballot measure designed to stop union political contributions from appearing on a low-turnout June 2012 primary ballot; instead, the anti-union Prop 32 was on the November general-election ballot and was soundly defeated.

Gauging the broader political context before pursuing the initiative route also requires groups considering campaigns to have honest discussions about money and volunteers. Tactical activists must anticipate that their initiative will face well-funded opposition. If the chief goal is victory, activists should assess their opposition's resources and not proceed if they believe that their grassroots campaign and messaging cannot overcome this spending advantage. I find it tiring to hear proponents of defeated measures claiming a "moral" victory based on getting the most votes per dollar—that is not the test for election campaigns. Similarly, post-election complaints about the opposition's campaign of lies or large spending advantage are pointless because such obstacles are to be expected; activists should not launch initiative drives designed for victory if they know they lack the resources to win.

Realism about Signature Gathering

One area for which honest discussion among activists considering initiatives is most vital regards signature gathering. It is harder than ever to qualify initiatives for the ballot using primarily unpaid signature gatherers. A major reason is that corporate interests seek to qualify so many initiatives with misleading titles that voters are much more distrustful than before about signing petitions. For example, the oil company backers that put Prop 23 on the November 2010 ballot called it the California Jobs Initiative. But its actual goal was to overturn the state's landmark 2006 law to reduce greenhouse gas emissions and global warming. (Opponents called it the Dirty Energy Proposition and it failed.) I was involved in California's "No on Prop 98" campaign in June 2008, a measure that qualified for the ballot after signature gatherers told voters it was limited to ending eminent domain. Petition signers were not told that it also invalidated rent control and affordable housing laws, an impact that, once publicized, led to the measure's defeat.

I supervised signature gathering for San Francisco ballot initiatives in 1992 and 1994, and it was said in those days that San Franciscans would sign any petition put before them. Today, San Franciscans are far more reluctant. This slows the signature-gathering process, frustrates volunteers, and increases the cost per signature of paid gathering (as gatherers get fewer per hour). A referendum drive to stop a San Francisco waterfront development project in 2012 paid gatherers $6 per signature, a cost feasible only for well-heeled interests (a condo owner near the site contributed $80,000).

That's why activists must honestly discuss money and volunteer resources before considering an initiative. And this assessment must address what is needed not simply to qualify the measure but also to win. Unfortunately, many activists rely on the "field of dreams" approach to initiative campaigns: if they circulate a progressive initiative on the streets, volunteer signature gatherers will come forward and money for enough paid signatures will emerge. The initiative world does not work that way. Organizational commitments to volunteer signature-gathering targets are commonly broken, and they cannot be enforced. Few groups want to douse the excitement that surrounds the early discussions of an initiative by saying, "Gee, it's a great idea. My group will endorse it, and tell our members to vote for it, but we are not willing to gather petitions, make phone calls, drop literature, or do anything that is necessary for the initiative to qualify or prevail."

To summarize: a progressive initiative should do well if it appeals to the self-interest of a significant portion of the electorate, is simple enough to be explained in one sentence, has been developed though a fair and open process involving key constituencies, is timed to appear in a high-turnout election, and has sufficient money and volunteer resources to withstand a big-money opposition campaign. I had the opportunity in 1992 to test this analysis at the ballot box. Our strategic planning for an initiative resulted not only in one of the biggest surprise victories in San Francisco political history but also, and more important, an unprecedented redistribution of millions of dollars in wealth from the rich to the poor and middle class. The initiative's story serves as an example of what tactical activists can accomplish by adhering to the rules of the initiative process.

SAN FRANCISCO'S PROPOSITION H: WINNING ECONOMIC JUSTICE AT THE BALLOT BOX

In November 1991 I had the misfortune of observing a ballot measure that violated every single rule discussed in this chapter—the vacancy control measure that contributed to the downfall of Mayor Art Agnos (see chapter 2). The measure asked voters to limit the amount by which landlords could raise the rent when units became vacant. To the surprise of many, it went down to a landslide defeat. I viewed the measure with the same trepidation and sense of helplessness one might feel when watching a brakeless train approaching a sharp curve. I was surprised by the margin of defeat, but I had always perceived a fundamental flaw in the measure that could be described in five words: vacant units do not vote.

The principal requirement for any successful progressive initiative— that a significant percentage of the electorate find a self-interest benefit—was entirely absent. Few people casting a ballot on Election Day could be sure of receiving any advantage from the measure's passage. All of the claimed benefits were conditioned upon a voter's moving within the city to a new apartment, whose initial rent might be lower if the initiative passed. Most voters understandably dismissed this remote possibility. Nor was the vacancy control initiative simple enough to explain in one sentence. The measure was so riddled with loopholes, "good landlord" exceptions, and complicated rent-increase mechanisms that the raw concept no longer said enough. Activists were willing to ignore the complexity of the measure and focus on the big picture; voters were not.

Because the vacancy control measure was not truly a creation of tenant groups, the necessary due process for ballot measures was also absent. Although all tenant groups endorsed the measure, their members had been entirely left out of the planning stages. This problem manifested itself in the absence of any grassroots election campaign, thus violating the requirement that progressive initiatives have the volunteer base necessary to offset the opposition's financial advantage. Finally, the measure was placed on the ballot in an off-year election, when the state and national races necessary for a large turnout of progressive voters were lacking. After the election I was contacted by reporters and activists eager for my opinion on the "death" of San Francisco's tenant movement. I replied that the vacancy control travesty did not reflect the real power of tenants and that I intended to prove as much by putting a winnable tenant measure on the November 1992 ballot. This vow led a cocky landlord leader to belittle me as "the mouse that roared." The remark encouraged me to begin immediately the time-consuming process necessary to create the first successful tenant initiative in San Francisco history.[5]

My first step was to refocus on the issue that I believed to be tenants' chief concern: high rent. San Francisco rents were extremely high, despite a decade of rent control, because the law guaranteed landlords rent increases of at least 4 percent annually. This automatic raise particularly hurt seniors, persons with disabilities, public-assistance recipients, low-income working people, and other people who either lived on fixed incomes or did not get an annual salary increase of at least 4 percent. The 4 percent increase was particularly unfair because the inflation rate in 1991 was about half that amount. To spark discussion of the issue, I authored an article for tenant newsletters (email and online communication not being options in those days) arguing for a citywide rent freeze.

The idea was that a one-year freeze would compensate tenants for years of rent increases that exceeded the inflation rate. The city's tenant counseling groups met to discuss the idea, and in order to involve the broadest possible constituency, each agreed to hold neighborhood "tenants' conventions." The conventions would facilitate participation by people who were not members of any tenant group and perhaps draw new energy into the movement. None of the conventions would have a rigid agenda; everyone attending would feel his or her input was not simply tolerated but strongly encouraged. We planned to hold the five events in March and April 1992. The top two recommendations for ballot measures from each event would proceed to a citywide tenants' convention in May. That gathering would vote on whether to proceed with a ballot initiative and, if so, on what issue.

The process, which gave equal decision-making power to all convention attendees rather than limiting voting to members of key constituency organizations, had its detractors. There was certainly something reckless about allowing people with no prior involvement in tenant activities to attend a meeting, vote for a particular issue, and then disappear, never to be seen again. There was also a risk that the staff members and governing bodies of organizations would chafe at having their own influence diminished by giving outsiders an equal vote. Tenant leaders were highly aware of these dangers but felt it essential to let every tenant in the city know that her or his participation was desired. A far different message is conveyed when you tell people you value their presence but not their judgment; it is a choice between a process of inclusion or exclusion. An open, inclusive process is always preferable, but it is mandatory when the people affected by issues feel estranged from activist leaders.

Many of us interpreted the lack of grassroots enthusiasm for the vacancy control ballot measure as a reflection of its authors' failure to listen to the concerns of actual tenants; an exceedingly open process would help rectify this shortcoming. An open process was also necessary to maintain unity among the convening groups themselves. Any process limiting voting to tenant group members would raise debate on the definition of membership; the relative political strength of groups emphasizing membership; the value of non-membership organizations focused on organizing or direct service; and many other issues that would have diverted energy from our objective. Because agreeing to an open, inclusive process does not require that groups formally endorse the outcome, the risk to organizational autonomy is not as great as it might appear. Our reliance on an open process succeeded in clearing the air and burnishing the image of the tenant movement.

Throughout the four-month convention process, the tenant groups engaged in a level of strategic discussion and proactive agenda setting that had virtually disappeared from the movement. This activity clearly raised the spirits of tenant organizations. Because high rents affected all tenants covered by rent control, this was, not surprisingly, the most frequently mentioned concern. Other issues raised at the conventions affected some tenants but not others. The tenant movement had resoundingly lost all four of its previous ballot initiatives and was in no position to advance a measure excluding any segment of the tenant population from its benefits; our proposed initiative had to appeal to the maximum number of tenants.

At the citywide tenants' convention in May 1992, a spirited debate broke out between those who wanted an initiative limiting annual rent increases and those who wanted to focus on both high rents and unfair evictions. Many people in the room had been unfairly evicted, and there seemed no way to reach unity without addressing their concerns. To satisfy those who, like me, strongly opposed combining two distinct ideas in one measure (remember: keep it simple), the convention voted to proceed with two separate initiatives.

This decision illustrated why many activist leaders oppose an open decision-making process. In voting to proceed with two measures, the convention did not discuss how the necessary signatures for both could be obtained, or how we could fund two initiatives or provide sufficient volunteers. Further, it subsequently became clear that some of the people voting to do two initiatives were unwilling to volunteer for either. Yet despite its politically naive outcome, the convention achieved something unprecedented: for the first time, every tenant group felt that the initiatives going to the ballot had been through a fair, democratic process. This was no small accomplishment for a gathering whose participants spoke three languages and whose organizing groups had very different political styles. Progressive initiatives do not often enjoy such unified support and legitimacy, as many activists prefer to draft their measures without consulting less politically sophisticated allies. Our ultimate success was a sharp rebuttal to those espousing the "father knows best" approach.

Following the convention, we had seven weeks to collect 15,000 signatures for each of the two initiatives. We learned a valuable lesson at the outset: many hardworking, committed activists do not like collecting signatures. People who are willing to work tirelessly dropping literature or making phone calls often do not feel comfortable stopping someone on the street and giving a quick sales pitch for a petition. Further, many volunteers from my organization, the Tenderloin Housing Clinic, simply lacked the verbal skills necessary for successful petitioning. Organization leaders must understand the limitations of fellow activists and be careful not to make people feel badly because they lack the ability to perform an important task.

Signature gathering is simply a means to an end. If leaders make extensive participation in the petition process a test of people's commitment to the cause, those unable to perform the task will feel guilty and distance themselves from the campaign. Later, when their skills are needed, they will be gone. We did not interpret our unexpected difficulty in getting volunteer signature gatherers as a sign of low interest in the effort. Neither did we view the signature process as a barometer of our capacity to run a strong grassroots campaign in the fall. We simply acknowledged people's unease over signature gathering and hired paid signature gatherers. Today's progressive initiative campaigns all use this tactic, as activists in every field of social change have had increasing trouble getting the necessary signatures strictly through volunteer efforts. The goal of signature gathering is to get the initiative on the ballot, not to educate voters (though some education naturally occurs). With key volunteers excused from the signature drive, the grassroots team enters the actual campaign rested and primed.

Although our volunteers eventually did gather a majority of the signatures necessary to qualify one measure, our need for paid gatherers made the pursuit of two initiatives fiscally unfeasible. Some advocates of the two-initiative approach had felt that the unfair-eviction measure would bring large numbers of new volunteers into the campaign. This influx of volunteers never materialized, however, so there was no chance of qualifying the measure without paid gatherers. Most volunteer petitioners had difficulty getting people to sign their name and address twice, so nearly everyone was relieved when we could focus only on the high-rents measure.

Our campaign ultimately gathered more than 16,000 signatures in seven weeks, easily qualifying the initiative for the November ballot. We also learned which individuals and organizations produced results and which produced little more than promises. Most important, we recognized that the initiative had primarily activated people already connected to existing tenant groups rather than bringing new people into the movement. We were initially disappointed by the absence of new people from the petition drive; we had hoped that the new faces so active at the conventions would continue their involvement. After repeated phone calls and letters brought little new participation, however, we realized that we should not count on newcomers. Our disappointment was more ideological than practical, as we had achieved our goal of creating a large volunteer base. It is always nice to say that you have developed an issue so exciting that new people are joining your cause in droves, but the reality was that the city's tenant-counseling groups already had a sufficiently large membership base. Like most social change organizations, the tenant groups had many inactive members; tenant leaders like Ted Gullicksen of the San Francisco Tenants Union succeeded in using the initiative to reenergize volunteers. Gullicksen's success confirmed that the convention process and resulting initiative had succeeded in rebuilding the tenants' activist base.

Initiatives often serve this purpose; in fact, a progressive initiative that fails to activate one's own base faces certain defeat. Unfortunately, in local elections in California the number of signatures necessary to qualify initiatives is so low that as few as five people working daily for months can obtain the necessary signatures. In other words, activists can qualify initiatives without broad-based constituency support. As tempting as it may seem to qualify an initiative in this way, it is ultimately a waste of everyone's time, because it will go down to defeat without any accompanying benefit. I emphasize this point because some activists wrongly equate ballot qualification with broad-based constituency support. Although we appeared to have the necessary support after our citywide convention, we would have had to abandon the high-rents initiative had we found the support lagging during the petition drive. Our goal was to win in November, not to prove we could simply qualify something for the ballot.

Prop H Campaign Strategy

As we began the actual campaign, we had already satisfied all of the requirements for success. First, our measure was simple. The existing law allowed annual rent increases equal to 60 percent of the overall inflation rate, the percentage that constitutes the housing portion of inflation. But the law also stated that "in no event shall the annual rent increase be less than 4%." Nearly every year in the late 1980s and early 1990s, inflation was less than 4 percent, so a formula designed to allow landlords to keep up with inflation was actually giving them a windfall. Our initiative ended rent increases above the inflation rate by simply deleting the 4 percent guarantee from the existing law. The measure not only could be explained in a sentence but also could be illustrated in handouts showing the text of the current law with the 4 percent guarantee crossed out. The simplicity of Proposition H prevented the traditional opposition tactic of focusing on ambiguous phrases or provisions—such as the school voucher proposal's implicit allowance for witches' schools—collateral to the initiative's purpose. Unable to confuse voters over the initiative's content, our opposition was forced to focus on our claim that Proposition H was "fair."[6]

Second, our measure appealed to the self-interest of a significant portion of the electorate: every tenant covered by rent control would save money if our measure passed. Under existing law a tenant paying $500 per month would be subject to automatic 4 percent annual rent increases; rent would increase to $520 a month after the first year, to $541 the next year, and so on. After five years the rent would be $608 a month, a little more than $100 above the initial rent. The tenant would be paying $1,296 more per year in rent than he or she had paid five years previously. Our initiative would save this tenant at least $120 the first year, and savings would increase every year because the rent increase percentage would be levied on a lower prior-year level. Further, many apartments in San Francisco rented for more than $1,000 per month, and their tenants would enjoy even greater savings from our initiative. These higher-end apartments housed people who regularly voted, whose political outlook was less favorable toward government regulation of the marketplace unless it affected their wallets, and whose financial future had suffered because of the lingering recession. Our initiative thus appealed to the economic insecurities and financial self-interest of middle-class and low-income tenants. It also appealed to upper-income people who might not identify themselves as progressive but who always voted in their own financial interest.

Third, and of central importance, our initiative was conceived with the full understanding of the political context of the November 1992 election. This context involved far more than an expected high voter turnout. Two significant factors stood out in my mind. First, the presidential campaign—Bush versus Clinton—would be a highly partisan contest. (California also had two hard-fought U.S. Senate races in that same election.) All national elections are partisan, but after losing a winnable presidential race in 1988, Democrats had a unified thirst for victory unparalleled since at least 1960. The high stakes of the 1992 election would give a boost to initiatives that could be portrayed in a partisan light. Second, it was clear from the primary debates of early 1992 that the Democratic presidential candidate, whoever it was, would base his November campaign on the economy. This focus would assist a local high-rents initiative in two ways. It would remind voters why the times required that landlords lower rents; also, the emphasis on the unfairness of Republican economic policies could be used to attack a law that unfairly raised rents at more than double the inflation rate.

We soon harnessed our campaign to the Democrats' national campaign by making our race—like the Clinton-Bush contest—into a plebiscite on economic fairness. Just as it was not fair that the rich got richer and everyone else got poorer in the 1980s, it was not fair that rich landlords received rent increases in excess of inflation at the expense of working people. Rather than talk about tenants' rights, rent control, or housing policy, our campaign focused on the savage consequences of trickle-down economics for the middle class, families, children, seniors, people with disabilities, and ethnic minorities. Whereas prior pro-tenant ballot campaigns had used the official voter handbook to make arguments related to tenant issues, ours had key groups make the case that Proposition H was essential for economic fairness. For example, groups representing seniors emphasized that the total yearly Social Security cost-of-living increase was less than the 4 percent annual rent increase and that seniors were suffering as a result. Children's advocacy groups noted that national economic policies had caused undue hard-ships for San Francisco's middle- and low-income families, many of whom were being driven out of their homes and the city by unfairly high rent increases. African American and Latino organizations empha-sized the damage caused to their communities by Reagan-Bush eco-nomic policies and explained how our initiative would help start to turn the process around. These arguments and others helped establish our campaign theme that Proposition H was essential not only for local economic fairness but also to rectify unfair national economic policies.

The focus on economic fairness was critical in attracting votes from homeowners and others who had no self-interest in the initiative. Although tenants constitute 70 percent of San Francisco's population, even in the highest-turnout elections they make up only 55 percent of the voters. Because this percentage includes those living in government-subsidized housing, newly constructed apartments, and other units exempt from the city rent-control ordinance, nearly half of the elector-ate would not immediately benefit from Proposition H. Our success thus required the support of liberal homeowners and others whose vote would be based on their overall political outlook. This group typically had supported liberal economic and tax policies at the national level, but failed to connect these views with the fairness of laws protecting the city's tenants. This failure was understandable, because the plight of local tenants had never been explicitly connected to national politics, and what little homeowners knew about rent-control initiatives tended to come from opposition campaign literature. By connecting our propo-sition to the Clinton-Gore economic fairness theme, we could win the support of this critical voting bloc.

We also sought to win disinterested voters by identifying Proposition H's opponents with the Republican Party. This kind of tactic can involve both controversy and risk. Controversy arises because many progres-sive social change activists are uncomfortable with identifying their causes with the Democratic Party. The reasons for this view are legion, but in essence the argument goes that Democrats represent the moderate side of corporate America while falsely claiming to speak for working people. The actual political orientation of the Democratic Party, however, is an issue separate from the tactical question of whether identifying with it will facilitate progressive social change. When your electorate is certain to vote overwhelmingly Democratic in a highly partisan presidential race, it only makes sense to use this association to your advantage. Our campaign emphasized less the universal support we had from the local Democratic Party and clubs and more the fact that the San Francisco Republican Party opposed our measure. Literature delivered in liberal homeowner areas focused entirely on our claim that the Republican Party opposed Proposition H because it was designed to help the victims of the Reagan-Bush years. I even sought to link California's then-unpopular Republican governor, Pete Wilson, to Proposition H's opponents. In my official campaign response to the *San Francisco Chronicle* editorial opposing Proposition H, I noted that the paper's position was not surprising in light of its unwavering support for both Reagan-Bush trickle-down and Governor Wilson's failed economic programs. I believed this argument would win us more votes than were lost by the paper's position.

Our effort to link Proposition H to the Democratic Party reflected the tactical principle of invoking the values and symbols that your target audience understands. Progressive social change is not achieved by winning the ardent support of only a small minority of the population; identifying progressive causes with widely accepted values and symbols is simply common sense. Despite the apparent obviousness of this strategy, however, many social change activists reduce their chances for success by ignoring, even attacking, popular cultural values. For example, Saul Alinsky considered 1960s antiwar demonstrators' attacks on the American flag disastrous, because the flag's role as a symbol for American values made the demonstrators, rather than the war, appear anti-American. Sponsors of progressive initiatives should carefully analyze the possible linkages between their measure and values broadly supported by the electorate.[7]

However, equating opposition to Proposition H with support for an unpopular Republican Party had its risks. As Thomas Ferguson and Joel Rogers amply document in *Right Turn: The Decline of the Democrats and the Future of American Politics,* the national Democratic Party of the 1980s was heavily funded by real estate interests. In Boston, New

York, Los Angeles, Chicago, San Francisco, and other major cities, battles over rent control or development primarily occurred among Democrats rather than between the two major parties. San Francisco's Democratic mayor, Frank Jordan, opposed Proposition H, and Democratic senator Dianne Feinstein had consistently opposed strengthening rent control while she was mayor from 1979 to 1987. In other words, our effort to transform Proposition H into a litmus test for Democratic Party loyalty could have provoked a mass mailing from "Democrats against H." Our landlord opposition could have self-righteously proclaimed their Democratic bona fides and attacked our cloaking of a "radical" measure in Democratic Party clothing. Rather than so responding, however, they chose to rely on confusion and scare tactics.[8]

Linking ballot measures to notoriously unpopular constituencies is an effective political tactic. If right-wing interests actively oppose your measure, it may be wise to focus your campaign on their agenda so that people will vote yes in order to say no to your adversaries. We always made sure to include a partial list of Proposition H opponents in our literature. This list was limited to real estate groups and the local Republican Party, entities highly unpopular with swing voters. We also emphasized hotel magnate–turned–tax evader Leona Helmsley's role as the leading contributor to the "No on H" campaign. (Helmsley owns one of San Francisco's largest apartment complexes.) A yes vote became a way for people to say no to Helmsley. Tactical activists must look for opportunities to use their opposition's goals, symbols, and even personalities as springboards for success at the ballot box.

Although Proposition H had all the characteristics of a successful progressive initiative—simplicity, self-interest benefits, due process, and a favorable political context—the measure could not pass without a sufficient volunteer and financial base. There is no formula for estimating what constitutes a "sufficient" volunteer base; a campaign has sufficient volunteers when it has people available to carry out all of the tasks necessary to win. With the signatures already collected and the initiative officially on the ballot, our grassroots effort swung into gear. Our campaign needed volunteers for two tasks: phoning and literature drops. We were able to meet our volunteer goals through the significant participation of unemployed single men receiving county welfare.

People living in desperate poverty rarely play such a decisive role in the outcome of an election. The Tenderloin Housing Clinic had long worked with single men living in low-rent hotels, but even we were surprised by the willingness of hotel tenants to drop literature in outlying neighborhoods almost daily. Unlike most progressive initiative campaigns, which rely heavily on Saturday mobilizations, our campaign could utilize people during the week. This made a big difference in our ability to reach voters, because our campaign had decided to forgo expensive mailings and signs in favor of cheaper but more labor-intensive phoning and literature drops.

Our volunteer base also included members of citywide tenant groups, but we did not enlist well-known progressive activists. Our reliance on people unknown to traditional activists and our focus on nuts-and-bolts phoning and literature dropping rather than high-profile media and fund-raising events contributed to the pundits' perception that Proposition H did not have a viable campaign. After we won the election, one City Hall "insider" told me she did not see how we could have won, because our campaign had been "invisible." Our goal had been to get information to voters, not prove something to the establishment by running a flashy media campaign.

Proposition H had advantages that most progressive initiatives lack in attracting low-income volunteers. The Tenderloin Housing Clinic had a strong institutional connection to hotel tenants, we had paid organizers focusing on this group, and we had an initiative that directly impacted the meager living expenses of those depending on public assistance. Notwithstanding these factors, social change activists miss out on a critical opportunity when they fail even to attempt to bring unemployed single adults into their campaign.

Many of our volunteers had a broad progressive political outlook that would lead them to participate in campaigns that might not directly involve their economic self-interest. Organizations that have no direct contact with such people can make connections through local anti-poverty groups. For example, if representatives of environmental, health care, or slow-growth initiatives were to express interest in reaching low-income tenants, the Clinic would happily schedule a community meeting to discuss the measures. Many unemployed single adults living in SRO hotels or studio apartments are desperate for human contact. They want to be involved in working with other people, but they are waiting for an invitation. They have learned not to go where they are not wanted and are unlikely simply to show up at an open campaign meeting and get involved. Tactical activists do not have the luxury of ignoring this key volunteer constituency. We could never have dropped nearly 100,000 pieces of campaign literature without the critical involvement of poor people in every facet of this effort.

For many progressive campaigns, however, the problem is money, not campaign volunteers. This is particularly true in statewide campaigns in large states such as California, whose very size has made television advertising almost a must. But as the case of Proposition 103, the auto insurance initiative, proved, a strong grassroots attack coupled with such factors as a widely publicized Ralph Nader endorsement can enable David to defeat Goliath. In local initiatives, costly television advertising is less effective, making the money differential slightly less determinative. Nevertheless, social change organizations often err by proceeding to the ballot without first achieving the minimum financial backing necessary to mount a winning campaign.

Proposition H was outspent by a twelve-to-one margin—we spent $25,000, our opponents $300,000—yet we prevailed. We won despite the fact that various "experts" had assured me it would take $50,000 to $75,000 to run a campaign with any potential for victory. For our $25,000 we dropped 100,000 pieces of literature, made several thousand phone calls, and distributed 10,000 specially made YES ON H doorhangers in a key swing neighborhood. We avoided costly glossy literature, used no expensive street signs, and did only one, narrowly targeted mailing. I repeatedly said before and during the campaign that Proposition H would not lose due to a lack of funds, and I remain convinced that we would not have done substantially better at the polls if our budget had doubled.

Many progressive initiatives become too caught up in imitating their opponents' expensive campaigns. In a San Francisco rent-control campaign in 1979, the ardor to create glossy color mailers equal in quality to the landlords' predominated over analyzing how our money could best be spent. That campaign spent more than $50,000 in 1979 dollars to win barely 40 percent of the vote. Some consultants insist that progressive campaigns need expensive literature to establish "credibility" with voters. Yet credibility is established by an initiative's content and how it is framed, not by fancy campaign materials.

Our first campaign expenditure was to hire David Binder, a local political pollster who would later work on Barack Obama's 2008 and 2012 campaigns, to evaluate which neighborhoods we should target. After receiving his report, we calculated how much it would cost to reach these target areas through literature drops and phoning. Based on this estimate, we felt confident that $25,000 would be sufficient. Most of the campaign was funded by my organization. I had learned in 1991 that 501(c)(3) nonprofit organizations are permitted to spend money on ballot initiatives; and I could not think of a better use of Clinic funds than to spend them on an initiative that would lower rents. The Tenderloin Housing Clinic generates unrestricted funds by representing tenants in lawsuits against landlords, so we had the money to spend. The fact that we were running a true "outsider," grassroots effort meant we would not attract significant funds from elected officials or well-off individuals who did not feel directly involved in our campaign. Neither did we want to squander precious time on small-scale fund-raising events unlikely to make much money. To reach the necessary budget, in addition to the Clinic funds, the campaign received a $5,000 contribution from one large tenants' organization and individual donations of an equal amount.

I am a big believer in nonprofit advocacy organizations' spending money on ballot measures. If an organization's mission statement or agenda can be fulfilled through a ballot initiative, choosing not to pursue this tactic raises questions about the value of the group's advocacy and its true commitment to achieving social change. Some groups' spending is restricted by various funding sources, leaving no funds for initiatives. But many self-proclaimed advocacy groups do have unrestricted funds that they invariably spend on additional staff or "services." Is spending from $5,000 to $15,000 on a portion of a staff salary a more effective form of advocacy than contributing the same amount to help initiatives that could, for example, reduce rents, prevent environmental hazards, or widen access to health care? People working in nonprofits need to examine this issue seriously. It should be a required discussion at the organization's annual retreat.

I found the question a simple one. If the Clinic had used the funds we spent on Proposition H to hire additional staff, the expenditure would have brought negligible benefits to the city's low-income, senior, and disabled tenants, who would have continued to suffer from steeply rising rents. Hiring a staff person to "advocate" for a goal that cannot be achieved without a ballot measure is not a strategic use of resources. With funding so precious, nonprofit social change advocacy organizations should participate in and be counted upon to help fund initiative campaigns seeking to benefit their constituencies. Some nonprofit staff view spending money directly on ballot measures as too "controversial" or "political." However, an organization that fears controversy or politics is not likely to achieve social change.

In the Proposition H campaign, we sought to stretch our funds by creating literature that would stick in the minds of voters. We knew that if our literature resembled the dozens of other campaign pieces voters received, our message might be quickly forgotten. Further, whereas our opponents could hammer their message home through several mailings, we would reach most voters with only one piece. We therefore created a campaign theme that raised eyebrows even among people whose judgment I usually trusted.

When I first learned that our proposition had been assigned the letter "H," I was upset. "Proposition H" sounded too much like "Preparation H," the heavily advertised hemorrhoid ointment. I then realized that we had the opportunity to make a memorable impression with voters by deliberately connecting Proposition H to that famous medication. After considerable discussion and debate, we came up with the slogan "Proposition H: For Relief of Rental Pain." Our first piece of literature included a picture of a female doctor, her accompanying words prescribing Proposition H. Our campaign insignia became a tube with the words YES ON H. We used both humor and an unusual message to pack our lone piece of literature with the punch of several. We hoped to further heighten the impact of our message by distributing this initial piece prior to the start of other campaigns. With this early start we also sought to sway absentee voters, who often cast their ballots before receiving the frenzy of end-of-campaign mailings.

One factor we never considered was the need to act quickly to preempt our opponents' use of the same advertising theme. Yet three weeks after we distributed our "Relief of Rental Pain" literature, bus shelters throughout the city sprouted lurid red and yellow posters depicting a large tube emblazoned "Proposition H Means Higher Rents." Dozens of billboards with the same design soon followed, and the Preparation H tube became the focal point of opposition literature. If any voters were offended by the linking of Proposition H to an over-the-counter ointment used for a very personal problem, they were surely more likely to blame our opponents than us. Indeed, the *San Francisco Examiner* editorial opposing Proposition H castigated our opponents for their unsavory attempt to portray tenants as needing a hemorrhoidal cream. No one in the media ever commented on our use of the same imagery, though we maintained it throughout the campaign.

Although Proposition H satisfied all of the requirements for a successful progressive initiative, very few people thought it would pass. When reporters asked me whether Proposition H would prevail, I responded truthfully that I felt it would. When I asked their opinion, the hemming and hawing would begin, frequently ending with the assertion that we had really done a good job and that the contest surely would be close. In fact, the skepticism over our grassroots, outsider campaign was so great that, to our disappointment, even alternative newspapers seemed to look forward to our defeat. Apparently they preferred seeing their predictions of Proposition H's failure fulfilled over achieving lower rents for tenants.

On election night, the first results came from the more conservative-leaning absentee voters. These ballots had us trailing only 48 to 52 percent, meaning we would most likely win. Our eventual margin of victory was 53 to 47 percent, a dramatic reversal of the 57–43 margin defeating the preceding November's tenant ballot measure. A review of voting totals by neighborhood showed that Proposition H did well even in conservative parts of the city that had strongly rejected previous progressive initiatives. The broad support for Proposition H reflected support from seniors and upper-income tenants; many of the latter subordinated free-market economic views to their personal desire to pay less rent. Although San Francisco's overall voter turnout in November 1992 was large, other local results did not reflect an unusually large or disproportionately progressive electorate. We had succeeded in winning the votes of political moderates on behalf of an initiative that would result in an unprecedented progressive redistribution of wealth in our city.

Prop H's Dramatic Long-Term Impact

After its passage in November 1992, Proposition H took effect on December 10, 1992. From March 1984 to Prop H's implementation in December 1992, landlords could impose annual rent increases of 4 percent. Since Prop H, the highest rent increase has been 2.9 percent, and that was during the height of the dot-com boom of 2000–2001. In the twenty years since Prop H's passage, annual allowable rent increases have been less than 1 percent on four occasions, and less than 2 percent on ten other occasions. During the economic downturn of 2010–11, the annual allowable increase was only 0.1 percent. We had told tenants that Prop H would cut annual rent increases in half, and it has provided even greater results. And while San Francisco rents on vacant units jumped 10 percent in 2011, Prop H limited annual rent increases in 2011 to tenants staying in place to 0.5 percent.

That's a staggering savings to tenants over time.

A tenant paying $500 per month in 1992 has saved thousands of dollars under Proposition H. Because most rental units in the city rent for far more than $500, the total Proposition H savings to tenants is in the billions of dollars. By giving tenants an immediate and ongoing economic benefit, Proposition H proponents kept faith with the electorate.

Prop H has also helped the local economy by keeping millions of dollars every year in the hands of tenants who live and shop in the city. This money would otherwise have been sent to the out-of-town landlords who own most of San Francisco's rental properties. We focused on this stark redistributive shift in resources during our campaign by referring to the late notorious hotel queen and convicted tax evader Leona Helmsley. Helmsley's Park Merced, at the time San Francisco's largest apartment complex, was a leading funder of the "No on H" campaign, and for good reason: most of her 1,000-plus apartments rented for more than $750 a month. A 4 percent rent increase on only five hundred apartments would bring her an annual gain of $180,000. Proposition H thus immediately cut Helmsley's annual profit from rent increases on these apartments by more than $100,000. Because Proposition H's rent savings multiply year by year, tenants' savings increase exponentially.

Proposition H has caused the largest redistribution of wealth in the history of San Francisco, and perhaps the largest any ballot measure has created in any city. And it took a ballot initiative to make this happen.

Prop H also reversed the prevailing view that San Francisco tenants could not win a citywide ballot measure. Prior to Prop H, most doubted that a pro-tenant initiative could ever pass; after Prop H created the strategic blueprint for victory, almost every tenant measure prevailed for the next two decades. A ballot measure in 1994 ended the biggest loophole in the original rent-control law by bringing previously exempt, owner-occupied buildings of four or fewer units under the law. Subsequent ballot measures greatly expanded protections against eviction. San Francisco continues to have some of the nation's highest rents, but tenants in place do not face steep annual rent increases. And nearly all of the major improvements in tenant protections have come through ballot measures, with the city's legislative process still incapable of overcoming the real estate industry's power.

INITIATIVES ARE PROACTIVE

Ballot initiatives are a proactive strategy that puts opponents on the defensive. That's why conservative and corporate interests put something on almost every California state ballot, and keep up the pressure through a "try and try again" approach. Losing initiatives appear again on future ballots, continually requiring progressives to run opposition campaigns. Initiatives requiring parental notification before a minor can have an abortion appeared on California's 2005, 2006, and 2008 ballots, and measures to restrict political contributions by labor unions appeared in 1998, 2005, and again in 2012. None of the six succeeded, but progressives had to divert resources from pursuing their own goals in order to defeat them.

Progressives have the resources to use the same proactive strategy, but in most cases they instead value legislative and political races that only potentially and indirectly bring the results that a winning initiative can achieve. It's as if progressives who oppose the initiative process have decided not to use this powerful strategy even when it clearly makes sense to do so. And their widespread belief that big money can defeat even the most popular measures means that potentially winning proposals to increase economic and social fairness never even reach the ballot. For example, California's Prop 217 in 1996 would have raised income taxes on the top 1 percent of earners and brought the state $800 million in additional revenue annually. Although it lost by fewer than 150,000 votes (50.8% to 49.2%), progressives did not put another initiative imposing an income tax hike on the wealthy until 2012, when voters passed the far more sweeping Prop 30 by a 54 to 46 percent margin.

Prop 30 was among many progressive ballot measures that won throughout the nation in the November 2012 elections. Cumulatively, these victories may increase progressive confidence in the initiative process. Prop 30 has national implications because it reversed the pattern of voters using initiatives to reduce taxes and government spending, and because what starts in California often spreads nationally. Similarly, after thirty-three consecutive state elections across the nation defeated gay marriage, measures in Maine, Maryland, Minnesota, and Washington all prevailed. In the wake of these victories progressives are sounding more positive about the initiative process than they have in decades, and this bodes well for their proactive future use.

DEFEATING CONSERVATIVE INITIATIVES

Progressives must do a better job of defeating conservative initiatives, which have reduced public services, denied civil rights to minorities, and stigmatized and even criminalized Latino immigrants. Some of these measures could have been beaten if progressives had done what was necessary to win. For example, a measure that sought to end affirmative action in California—Proposition 209, which conservatives misleadingly named the "California Civil Rights Initiative"—appeared on the November 1996 ballot. In *The Color Bind: California's Battle to End Affirmative Action,* Lydia Chávez describes how conflicts over campaign messaging between civil rights activists and political staff, as well as conflicts within the civil rights community, prevented the "No on 209" campaign from using the strongest message to defeat the measure.[9]

Similarly, the campaign to defeat Prop 8, the anti–gay marriage initiative on California's 2008 ballot, was hurt by conflict between political consultants and activists in the gay marriage struggle. The latter were unhappy that Democratic presidential candidate Barack Obama did not then support gay marriage, so did not want to highlight his opposition to Prop 8 (which would have repealed California's constitutional right to gay marriage) in their appeals to African American voters. Obama was expected to win California handily and generate a large African American turnout, so that publicizing his opposition to Prop 8 would increase black votes against the initiative. While erroneous post-election reporting claimed that African Americans strongly backed Prop 8, the No campaign clearly made a strategic error in not using Obama's opposition to help defeat the measure. (Marriage equality activists in Maryland learned from this mistake and made sure that President Obama's support for a gay marriage measure in November 2012 was highly publicized among African American voters; the measure passed.)

NEW YORK CITY: A LAND WITHOUT BALLOT INITIATIVES

Those yearning for a political jurisdiction without grassroots-initiated ballot initiatives need look no further than New York City. One reason real estate is king in New York City is that activists cannot use the ballot initiative to stop or revise destructive development projects. Consider the Atlantic Yards project in Brooklyn, now best known as the home of the Barclay Center. Announced in 2003 by the powerful Forest City Ratner development group headed by Bruce Ratner, Atlantic Yards was initially proposed as a mixed-use commercial and residential development project of sixteen high-rise buildings. The centerpiece of the project was a basketball arena, which today hosts the Brooklyn Nets. The Atlantic Yards project was projected to fill seven large blocks, and its fifty-three-story towers would dominate the Brooklyn skyline.

The struggle over Atlantic Yards went on for nearly seven years, and is detailed in a remarkable documentary, the *Battle of Brooklyn*. The story is a case study of how powerful real estate interests can bypass voters and the traditional legislative process entirely—something that can occur only in the absence of an initiative process. No New York City elected official ever voted to approve this massive development project, and it was authorized by state agencies even though Brooklyn's state representatives opposed the project. In a land without local ballot measures, Atlantic Yards was approved by state political appointees unaccountable to the electorate.

Atlantic Yards would not have been constructed as currently planned—if at all—had activists been able to put an initiative on the ballot to stop the project. Had Forest City Ratner known that its project would face voter approval, it would have created a plan far more acceptable to the Brooklyn community. But in the absence of an initiative threat, developers in New York City have no reason to consider community concerns; they can rely on the same insider processes that allowed unelected Robert Moses to displace and demolish the city's working-class neighborhoods from the mid-1920s to the late 1960s.

You can be sure that if powerful real estate interests thought that ballot initiatives were a great tool to "screw the people," New York City would have authorized such measures decades ago.

5

The Media

Winning More Than Coverage

Social change activists today confront a media landscape very different from the pre-Internet, pre–social media days. Whereas wealthy media owners long ruled as "gatekeepers" for the news, activists can now break their own stories through email, websites, Facebook, or other social media. As a result, by the time Congress in 2012 sought to weaken Internet privacy through the Stop Online Piracy Act (SOPA) and PROTECT IP Act (PIPA), activists no longer depended on newspaper coverage; they got their point across when English Wikipedia and 7,000 smaller sites shut down in protest, with opposition websites drawing more than 160 million page views on the single day of January 18, 2012. When antiwar protesters in the 1960s chanted that the "whole world was watching," they were referring to the CBS, NBC, and ABC *Evening News;* today, it is the Internet that creates national and world-wide audiences, with national television news reaching a tiny fraction of its former audience. New media have created an even greater decline in daily newspaper readership. Print media still search for a strategy to attract new generations accustomed to getting their news from the increasingly crowded information superhighway.

Today's new media world offers enormous opportunities and formidable challenges. The constant demand for "breaking news" puts a greater premium on gossip, scandal, and celebrity than on more complex stories. Many are too busy publicizing their own causes online or via social media to read other people's writings. The sheer number and variety of informational tools combined with the massive volume of news available make it harder to get sustained attention for your story. Activists in the old media days knew that getting a front-page newspaper story, a magazine exposé, or coverage on *60 Minutes* would reach a broad audience. Today's infinitely more fragmented media audiences make this much more difficult, regardless of how many YouTube visits your video gets or how viral your story goes.

In some respects, the old media era was much easier for activists to navigate. In the 1980s I knew that if the *San Francisco Chronicle* covered a story related to my work in the morning, I could expect follow-up calls from radio and television stations later that day. Similarly, when national network news shows or the *New York Times* prominently featured a story, other news outlets throughout the nation followed up on it. Today, media outlets prioritize their own reporting and breaking stories and are less likely to report on what has been covered elsewhere.

Advertising dollars still drive the traditional media system. As Ben Bagdikian, a former *Washington Post* reporter and retired dean of the journalism school at the University of California, Berkeley, explained in his 1983 book, *The Media Monopoly:* "Most [newspaper] owners and editors no longer brutalize the news with the heavy hand dramatized in movies like *Citizen Kane* or *The Front Page.* More common is something more subtle, more professionally respectable and more effective: the power to treat some unliked subjects accurately but briefly, and to treat subjects favorable to the corporate ethic frequently and in depth."

Bagdikian made that comment thirty years ago, but it still applies to today's coverage of social change issues. For example, the media, particularly during the Christmas season, run frequent "hard luck" stories about homeless families or people living on ever-decreasing state disability payments. These mainstream media outlets are careful, however, to link the subject's plight to personal misfortunes rather than social and economic policies. Such stories routinely fail to call federal or state elected officials to account for cutting welfare or disability benefits. Once again, Bagdikian succinctly sums up the problem: "Large classes of people are ignored in the news, are reported as exotic fads, or appear only at their worst—minorities, blue-collar workers, the lower middle class, the poor. They become publicized mainly when they are in spectacular accidents, go on strike, or are arrested. . . . But since World War I hardly a mainstream American news medium has failed to grant its most favored treatment to corporate life."[1]

DEVELOPING A STRATEGIC MEDIA PLAN

For all these reasons, social change activists seeking positive media coverage must prepare a strategic plan. As when dealing with elected officials, activists must have clearly in mind demonstrable results they want to achieve through publicity. Contrary to what many activists believe, "media coverage" in and of itself is not a demonstrable result. When I have questioned activists in various fields as to why they are planning a particular event, the all-too-typical response is "to attract the media." If my relationship with the activists is sufficiently close, I gently ask what results they hope will come out of such coverage. Often the response is that it will help "the public" understand and support the activists' position on the particular issue. The activists rarely assess the true capacity for such coverage to assist in achieving their goals; nor do they usually have a strategic plan that connects the coverage to fulfillment of a specific agenda. Ironically, activists who place their faith in media coverage per se generally understand that the traditional media are not allies of social change. From this premise, it should follow that those media cannot be trusted to cover an event in a manner likely to prompt broad and immediate support for progressive causes. As I show in this chapter, events designed solely for media coverage of their issues can even result in a story that generates public anger against the activists' position.

In urging activists to create a strategic media plan, I am talking about something altogether different from maximizing public exposure of an issue or campaign. Activists typically want to reach the broadest possible audience for their news events. But if your campaign target will not be swayed by broad appeals, then that's not a winning strategy. It's easy to launch a blizzard of Facebook postings, tweets, emails, text messages, and phone calls about your issue, but casting the widest possible net is not always an effective strategy. This is particularly true in campaigns targeting politicians, who remain far more susceptible to in-person protests and other forms of public attacks than they are to negative postings about them online or in social media. Activists need to think beyond "getting the word out" and focus on assessing what this media barrage is designed to achieve.

Developing a strategic media plan takes time. It means thinking carefully about timing, targets, messaging, and how to proactively use the media to control the agenda for your issue or campaign. A blizzard approach relying primarily on the Internet and social media is quicker and easier, but as the legendary organizer Fred Ross put it, "short cuts lead to detours and dead ends." Working for progressive change has never been fast or easy. That's why the traditional tactics for drawing media attention such as personal confrontations, picket lines, mass protests, and civil disobedience continue to prove effective. The personal commitment involved in such events sends a powerful message to their targets about the movement's strength. The same message is not conveyed when support is registered simply by clicking on a link to show support.

The central rules for successful activism include using media coverage to win a specific, implementable result; selecting the proper media contact; utilizing the skills of trained investigative reporters as a component of a broader campaign; remaining guarded with most journalists and developing key relations with sympathetic reporters; knowing how and when to respond to media bias and stories generated by conservative think tanks; and understanding how best to use the alternative media to accomplish tactical goals. Following these rules will help activists overcome the ever-increasing institutional media opposition to campaigns for progressive social change.

Use the Media for Results, Not Coverage

By using the media not for coverage alone but rather to achieve a specific, implementable result, tactical activists can gain support for their goals. I begin with some examples from the "old media" days that still apply today.

I began working full-time at the Tenderloin Housing Clinic in October 1982. Paid through a $12,000 grant from the Berkeley Law Foundation, I was soon talking to dozens of tenants who lived in a wide variety of residential hotels and shared a serious problem: no heat. I went to hotel after hotel during the cold November evenings to verify personally that thousands of San Francisco's poorest tenants, including elderly and disabled people, were living without heat. When three elderly women came to my office complaining of this problem, I figured we had the perfect opportunity to attract media attention to the scandal. Although many of the residents of the heatless hotels were seniors, hotel residents primarily consisted of single men living on welfare, disability checks, or some other sort of fixed income. Some had drug or alcohol problems. Although all of them needed and deserved heat, the image of shivering seniors was the most likely to provoke the collective outrage of the media and the public.

Finding sympathetic subjects can be an essential part of an activist's media strategy. I sent out a press release headlined "Why Must Seniors Freeze?" and scheduled a heat protest in front of the women's hotel for the next day. My release attracted the immediate attention of former *San Francisco Chronicle* reporter Warren Hinckle. Hinckle, former editor of the 1960s magazine *Ramparts,* wrote dramatic exposés on an occasional basis for the *Chronicle.* I took him on a tour of the city's "heatless hotels" on one of the coldest December nights, and we did not find a single warm radiator. Hinckle's story—"Our City's Shame"— galvanized San Francisco residents in a way that has not been replicated on poor people's issues to this day. The day Hinckle's article appeared, the Tenderloin Housing Clinic staged a protest with senior citizens and other hotel residents, bringing coverage from nearly every television and radio station in the Bay Area. The story of seniors living without heat was the lead story on all the television news shows, and Hinckle wrote the lead article on the *Chronicle*'s front page for the rest of the week.[2]

The widespread publicity about "heat cheats" led to a variety of actions. Mayor Dianne Feinstein, herself a residential hotel landlord, had been attacked by Hinckle during the 1979 mayor's race for allegedly abusing her tenants. Perhaps to avoid renewed charges of insensitivity, Feinstein ordered immediate citywide "heat sweeps" for all residential hotels. The district attorney vowed to prosecute landlords who refused to provide heat, and various members of the Board of Supervisors called for hearings on the heatless hotels. This initial response was not unusual; when the media uncover a scandal, elected officials often call for crackdowns, sweeps, hearings, and prosecutions. Regrettably, such calls often represent the climax of media focus on the issue. Journalists, satisfied they have done enough by uncovering the scandal, soon forget about the story before putting sufficient pressure on government officials to solve the problem. Abandonment of an issue by the media often leads to abandonment by elected leaders.

To prevent the media's departure prior to achieving an effective solution to heatless hotels, I emphasized to Hinckle and other reporters that their publicity was meaningless if it did not lead to concrete changes in city enforcement of heat laws. Faced with my position, reporters had to concede that they could not claim their stories made any difference unless new legislation was enacted. The media thus became vested in supporting activists' demands for a concrete solution to the heat problem. I then drafted a new heat law that closed the loopholes preventing effective enforcement and created tough criminal penalties for heat cheats. Because I was ready with a specific, implementable measure to end the heatless hotel problem, City Hall could not resort to the usual diversionary tactics, such as lengthy hearings, task forces, and "white paper" commissions. The *Chronicle*'s Hinckle was particularly insistent that the new legislation be promptly enacted. He contacted various supervisors regarding their willingness to support the proposed measure, serving notice that the city's leading news source would be closely monitoring their position on the issue. When one supervisor tried the oft-used opposition tactic of expressing support for a measure while using procedural methods to derail it, Hinckle wrote an entire column vilifying the official for engaging in "damage control" for slumlords.

To keep the media, especially television, pushing for stronger heat laws, tenant advocates had to make the legislative process unusually interesting. We accomplished this by attracting a large turnout of hotel residents to the first Board of Supervisors hearing on the proposed legislation and stationing a person dressed in a polar bear costume to hand out flyers demanding heat. Costumed protesters at hearings garner so much press attention that it's a wonder activists do not use this tactic more frequently. The polar bear gave television cameras some eye-catching footage, something other than the typical clips of speeches. A decade later, the Tenderloin Housing Clinic rented a rat costume for a hearing on housing-code enforcement. The rat ended up on the front page of the *San Francisco Independent;* it also allowed me publicly to make fun of the city's senior housing inspector, who once stated she had never seen a rat in San Francisco.

We followed up our polar bear appearance at a subsequent hearing by distributing badges that showed penguins marching to demand heat. Our emphasis on visuals, combined with the media's sudden interest in running "day in the life" profiles of elderly hotel residents, kept the heat legislation on the media's front burner for over a month. The story went national; offers of blankets and other support came in from across the nation. We received letters from Alaska with advice on how to keep warm. Don Feeser, a seventeen-year Tenderloin resident who was profiled both locally and nationally, received marriage proposals from several women promising to keep him warm.

Ideally, tactical activists should use the media both to generate a scandal and then to demand a specific, concrete result. My experience with the heatless hotels was not entirely typical, because the extent of publicity and the strong pressure for legislation that Hinckle and the *San Francisco Chronicle* helped generate do not often occur. The pressure for action was so great that the new heat and hot-water laws, which mandated civil and criminal penalties for violators, were passed as emergency legislation, meaning they took effect in three days rather than the usual thirty days. Nevertheless, many people noted that city officials had long known of the lack of heat in residential hotels; until the media pressure mounted, they simply did not care about this problem faced by its poorest residents. Without the strategy of equating media success with the enactment of critically needed legislation, the "heatless hotel" scandal, like so many others, would simply have provided a few days' news and then been forgotten.

The need for a specific, implementable solution is also demonstrated by cases in which such a programmatic response is absent. For example, in San Francisco and many other cities, homeless families have been housed in SRO hotels. These small, undivided rooms are obviously inadequate to house families for other than emergency situations; their unsuitability for young children is worsened by the lack of kitchens and, often, private bathrooms. From 1983 to 1989, San Francisco housed homeless families for months and even years in two SRO residential hotels. During this period, local television news frequently showed footage of the squalid conditions in which these families lived. Filming was often done over a period of days, and the media clearly viewed the situation as an outrage. However, the social workers and children's advocates who brought the media to the hotels had no specific set of demands. As a result, the villains in the stories became the hotel owners, who typically were accused of getting rich at the expense of vulnerable women and children.

The real culprits weren't the hotel owners, whom the city had begged to house the homeless families; those responsible for the deplorable situation were city officials, whose policy was to shelter homeless families in hotels—the cheapest possible housing source—rather than apartments. Because the social workers did not focus media attention on the city's policy, the "solution" to the scandal thus became linked to the landlords' alleged misconduct. Like the Claude Rains character in *Casablanca,* who is "shocked" to find gambling at Humphrey Bogart's nightclub, local politicians responded to this media coverage by demanding more hotel inspections and threatening to cut off funds to uninhabitable hotels. The media, having won their "victory" with City Hall promises, moved on to other stories, while the families continued to live in completely unsuitable housing.

The differences between the media tactics used in the "heatless hotels" case and those used in the "homeless families" story could not be clearer. In the former, activists persuaded the media to pressure City Hall to take definite actions that would—and in retrospect, did—permanently end the widespread lack of heat in residential hotels. Advocates for the homeless families, however, failed to use the media spotlight to press for the only real solution: ending the city's practice of transforming residential hotel rooms into long-term family housing. Whereas the heat campaign shifted the focus away from landlord misconduct and toward the city's complicity, the coverage of homeless families made City Hall the hero for its vow to crack down on profiteering slumlords. The city's failure to monitor conditions in hotel rooms paid for with public funds was lost amid the footage of crying children, angry mothers, and decrepit rooms.

The ability to generate media coverage and then provide a specific, implementable solution obviously depends on the issue. Stories on hunger in the United States, which run with particular frequency between Thanksgiving and Christmas, utilize powerful images and evoke viewer sympathy. Many newspapers promote versions of the *New York Times*'s "Neediest Cases Fund" during this period to solicit donations to reduce poverty and hunger. But even though activists have responded to such stories by urging more public jobs, larger welfare payments, and wider availability of food stamps, in the past two decades, federal, state, and local governments have done exactly the reverse. Conservatives have succeeded in framing poverty and hunger as beyond government's ability to solve, a stance boosted by the failure of these neediest-cases campaigns to blame specific policies or politicians for the plight of the poor persons profiled.

Choosing a Media Contact

Although social change activists and organizations cannot totally control the traditional media's final product, we can significantly influence it by choosing a skilled media spokesperson. There are two contexts in which such a person is essential: when a reporter wants to speak to a member of the affected constituency group, and when the reporter talks to organization staff. A third critical point is whether an organization member or a staff person does the speaking. The first context is usually not a problem; the affected constituency typically includes at least one excellent spokesperson, someone whose communication skills have become evident during the organizing process.

Many groups devote great effort to preparing residents for media contact, as recommended in standard organizer-training manuals. However, I have never had a problem letting a homeless person, an elderly tenant living without heat, or a similarly situated individual with no prior public speaking or media training to simply tell his or her story to reporters. These people need no training or briefing; all I ever tell them is not to hesitate to describe fully how much they have suffered from the problem at issue. On the rare occasions when I feel reporters will be hostile but the interview cannot be avoided, I warn the interviewee to talk to the reporter as if speaking to an enemy. Otherwise, I have found that many people are natural communicators who would only be made nervous by instructions on what they should say.

Many people use media role-playing and mock press events to prepare untrained community speakers; I have found this unnecessary. Reporters enjoy interviewing real people with real problems, because so many of their interviews are with skilled spin-control experts. The natural demeanor of community speakers, combined with reporters' sympathy toward them, generally produces a positive story. For example, in the twenty-five-day sit-in by disabled protesters discussed in chapter 7, many if not most of the participants were interviewed. The activists needed no training to convincingly explain the meaning of their protest; their open discussion of their own life experiences proved a potent weapon in winning public support for their cause.

Staff members of activist organizations, on the other hand, should not deal with reporters until they have been trained. Some groups route all media contact through a designated spokesperson, but this deprives other committed staff of the fun and glory of speaking to reporters and seeing their names in print. It also may prevent the person most knowledgeable about an issue or most responsible for a campaign's success from getting the public credit she or he deserves. A better strategy is simply to have the most media-savvy staff person discuss the ins and outs of the reporting or interviewing process beforehand with other staff members.

The key media rule is to establish at the outset the message you want conveyed and then make sure staff remarks bolster this message. People often have many comments to offer about a particular issue or event. However, some of these may detract from your central message, so raising them with the press could result in a story that misses or undermines your main point. Staff members inexperienced with reporters get into trouble when they ignore this critical rule. By engaging in lengthy discussions, they allow the reporter to direct their attention away from the central message. A good reporter gets activists to let down their guard and to talk as if addressing a trusted friend. Think how often we read controversial quotes whose source complains that they emerged during a long, on-the-record discussion that veered from the reporter's original inquiry. There is no law requiring activists to talk at length to reporters or to provide comments on topics on which they are unprepared to speak. By training staff to stick to the central message, the organization fulfills its media strategy and reduces the risk that its mission or principles will be misrepresented.

Over my career I have become far less trustful of reporters. I spent the 1980s and 1990s dealing with veteran reporters who were not interested in playing tricks with gotcha quotes, knew the background of the issues discussed, and saw a benefit in maintaining relations with someone who could provide them with stories for years to come. But shrinking traditional news staffs in the twenty-first century changed this dynamic. The constant turnover in smaller newsrooms means activists are more likely to deal with reporters with whom they have no track record. Inexperienced reporters lack the background knowledge to write strong stories advancing activist campaigns, and are more likely to write what their editor tells them than what activists want emphasized

Using Investigative Reporters

In today's media environment, "investigative reporting" often means getting the scoop on the latest celebrity to enter rehab or photos of a movie star in the corner of a restaurant kissing someone other than their romantic partner. Celebrity investigative journalism now dominates a field whose exposés about defective products and political corruption once inspired many to become journalists, and that uncovered facts impacting people's lives. But thanks to fierce competition for "breaking news" and to online sources churning through stories at breakneck speed, serious investigative reporting is on the rebound. Activists should consider using investigative reporters to help achieve their goals.

My own experience working with the nationally acclaimed Center for Investigative Reporting (CIR) has led me to conclude that investigative journalists can have such a powerful impact on social change efforts that organizations should always consider calling upon them. I learned firsthand of the value of investigative journalism during the Tenderloin Housing Clinic's battle with the late Guenter Kaussen, a man characterized in various news reports as "the world's largest slumlord." This battle began with a small Tenderloin press conference, grew to an international story that received coverage on both West German national television stations and on CBS's 60 *Minutes,* and ended with Kaussen's suicide as his real estate empire slid into bankruptcy.

Although there is a certain glamour and excitement that come from such big-time coverage, attracting the likes of 60 *Minutes* to the story didn't yield any special victories for Tenderloin residents or help accomplish any strategic goals. The intense local coverage, however, apparently inspired the German television coverage, all of which contributed to the downfall of Kaussen and the improvement of conditions for his tenants in the Tenderloin, which was our goal. The genesis and development of the story is instructive.

Known as the "German Howard Hughes" for his secretive business practices and his estimated $500 million fortune, Kaussen was Germany's largest apartment owner when the Clinic began its fight with him in 1983. He also had significant holdings in Vancouver and Atlanta and owned twenty-three large apartment buildings in San Francisco, including fourteen properties containing more than 1,100 apartment units in the Tenderloin neighborhood. I became involved with Kaussen after Cambodian tenants living in one of his buildings contacted me. Kaussen's management company had issued eviction notices for nonpayment of rent to many of the Cambodian families. However, all of the families had paid their rent and had the receipts to prove it. The Clinic and some Cambodian tenants held a press conference and rally in front of the apartment building to demand that Kaussen rescind the eviction notices. There was certainly nothing innovative about this strategy, but as a protest by Cambodian tenants—widely but falsely viewed as afraid to fight for their rights—the event had enough of an angle to attract one television reporter.

When I saw the TV crew (more intimidating to wrongdoers than print reporters wielding mere notebooks), I assumed we would win a quick victory: management would withdraw the notices and apologize for the error, and the tenants would go on with their lives. But events took a different turn. Kaussen's staff refused to speak to the reporters, then barred the television crew from photographing the building's interior. The result was that instead of an unremarkable clip of yet another landlord-tenant dispute, the evening news showed dramatic footage of apartment managers denying a TV crew access to the building. Interspersed with the footage were shots of Kaussen's staff giving evasive "no comment" answers and teary Cambodians holding eviction notices. Something strange was going on, and given that Kaussen had quietly become the Tenderloin's leading property owner, I felt that further investigation into his empire was necessary.

After doing a property search and comparing the list to tenant complaints I had received, I concluded that Kaussen operated his properties unlike any other San Francisco landlord. His rents were the highest in the neighborhood, roughly equivalent to the pricier rents of lower Nob Hill, on the Tenderloin's border. I could not figure out how Kaussen got tenants to pay such high rents until I discovered that the rent stated in the lease was a myth. Kaussen had an "every sixth month rent-free" policy. A tenant agreeing to pay $600 per month for a studio would actually pay a monthly average of $500 over a year's period. It seemed to make no sense for Kaussen to inflate his rents, then negate his gains by charging *no* rent one month out of every six. Kaussen also had a unique strategy for attracting potential tenants despite the high initial rents: he established a free service for tenants seeking apartments in the city. The service, known as Mr. Apartment, differed from other such services in that it imposed no fee; however, Kaussen owned all of the units available through Mr. Apartment.

The inflated rent roll, Mr. Apartment, and other oddities convinced me to seek assistance in ferreting out Kaussen's operation. Fortunately, located barely a mile from my office was the CIR, which by 1983 had established a solid track record for investigative journalism. When I met with CIR director Dan Noyes, he immediately expressed great interest in investigating the secretive German multimillionaire. The CIR had a contract with the local NBC television affiliate to develop stories, and the station's reporter, Evan White, was excited about pursuing the story. I gave Dan all my notes and sources and let him go to work. Eventually, Dan would persuade a *60 Minutes* producer that Kaussen was worthy of attention. As depicted by *60 Minutes,* Kaussen was "the world's worst landlord," a reclusive eccentric who had successfully avoided publicity for years while pioneering condo conversions in his native West Germany. Now he was suddenly the subject of two or three television news reports per week.

The Clinic sought to emphasize Kaussen's strategy for building his real estate empire—a point ultimately deemphasized by *60 Minutes*. Research into the financing of Kaussen's properties revealed three critical facts. First, Kaussen used his buildings as collateral to obtain loans to acquire new properties. He was particularly adept at using the same property as collateral for several different loans. One such property, a 364-unit apartment building located in the heart of the Tenderloin, was worth at most $8 million in 1983; yet Kaussen had used this property to secure nearly $18 million in loans, including a multimillion-dollar guaranteed loan from the U.S. Department of Housing and Urban Development. Second, Kaussen inflated the value of his properties through his "sixth month free" policy, which exaggerated the rental income from each building by $15,000 to $20,000 a year. The inflation in value enabled him to obtain loans that could not be supported by actual revenues. Third, Kaussen's North American empire was created when the West German mark was at a historic high in relation to the dollar. As this margin contracted in the early 1980s, so did Kaussen's cash flow.

Simply put, Kaussen was an early practitioner of the type of real estate chicanery that led to the savings and loan scandal. S&Ls lent him money without paying attention to his lack of up-front capital, without determining the actual income from or operating expenses of property used as collateral to secure loans, and without investigating whether such property had been similarly used for previous deals. Guenter Kaussen became the Tenderloin's largest property owner solely on the strength of his name; his vast international holdings—rather than proof of equity—were all he needed. Kaussen also made use of shady post-deregulation financing vehicles such as the creatively named Consolidated Capital. These small, speculation-fed institutions must have been thrilled to attract someone of Kaussen's stature.

The publicity we generated about Kaussen's financing practices made some of his more traditional lenders nervous. They began monitoring their Kaussen loans closely, refusing new refinancing efforts, and cracking down on delays in mortgage payments. The lenders' concern intensified when they learned from the media that the rent schedule they relied upon in granting Kaussen financing was falsified.

By mid-1984, the San Francisco media were all over the Kaussen story. For several months I had been in almost daily contact with Dan Noyes, and the Clinic had helped fan the flames by filing highly publicized lawsuits over Kaussen's failure to return tenant security deposits and to make necessary repairs. As time went on, stories about Kaussen increasingly involved foreclosures and sales of his properties. Kaussen's problems in San Francisco became a major story in West Germany, and

I was repeatedly interviewed at length by the two West German national TV stations. The German media had long been frustrated by Kaussen and were excited at the prospect that events in San Francisco might spell the end of his empire.

Then *60 Minutes* came to town. I found myself hosting Morley Safer at my office, where we talked for a few hours, and taking him on a tour of the Tenderloin. His producer's interest in the story was not shared by Safer himself, who became animated only when the off-camera discussions turned to rising Manhattan real estate values. My own excitement over the prospect of national attention waned as soon as I saw the finished product, which didn't air until several months after the filming, by which time Kaussen's empire was in free fall. Significantly, the *60 Minutes* report virtually ignored the real estate practices that Kaussen used to create his empire. Instead, Safer focused on former employees' remarks about Kaussen's bizarre employment and management practices. The segment did not examine in detail the context of Kaussen's rise—his leveraging of properties through doctored rent schedules and overcollateralization of properties. Although Kaussen's empire was headed inexorably toward collapse when the *60 Minutes* episode finally aired, the show seemed to take credit for pushing him over the edge when, a month after the episode's airing, it announced his suicide.

The main impression left by the *60 Minutes* story was that Kaussen was one strange multimillionaire. I was obviously naive in thinking that his rise and fall would be portrayed as a cautionary tale for the real estate industry of the mid-1980s. As it stood, Kaussen's empire disintegrated three years before the savings and loan scandal toppled other real estate magnates of the 1980s. Had *60 Minutes* compared Kaussen's real estate acquisition strategies to those of American entrepreneurs, the program could have foreshadowed, if not predicted, the urban real estate crash of the late 1980s.

The rapid demise of Kaussen's empire was not an inevitable result of adverse publicity. Kaussen had been subject to media attacks before, including a cover story in *Der Spiegel* (the German equivalent of *Time*), with the cover drawing depicting him as a vulture. Our media strategy achieved greater results because the Center for Investigative Reporting produced one new gem of information after another, keeping the media focused on the story for months. I helped by timing the lawsuits against Kaussen to maximize media coverage (our filing was often the lead story on the local evening news).

Kaussen's real estate empire might have fallen eventually, but CIR's work ensured this outcome.

Tactics for Dealing with Reporters

To quote pioneer environmental activist Henry David Thoreau, today's tactical activists must "forever be on the alert" in dealing with reporters. No matter how sympathetic reporters appear, or how much time they spend interviewing you, you cannot assume that the resulting story will advance your cause. In case anyone still doubts this necessity for eternal vigilance, it's worth describing the worst media betrayal of a social change activist that I have ever witnessed.

Not surprisingly, the story involved the homeless. After an initial burst of highly sympathetic coverage of the re-emergence of widespread visible homelessness in the United States in the early 1980s, some of the media sought a new angle on the story by blaming those without homes for their own plight. Some of this coverage came to resemble the newsreels used by movie studios to attack Upton Sinclair's 1938 populist campaign for governor of California. In the trailers, actors dressed as hobos were asked where they were headed. "To California," they answered, "because when Upton Sinclair is elected he's going to raise taxes on working people so that I can be housed and fed." The newsreel audiences, not knowing the hobos were actors reading a script, believed their own scant savings would be taken to support the shiftless if Sinclair were elected. The tactic of using the words of hobos themselves to defeat Sinclair proved successful.

It is no longer unusual for stories about homelessness to quote self-identified homeless people stating such things as, "Ninety-five percent of the homeless are drug addicts or drunks who voluntarily choose to live on the streets." The media are far less interested in reporting on how the federal government's severe cutbacks in spending on affordable housing since the 1980s has caused and perpetuates widespread homelessness. Nor are there pieces noting that the overwhelming number of homeless people—particularly families with children—are in shelters or on the streets because they cannot obtain housing they can afford. Rather than relying on facts in the form of statistics and other empirical data to explain homelessness—which would require reporters to find, collect, and read such information—it is far more common for stories to quote homeless people themselves to define the problem. And since reporters can choose which homeless persons to quote, these interviews of "real" people have been used to shift the blame from a social problem to one of individual pathology; blaming homeless persons for the problem has become a media staple, even among reporters who personally understand the broader policy issues.

My example of media betrayal involves a 1993 Bay Area television news report on the homeless. The report centered entirely on a quote from one homeless advocate, an individual who had no prior media experience and worked full-time for the homeless despite receiving only a small stipend. This individual was not known outside a small core of activists, did not head any organization, and certainly never thought he would become the focus of a two-part series or that one of his quotes would run all week in promotional ads.

The activist was quoted as saying, "The homeless are just like you and me." Homeless advocates often make this statement, generally to convey the idea that homeless people, like everyone else, have dreams, aspirations, hopes, fears, and emotional and physical needs. This activist, however, was not "forever on the alert." He did not realize that the producer of the piece, for all his professed concern for the homeless, needed such a quote for his own agenda. The producer juxtaposed the quote "The homeless are just like you and me" with a video montage of drunks sprawled in gutters and guzzling cheap wine. Added to the montage were quotes from homeless people belittling the idea that the homeless were like "you and me." The entire series attacked homeless advocates for intentionally misrepresenting their constituency to the public. No sympathetic homeless person was included in the series. Such an omission was particularly striking coming from a news outlet that only a few years earlier—using different personnel—had run a five-minute report on how "people like you and me" end up homeless.

Although homeless advocates and media commentators attacked the series' depiction of homeless people as intoxicated lowlifes, it won a Peabody Award for best investigative local television news story. Whereas a series that exclusively portrayed members of an ethnic group drinking, shooting up, and lolling in gutters would be considered racist, a similar attack on the poor brought an award. The producer took advantage of an activist's attraction to television coverage of homelessness and used him to hurt his own constituency. The episode is a cautionary tale for all activists.[3]

Activists have no obligation to assist a journalist with what could well be a negative story. Some reporters are expert at making activists feel guilty about refusing to give quotes or to provide information; they claim they want only to hear your side of the story and emphasize their commitment to "the facts." They may warn that if you fail to speak, only your opponent's views will be expressed. Ignore their pleas. If your instincts tell you that a reporter cannot be trusted, he or she should be rebuffed.

Cultivating Media Allies

I prefer relying on reporters known to be sympathetic. Increased news-room turnover has made this more difficult, but most large media out-lets have at least one reporter interested in producing stories favorable to your constituency's interests. These reporters are readily identified from their prior coverage of similar issues or discussions with activists. They may not share a progressive political ideology but are simply com-mitted to honest reporting on social or economic unfairness. These reporters should be given the first crack at all stories you view as having major public interest. Many activists rely on the hit-or-miss method of issuing press releases to all media and trying to get good stories from unfamiliar reporters. This can produce good results, but it is more stra-tegically sound to work with the reporters most likely to produce the story that best promotes your cause.

Sympathetic reporters are far more likely to produce the necessary follow-up coverage and to include the quotes and overall spin you desire. You can also turn to these media allies when you or your orga-nization comes under unfair attack—assistance that cannot be counted on from reporters with whom you lack such a trusting relationship. Extensive reliance on sympathetic media sources may leave some stories with less exposure, or with no coverage at all if the reporter unexpect-edly fails to come through. Nevertheless, depending on a few key media allies will produce significantly better results over time. And if you face a situation in which issuing a broad release is essential, give your media ally a heads-up so she or he knows and is not taken by surprise.

A great strategy for cultivating media allies is forming relationships with columnists. Columns are often widely read pieces and are not sub-ject to the editorial control that can prevent sympathetic reporters from covering your stories. In the campaign against Nike sweatshops waged by Global Exchange and other groups in the late 1990s, *New York Times* columnist Bob Herbert played a critical role in publicizing the struggle. From June 1996 to June 1997, Herbert devoted eight entire columns to Nike's labor practices, ensuring that the critical struggle was covered in the nation's most influential newspaper. Herbert's pieces were so influential in spurring other media to cover Nike sweatshops that Nike CEO Phillip Knight met with the *Times* after the fourth column appeared. Knight asked the *Times* to stop Herbert from writing about Nike's practices, but the *Times* said it did not tell columnists what to write and denied his request. While declining news readership and the explosion of online commentators mean that fewer columnists can have such a national impact, the role of local columnists may be even greater today. As there is less space for reportage, columns are often the only place readers learn about certain issues.[4]

I came to appreciate fully the tactical value of relying on media allies when a 1993 front-page story in San Francisco's daily afternoon newspaper, the *Examiner*, attacked the Tenderloin Housing Clinic and me. The story accused the Clinic of referring homeless persons to a residential hotel that was known to be a firetrap. A blaze had occurred at the hotel, resulting in one death. I was quoted extensively in the story, but some passages were entirely fabricated, and most of my quotes were placed at the tail end of the piece (an increasingly common tactic). The key message of the story was that the Clinic, an organization claiming to care about low-income housing conditions, ignored city warnings about the hotel's dangers and intentionally put the lives of tenants in danger.

A front-page newspaper story offering a new angle on an issue often prompts a feeding frenzy from other media sources, because reporters take heat from their editors and news directors for missing the new angle themselves. The Clinic averted a full-fledged media assault on its credibility because I got in touch with all of our trusted media contacts and explained why the *Examiner* story was wrong. I also faxed documents to the media to confirm our position. Reporters with whom I had worked on prior stories and established a relationship of trust were not going to produce false articles about the Clinic. As a result, not a single radio or television station ever followed up on the *Examiner*'s angle. Instead, I diverted the media frenzy toward the city's dismal failure at housing-code enforcement. As media attention shifted from the fire to the city's inadequate housing inspection process, even the *Examiner* was forced to redirect its own coverage accordingly.

The best was yet to come. On the morning of the fire, I had received a call from Mayor Frank Jordan's office requesting all Clinic documents relating to the burned hotel. Sensing a hidden agenda, I immediately warned city officials against trying to connect the Clinic to the fire. When I saw the *Examiner* story, it was obvious that the Jordan administration had fed the reporter this material in order to undercut me, a vocal critic of administration policies.[5]

I promptly contacted a reporter for an alternative weekly newspaper with whom I had worked on several stories. In the next issue, she revealed how the mayor's chief of staff sought to use the fire to tarnish the Clinic's image as a zealous advocate for the poor. When the article came out, the mayor's chief of staff promptly called me to deny any connection to the *Examiner* story or any effort to harm the Clinic. I saw as never before how sympathetic coverage can transform even the worst media attack into an advancement of organizational interests. The fact that the fire resulted in prompt passage of Clinic-supported code enforcement legislation (previously stalled for lack of votes) only added to my satisfaction.

RESPONDING TO MEDIA BIAS

Activists often debate whether to respond to unfair stories about their causes. The typical scenario does not involve a direct attack on activists or their organizations—which makes responding essential—but rather occurs when stories are premised on unrepresentative sources, miss or confuse key facts, or unfairly frame issues in a manner designed to undermine support for the group's agenda. Since responding to such bias risks further publicizing the unfair comments, careful consideration must be paid before activists publish an angry response that elevates a story that would otherwise have no impact.

I recommend the following thought process. First, consider whether the piece has caused any real harm to your cause or constituency. If not, the best response is no response; people are so overloaded with information that one unfair story is usually soon forgotten. A nonresponse is particularly appropriate when the story's author has the right to reply; this only gives him or her a second chance to make unfair assertions against your cause.

Assessing real harm to your constituency first depends on the author and forum. For example, some bloggers routinely post completely untrue and defamatory statements (often anonymously) about activists and progressive organizations. Responding is unnecessary because their comments have no impact. The same rule applies when the forum is legitimate but the author has little public influence. The *San Francisco Chronicle* has long employed a Republican columnist whose conservative views are out of touch with San Francisco. Calling attention to her writings only gives them attention they otherwise lack.

Sometimes the unfair media coverage comes from a credible source in a legitimate medium. In these more critical cases, activists must assess whether the bias is central or collateral to the story's purpose. For example, stories often include references—entirely unrelated to the article's primary thrust—intended to portray social change advocates negatively. For instance, stories about Alaska in the travel section of a newspaper may include a sentence criticizing environmental groups for seeking to preserve an area they have never visited. Restaurant reviews may include brief attacks on animal-rights activists who preach against meat but wear leather belts. Perhaps most common are articles criticizing activists battling global warming for flying to conferences on jet-fuel-burning airplanes (a silly charge often leveled against Al Gore). Such attacks are unfair, but do not cause harm and are best ignored.

In contrast, a response is definitely appropriate when media outlets with public credibility feature unfair stories *focused on your agenda*. In such cases, after establishing that unfair media bias has caused real harm, a tactical activist must decide how to react. Many respond through letters to the editor or, if possible, by posting a comment on the website where the offending story appeared. But letters addressing newspaper bias are missed by online readers, and either may be shortened for publication in the print version or may not get published there at all. Online newspaper comment sections are particularly ineffective for challenging unfair stories, because they allow anonymous postings and are edited only to exclude profanity and other clearly improper speech. Since they tend to be filled with racist, sexist, and other hateful comments, such forums are not the place for a substantive response to a biased story.

Some activists ask editors to run their response to an unfair column or feature story as a guest editorial. I don't favor this strategy. Editorial page editors often impose so many restrictions on the op-ed that it becomes ineffective and untimely. Further, even if timely printed without revisions, the response is still identified as an opinion piece whereas the offending story appeared as "objective" news.

A far better strategy is to publish a response to unfair media stories online, and then use new media tools to distribute it widely. As I discuss in the following chapter, the rise of the new media has made it much easier for activists to combat unfair stories in whatever format they appear. I have written countless pieces for BeyondChron.org exposing falsehoods and bias in local and national news stories, thereby setting the record straight and helping deter future unfair pieces. One of my pieces described how a *New York Times* reporter had relied on anonymous sources in violation of the paper's written ethics procedures; he had also used sources as "neutral" experts without disclosing their financial ties to those whose position their comments backed. While my reporting drew a heated response from the reporter, he was careful to avoid such sourcing problems in future stories.

To forestall future unfair stories, activists should also contact the reporter directly to express their concerns. This process is greatly facilitated by the inclusion of reporter's email addresses at the end of online and many print stories. Reporters resent being accused of writing unfair stories, and since editors or the writers' personal agendas often drive these pieces, the chances are slim that they will concede their story was unfair. But once activists tell reporters about facts omitted from the challenged story, expose the financial conflicts of the story's "impartial" academic expert, or provide contact information of those with expertise with whom the reporter should speak, it makes it much less likely that the reporter repeats these errors. So contacting reporters has little downside: it either improves future stories or at least ensures that the specific mistakes activists highlighted are not repeated (and if they are, activists have an even better story to send out through the new media!).

Correcting television news bias is more difficult. The best strategy is to respond with your own online critique as discussed above. Although television is a powerful medium, I have never believed that unfair television news stories can do as much harm to my constituency as print media bias. Fewer people now watch a particular news show than in the pre-cable, pre-Internet days, and many view television news while eating or doing something else. When people tell me they have seen me interviewed on the news, they invariably do not recall more than the general subject matter of the story. If people cannot remember the views expressed by someone they know, it's doubtful that they pay close attention to other stories.

RESPONDING TO THINK-TANK MEDIA STORIES

Activists must respond to corporate- and conservative-backed media campaigns using "think tanks" to promote major policy shifts. Since the 1970s, such elite-funded "research" institutions have produced an endless stream of studies and reports designed to advance wealthy interests. The resident "scholars" in these think tanks are employed full-time to write stories, editorials, columns, and "news analysis" on political issues. The first generation of such groups included the Heritage Foundation, widely seen as providing the policy blueprint for Ronald Reagan's first term. Other early examples include the libertarian Cato Institute and the American Enterprise Institute, both of which routinely issue reports and provide speakers supporting a conservative ideological agenda. The media typically identifies such "experts" by their think-tank affiliation, rather than by the corporate polluters and Wall Street interests that indirectly pay their salaries.

Think-tank scholars shape the political environment when newspapers, magazines, and particularly television news shows give them ample space in all media formats to express their views. A lengthy article in a Sunday newspaper or a prominently placed article on an editorial page often triggers follow-up news stories and editorials supporting the "scholar's" view. Conservative think-tank articles echo through media outlets like almost no other, as ideologically sympathetic corporate news owners recognize their potential policy impact. The appearance of objectivity coupled with wide access enables conservative think tanks to increase public acceptance of elite political positions while also undermining the progressive agenda.

Following are two contrasting examples of how activists responded to two of the largest elite-driven uses of think tanks to change public policy: the nation's adoption of "supply side" economics in the 1980s, and the ongoing battle over "school reform." The former shows the destructive consequences of progressives' failure to mount an aggressive counterattack against conservative policies promoted by think tanks, and the latter struggle, while still ongoing, shows that progressive activists can reshape the debate when they fight back.

Supply-Side and Think-Tank Voodoo

Elite investment in think tanks has paid the greatest dividends—literally—in changing the national political environment regarding tax policy. The emergence of "supply side" economics in the late 1970s ushered in an almost uninterrupted three-decade shift away from progressive taxation and toward lowering taxes on the wealthy at the expense of everyone else.

The phrase *supply-side economics* first appeared in the *Wall Street Journal*, which began aggressively promoting federal tax cuts for the rich in 1978. The idea was the centerpiece of former *WSJ* editorial writer Jude Wanniski's book *The Way the World Works*, which argued that cutting taxes on the wealthy was the key strategy underlying nations' economic successes throughout history.[6]

Supply-side economics burst onto the national agenda during Ronald Reagan's 1980 presidential campaign and, upon his election, became the dominant U.S. economic policy. It appeared to offer something new to an electorate battered by both inflation and unemployment. In those days, Republicans felt they could not openly support reducing taxes for the rich without losing support among blue-collar voters. Nor could Reagan describe his plan as "trickle-down economics," a policy that would alienate working people. As a result, conservative scholars such as Wanniski and George Gilder—the latter affiliated with the Lehrman Institute's Economic Roundtable and the Manhattan Institute—joined with the *Wall Street Journal* to make an economic policy geared entirely toward helping the rich appear populist and even revolutionary. *Wall Street Journal* editor Robert Bartley, an ardent advocate of supply-side theories, strategized with Wanniski to broaden the audience for his proposal. In a 1989 preface to the third edition of Wanniski's book, Bartley noted that the "*Journal* op-ed page provided a daily bulletin board for such ideas."

It may sound hard to believe today, but during the 1980 campaign for the Republican presidential nomination, the strongest attack on the economic viability of Reagan's supply-side plan came from George H. W. Bush, who was later selected as his running mate. During the primary season, Bush decried supply-side as "voodoo economics" in a famous exchange. With incumbent Democratic president Jimmy Carter having alienated the party's liberal wing and abandoned progressive economic policies, activists felt they had no ability to pressure Carter to condemn Reagan's tax agenda. With Carter ineffectively challenging supply-side's extraordinary windfall for the rich, and activists disconnected from his campaign, the media saw no major political forces attacking this rebranded elitist economic program, and it was given a credibility never warranted.

When Reagan made supply-side economic policy the centerpiece of his historically regressive 1981 tax bill—cleverly named the "Economic Recovery Act of 1981" so that opponents would be accused of opposing recovery—activists had another chance to mobilize public opposition to the measure. Since Democrats still controlled the House of Representatives, they could have defeated the regressive tax bill. But the Democrats folded. The Internet's power to influence politics was still two decades away, and in the absence of the independent activist voices of still-non-existent social media, the Democratic Party joined in the tax-cutting frenzy. The House ratified the core economic principle of trickle down that still governs the Republican Party today.

Activists have paid dearly for not engaging in a full offensive against supply-side from the start. In William Greider's famous December 1981 *Atlantic* interview of David Stockman, Reagan's budget chief, Stockman admitted that *supply-side* was simply another name for trickle-down economics. Stockman's admission of this obvious fact became a national cause célèbre. The media were furious, acting as if they too had been deceived. But the damage was done. The Republican Party credited supply-side—rather than Reagan's massive Keynesian-style, budget-deficit-expanding defense spending—for taking the country out of the Carter economic stagnation and into a brief mid-1980s economic boom. The shortness of this economic success, whose decline culminated with the 1987 stock market crash and savings and loan fiscal meltdown, was never blamed on supply-side.

The elite-backed policy had enough clout that in 2001 George W. Bush could promote tax cuts for the wealthy without even claiming it was part of supply-side or any other economic "theory." And when Bush's repeat of Reagan's elite-driven policies plunged the nation into a new financial crisis in 2008, it made no difference to the interests that initially promoted supply-side. Every Republican running for the party's nomination in 2012 argued that cutting taxes for the wealthy would trickle down to benefit the middle class, the working class, and even the poor. Mitt Romney, the party's 2012 presidential nominee, made lowering taxes on the wealthy the centerpiece of his campaign.

President Barack Obama made raising taxes on the wealthy central to his 2012 reelection effort, and his victory was widely interpreted as reflecting a shift in American attitudes toward taxes. If so, the political success of supply-side economics had a remarkable three-decade run, even surviving in the face of the economic boom helped by President Bill Clinton and Congress's raising taxes on the wealthy in 1993. But activists have paid dearly for not challenging supply-side when it first moved from conservative think tanks to the political arena.

Teachers Fight Back

Just as elite interests promoted supply-side economics in response to a troubled economy, powerful forces outside the classroom are using the illusion of data-driven proposals to press for reforms in our nation's troubled public schools. Billionaires like Bill Gates and Eli Broad are among those engaged in a heavily funded school "reform" initiative that often blames teachers unions rather than inadequate public funding for achievement problems in public schools. Pointing to declining test scores, rising dropout rates, failing schools, and ample research from elite-funded think tanks, these school reform efforts gained momentum after 2000 as the Bush administration underfunded education and state school budgets were slashed. But teachers and public school advocates are vigorously fighting back, and, unlike supply-side opponents, have mobilized grassroots support for their own reform agenda.

Just as Jude Wanniski and economist Arthur Laffer provided convincing public faces to promote supply-side economics, Michelle Rhee, chancellor for Washington, D.C., public schools from 2007 to 2010, is the front person for elite attacks on teachers unions and public schools. Local school superintendents rarely become national figures, but Rhee appeared on the cover of *Time* magazine holding a broom to signify her plans to sweep away teacher tenure. She was also on the cover of *Newsweek* and even appeared on Oprah Winfrey's widely watched nationally syndicated show. The latter was part of the chancellor's strategy to convince African American parents that their children are suffering because of bad teachers.

In 2012 Rhee toured the nation promoting charter schools and vouchers, assessing teachers based on their students' test scores, and, most important, condemning the evils of teachers unions. Rhee made more than 150 public appearances in 2011–12, reportedly getting as much as $50,000 per speech plus "first-class expenses." It's a pretty good deal for an educational "reformer" whose reputation is based on her controversial tenure as D.C. chancellor. Rhee closed schools, fired over half of the teachers, and tried to eliminate tenure. She justified her actions by pointing to statistics that showed sharply rising test scores in the district—until the same type of cheating found in Atlanta, several Texas school districts, and other reform "models" emerged to undermine her sole claim to achievement. Rhee may be the only school chief in history whose tenure was the central issue in a big-city mayor's race; the 2010 Washington, D.C., mayoral election was seen as a referendum on Rhee, and the mayor who appointed her was defeated. Rhee resigned from her position (before the new mayor could terminate her) in October 2010.[7]

Prominent educator Diane Ravitch has explained the Rhee phenomenon:

> Her celebrity results from the fact that she has emerged as the national spokesman for the effort to subject public education to free-market forces, including competition, decision by data, and consumer choice. All of this sounds very appealing when your goal is to buy a pound of butter or a pair of shoes, but it is not a sensible or wise approach to creating good education. What it produces, predictably, is cheating, teaching to bad tests, institutionalized fraud, dumbing down of tests, and a narrowed curriculum.
>
> This formula, which will be a tragedy for our nation and for an entire generation of children, is now immensely popular in the states and the Congress. Most governors embrace it. The big foundations endorse it. The think tanks of D.C., right-wing and left-wing, support it. Rhee helped to make it fashionable. If she doesn't pause to consider the damage she is doing, shame on her. If our policymakers don't stop to reflect on the damage they are doing to public education and to any concept of a good education, then our nation is in deep trouble.[8]

The membership roll for Rhee's "StudentsFirst" national lobbying and advocacy group reads like a donor list to Super PACs. This is fitting, given that Hari Sevugan, StudentsFirst's vice president of communications, said in late 2011 that the group "plans to raise $1 billion over five years." Its donors include billionaire New Jersey hedge-fund trader and major Republican donor David Tepper, and the Texas-based Laura and John Arnold Foundation, whose grant to Rhee's group was reportedly in the tens of millions of dollars. The Broad Foundation, the philanthropy funded by Los Angeles billionaire Eli Broad, is also a donor. The Broad Foundation has poured billions into education "reforms" such as charter schools, and Eli Broad has spent hundreds of thousands of dollars backing Los Angeles and San Diego school board members who support his vision. In 2011 and 2013, Broad's Coalition for School Reform joined other billionaire donors (New York City mayor Michael Bloomberg contributed $1 million to the March 2013 race) in backing a Los Angeles School Board slate opposed to the teachers union–backed candidates (the key billionaire-backed candidate was defeated). The infusion of big donor contributions into historically low-budget school board races can easily tilt the election to the billionaire-backed candidates, effectively giving wealthy outsiders significant input in, if not control of, school board policies.[9]

These attacks on teachers and public schools are particularly daunting because Broad and other billionaire school "reformers" also provide financial backing to Democrats. This leaves some activists less willing to challenge political allies over support for linking teacher performance to standardized test results, for charter schools, and for other portions of the "reform" agenda that do not directly attack unions. Meanwhile, Rhee and others who bash teachers unions have found allies in the anti-union agendas of Republican governors. For example, Rhee joined notoriously anti-union Wisconsin governor Scott Walker at the 2011 convention of the American Federation for Children, a right-wing "education reform" organization funded by religious-right multi-millionaire Betsy DeVos to support vouchers for Christian schools and the ending of public employees' unions. Rhee has also appeared with Florida Tea Party favorite Rick Scott, a strong opponent of unions.

Never before have so many resources gone toward increasing public opposition to teachers unions and public education. The "reform" campaign has funded studies, media appearances, books, the feature documentary film *Waiting for Superman,* and in 2012 even a major Hollywood movie, *Won't Back Down* (in which parents "won't back down" from battling evil teachers unions trying to wreck public schools; the film bombed). Despite this onslaught, grassroots school activists and teachers unions continue to mobilize for school reforms that do not excessively elevate misleading test scores and blame teachers for all problems. And they appear to be making headway. Here's how they have done it.

School Activists Create a Counternarrative

The most important strategy used by opponents of think-tank-led school reforms was establishing a counternarrative. Ironically, some credit for teachers' aggressively setting forth an alternative analysis for failing schools might go to someone not on most progressive lists of heroes: former longtime New York City teachers union chief Albert Shanker. Starting in the 1960s, Shanker's United Federation of Teachers paid to have a weekly column in the Sunday *New York Times* Week in Review section. Intended to set forth the union's positions on issues, the column and its high visibility made Shanker among the nation's best-known labor leaders. His successors continued the column, demonstrating that teachers have long been way ahead of other labor unions in understanding the importance of connecting to the broader public and winning its support.

This legacy is important in that it helps explain why teachers understood that these elite-funded attacks against them could not simply be opposed, but had to be responded to with a counternarrative explaining troubled schools. Central to the teacher counternarrative was disproving "research" claiming that students in nonunion charter schools had test results superior to those attending traditional, unionized public schools. Teachers recognized that despite questions about what test scores actually prove, many parents see standardized test results as critical to their children's future. This meant that teachers could not simply argue, for example, that a school's preponderance of immigrant children with limited English proficiency distorted test scores, or that it made no sense to deem a middle school "failing" for low test scores from kids who had arrived from their prior schools well below grade level in reading and math. Opponents of elite-driven reform had to accept the public's support for testing, and take on the issue directly. This was a crucial strategy because Michelle Rhee's own credibility was built on her claims to having achieved both astonishing improvements in test scores during her second and third years as a teacher, and smaller but still significant increases while D.C. chancellor.

The teachers and their activist allies soon discovered that claims by Rhee and other "reformers" that their educational strategies produced higher test scores were not supported by the facts. Guy Brandenburg, a retired math teacher, struck a powerful blow when he investigated the actual test results from Rhee's Baltimore tenure and found that her increases were less than half of what she claimed. "It's important for the public to know," Brandenburg concluded, "that the main spokesperson for the movement for additional dumb standardized testing, for teaching to the test, and for firing teachers based on those dumb tests would herself have been fired under those criteria." In fact, Rhee's Washington, D.C., gains became subject to a federal investigation because of excessive erasures on tests from thirty-five classrooms.[10]

Similar flawed testing results allegedly supporting the advantages of nonunion charter schools were also exposed. The Atlanta Federation of Teachers exposed a test cheating scandal in December 2005, but the union's complaint was ignored and whistle-blowers in the district were punished and silenced. Ultimately, the union's charges were confirmed, and nearly 180 Atlanta district employees were found to have participated in altering student test results. A *Los Angeles Times* study in 2011 found that in L.A. Unified, "struggling schools under district control saw test scores rise more than most operated by the mayor, a charter organization and others." This was after Mayor Antonio

Villaraigosa, strongly backed by billionaire education reformer Eli Broad, had spent years bashing teachers unions (for whom he once worked). Teacher advocates also pointed out that "many of the nation's worst-performing schools (according to the National Assessment of Educational Progress) are concentrated in Southern and Western right-to-work states, where public sector unions are weakest." A 2009 study of about half of all charters nationwide, financed by the pro-charter Walton Family Foundation (of Walmart fame) and the Michael and Susan Dell Foundation, "found that more than 80 percent either do no better, or actually perform substantially worse, than traditional public schools, a dismal record."[11]

Teachers and other progressive reform advocates enlisted media allies in publicizing the actual facts about charter schools and other conservative goals, and the resulting stories echoed through the traditional and new media. As parents noticed that art, music, and other cultural programs were being sacrificed for student standardized test preparation, the reality of the Rhee agenda aroused a parent backlash that continues to grow. Progressive school reformers also created their own media vehicles for countering the attacks on teachers and public schools. These include publications from Rethinking Schools and from Teaching for Change, whose Washington, D.C., bookstore, Busboys and Poets, provides public education for parents and others who want to turn schools into centers for social justice.

Some diminish the success of school activists battling corporate control of schools by noting that teachers unions have money to combat such attacks, that teachers are college graduates who understand how to use the traditional and new media, and that teacher organizing is more easily done because schools promote close interactions between teachers and parents. But none of these factors alters this key fact: teachers, parents, and other opponents of regressive reforms have effectively used media and grassroots organizing to create a powerful counternarrative about what is ailing our schools. In contrast, progressive activists who challenged well-funded conservative think-tank policy initiatives on such issues as supply-side economics, attacks on unions, and the "virtues" of deregulation, to name but a few, failed to create powerful counternarratives until it was too late.

The billionaires funding Rhee-style school "reforms" are not giving up, and it is far too soon to declare victory in their war on public schools. But progressive school activists have already created a critical model for others battling potentially transformative "reforms" initiated by elite-driven think tanks. Progressives have also invested in their own influential research centers to promote progressive policies and challenge conservatives—including the Center for American Progress, the Economic Policy Institute, and Media Matters—ensuring that never again will the elite's funding of research to support policy changes go unchallenged.

6

The Internet and Social Media

Maximizing the Power of Online Activism

For many activists, particularly those under thirty, the traditional media are less relevant than the Internet, email, Facebook, Twitter, and other so-called new media. New media's rapid growth in political influence has been astonishing. During the 2000 election, only 41 percent of households even had Internet access, and very few activists had laptops facilitating instant communication. Markos Moulitsas did not found Daily Kos, perhaps the nation's preeminent progressive activist electoral site, until May 2002. Arianna Huffington's widely followed *Huffington Post* did not exist until 2005, the same year that YouTube, now one of activists' most common tools, emerged. While new media have not changed the fundamental rules of organizing and activism, these tools have dramatically expanded tactical and strategic possibilities. The challenge for activists lies in maximizing the potential of new media by harnessing them to traditional organizing and media strategies; too many campaigns still fail to seize upon this synergy.

This chapter describes how to use new-media tools to expose issues and mobilize grassroots support. I also discuss how new media foster progressive electoral activism, particularly through "nationalizing" local and state campaigns. The rise of the "Netroots" has greatly benefited progressive activism and has clearly boosted campaigns for greater social and economic justice.

EXPOSING ISSUES AND CAMPAIGNS

In the old media days, the failure of leading newspapers, television news stations, or radio outlets to cover a news event was like a tree falling unobserved in the forest—it effectively did not occur. And while some news stories got ample coverage in progressive media or limited circulation publications, activists had limited capacity to propel the story out to a broader audience.

New-media tools changed this dynamic. Tactical activists can now turn stories that would have remained buried in the past into national headlines. In December 2006, five African American students in the small town of Jena, Louisiana, were charged with attempted murder after a school-ground fight with a white student. Such school fights are common, and activists saw racial bias in the decision to charge the African American students with committing major felonies. While local media covered the story, it did not get out to the rest of the country until the website Color of Change (colorofchange.org) launched a major online campaign in 2007 to highlight the case.

Founded by former Obama Green Jobs "czar" and Rebuild the Dream founder Van Jones and James Rucker, a former director of MoveOn Political Action, Color of Change was created to use online resources to strengthen the political voice of African Americans and to advance racial justice. Jones and Rucker recognized a key fact about the Jena prosecutions that other activists might have missed; namely, that getting broader publicity for a story coming out of a little-known Louisiana town could take time. As a result, the duo persisted in pounding the story on its Color of Change site even after a month of promoting the Jena case failed to bring broader coverage. The "Jena 6" prosecutions did not get coverage outside Louisiana until May 2007, and it was not until September 20 of that year that 15,000 to 20,000 protesters from across the nation descended on Jena for one of the era's largest civil rights protests. Color of Change used new-media tools to expose this racial injustice, and its website also raised more than $200,000 for the students' legal defense.

In a more prominent example of new media's potency, on February 26, 2012, Trayvon Martin, an unarmed African American teenager, was shot and killed in a gated community in Stafford, Florida. His assailant was questioned by police but not arrested. Despite these facts, the story did not reach beyond Florida media until March 8. Martin's parents then launched a petition on the website Change.org that explained the facts of the case and requested support. The online petition galvanized concern and garnered more than 2.3 million signers by April 11, when the independent state prosecutor announced the arrest and prosecution of Martin's killer. The parents' attorney was among those who credited the petition for bringing this case to the national spotlight, as media coverage snowballed after its launching. The petition built support for rallies across the country and for a major event on March 22 in Stafford attended by civil rights leaders. According to the Project for Excellence in Journalism, Martin's killing became the first story in 2012 to exceed coverage of the presidential race.

Change.org's publicizing of Martin's case and its building of grass-roots support for action reflected its broader mission. Through its "Featured Petitions," Change.org creates vehicles for activism on issues—such as pressuring Secretary of State Hillary Clinton to support Saudi Arabian women's campaign for the right to drive—that otherwise would have difficulty building broad support. And by promoting campaigns that lack other major organizational backers, Change.org expands the "people power" devoted to the cause rather than duplicating other efforts. The website also focuses on specific, winnable fights. Online petitions are less effective in securing structural change, but mobilizing people to persuade Bank of America to cancel a planned $5 debit fee, or to stop banks from foreclosing on individuals' homes, encourages those involved to take on bigger struggles.[1]

Like all tactics, activists' efforts to expose issues and campaigns via new media can be misused. The risk is greatest when these tools purport to expose a huge injustice to an audience that lacks information about the underlying issue. In the same month that Change.org propelled Trayvon Martin's killing into a national story, a twenty-eight-minute YouTube video went viral that described a long-running military conflict in northern Uganda. The video portrayed the violence as having been entirely caused by Joseph Kony, leader of northern Uganda's Lord's Resistance Army. The particular angle that outraged millions was the video's discussion of Kony's kidnapping of children to serve as sex slaves and forced soldiers; this compelled viewers to demand action to stop these wrongs. According to narrator Jason Russell, the problem "is 99 percent of the planet doesn't know who he is. If they knew, Kony would have been stopped long ago."

In the space of only a few days, the video moved a formerly obscure issue to the *New York Times*'s front page and forced the White House and Pentagon to respond. Many concluded that the San Diego–based organization Invisible Children and its leader, Jason Russell, who produced the Kony video, had accomplished an incredible feat of new-media activism. And if the only measure is coverage, getting 100 million views was a brilliant activist strategy.

But a different perspective soon emerged. Scholars noted that the video did not disclose that President Obama had already sent one hundred troops to Uganda. Nor did it reveal that Kony was no longer in Uganda, or that the size of the Lord's Resistance Army had been reduced from thirty thousand to a mere hundreds. In fact, the video explained nothing about the Ugandan political situation, the United States' role in Uganda, or any wrongs other than Kony's. While the video led many to demand U.S. military intervention to protect "invisible" kids, it ignored ongoing human rights violations by the U.S.-backed Ugandan president, Yoweri Museveni—who would have been the chief beneficiary of greater U.S. military aid.

Russell's video did spotlight Kony, but ultimately confused rather than educated millions about the actual causes of Uganda's ongoing violence. This is a classic example of what longtime human rights activist Matthew Kavanagh described as the "over-simplistic [sic] media framing" that particularly takes root when a lack of public knowledge or historical context regarding an issue leads to questionable policy "solutions." By focusing solely on Kony, the millions exposed to the issue were not led to pressure the Ugandan government to reduce violence or to pressure the United States to reassess its support for the brutal Ugandan army.

Within weeks of making Kony's name known to millions, Russell was found naked on a street corner in San Diego. He was talking to himself and making sexual gestures, and was placed in a psychiatric facility for observation. That does not appear to be someone who feels he has just achieved a great advance for social change.[2]

Further, unlike the examples of the Jena 6 and Trayvon Martin, the mass exposure of Kony did not build a broader campaign. Barely a month after the video led to more than 7 million page views of Wikipedia's article on Kony in only three days, the number of daily readers fell to 15,000. Stories about Kony or Uganda were as absent from the news media as before the video. Social media can turn a little-known injustice into an international story almost overnight, but that's different from the story becoming an agent for enhancing social justice and human rights.[3]

ACTIVISTS PROMOTING ACTIVISM

During the 1960s, an alternative medium emerged in response to traditional outlets' inadequate coverage of the anti–Vietnam War movement and of youth culture generally. For several years, activists wrote stories for alternative weeklies or used their reporting to mobilize support for a broad range of social movements. But as corporate outlets expanded coverage to capture advertising dollars once spent on the alternative press, activists again lacked media vehicles to break stories and mobilize large numbers for progressive causes.

The Internet changed this. It enabled progressives to create their own alternative news sites, which now range from daily blogs to such widely read sources as the *Huffington Post* and Daily Kos. In April 2004, my organization launched a daily alternative news website, BeyondChron. org. The site sought to go "beyond" the conservative, pro-landlord, pro-downtown coverage found in the Bay Area's dominant media outlet, the *San Francisco Chronicle*. Whereas the *Chronicle* billed itself as the "Voice of the West," *BeyondChron*'s masthead proclaimed it the "Voice of the Rest." We believed our own news site could promote progressive causes and activist stories the *Chronicle* was likely to ignore.

BeyondChron has taught me a lot about how activists should use the Internet. I have learned that online stories can reach a national and even international audience regardless of their original source. Whereas a front-page *Chronicle* story in the pre-Internet era would rarely be read outside the Bay Area, *BeyondChron* stories on labor, immigration, national and California politics, and other topics are picked up via Google or other sites and reach a national readership.

Many activists do not understand how online stories echo through other new and traditional media. Notwithstanding the Color of Change and Change.org campaigns described above and many other successful efforts, some organizers maintain the old-media mind-set that the first place the story appears is most critical. Obviously, campaigns benefit from a sympathetic *New York Times* story or an activist account prominently displayed on the *Huffington Post*'s homepage. But unless this option is readily available, activists are typically better off getting a story posted quickly on a reputable site so that it can immediately be Googled and distributed through social media, email lists, and other websites. Such dissemination often leads traditional-media reporters to cover new angles or developments. Many influential websites welcome breaking news submissions by activists. The online world is constantly hungry for quality content—yet too few activists, labor unions, and community organizations take advantage of this opportunity to promote their campaigns.

I want to highlight this last point: *too few activists, labor unions, and community organizations effectively use new-media tools to promote their campaigns. BeyondChron* regularly offers space for activists who want to write about their campaigns, yet surprisingly few follow through. It's not that they place the story elsewhere; rather, they simply do not make promoting their work a sufficient priority. Activist campaigns that harness new media become widely known, while those that miss these opportunities are often heard blaming "the media" for their lack of coverage. That excuse is harder to justify in today's new-media world.

NEW MEDIA AND LABOR

Consider organized labor, a leading force for progressive change. Most labor unions have failed to effectively exploit new-media tools despite repeatedly pledging to make this a priority. All too typical was a radio report I heard some years ago about a labor-community campaign to improve Walmart workers' wages. When the reporter asked the campaign spokesperson for a website that listeners could go to for more information, the spokesperson replied that the website was still being created. I thought, "These folks think they can take on Walmart, and they don't even have a website in place before launching their campaign?" Fortunately, labor learned from this experience. The "OUR Wal-Mart" campaign was launched in 2012 with its new-media operation in place—one reason it quickly had greater success than the prior effort.

Labor's' failure to take advantage of new-media opportunities was particularly evident after President Obama took office in January 2009 and unions mounted a major drive to secure enactment of the Employee Free Choice Act (EFCA). The legislation was widely viewed as essential to labor's membership growth. But the campaign for EFCA's passage made little use of new media to mobilize progressives and worker advocates who were not union members. I am on many labor and progressive email lists, yet heard little after Obama took office regarding EFCA's progress. I learned for the first time during the AFL-CIO's national convention in September 2009 that the federation had been very active on the ground for EFCA in a number of key states. Because new media were not used to publicize the grassroots momentum for EFCA's passage, the issue was widely seen to be on the legislative back burner. While EFCA might not have become law in its original form under any circumstances, new media would have at least let labor supporters know that unions were waging a powerful fight.

The power of new-media tools in labor struggles was demonstrated in the February 2011 "uprising" in Madison, Wisconsin, following Republican governor Scott Walker's announced plan to eliminate collective bargaining for public employees and teachers. New-media activism by community allies of labor was central to the Wisconsin protests. New media sustained daily rallies for weeks and repeatedly built large crowds on short notice. When filmmaker-activist Michael Moore announced he was coming to Madison on only a few hours' notice, activists used social media to get 50,000 people to the Wisconsin Statehouse for his speech. Teachers, nurses, students, and other activists used Facebook, Twitter, and local progressive blogs like BlueCheddar.net to mobilize opposition to Walker's plan, and new media kept activists constantly updated on the struggle. The website for the Madison-based Center for Media and Democracy (prwatch.org) became the place to go for those seeking videos, updates, blogs, and other information about the ongoing events.[4]

Some organizations are not using new-media tools that could increase their political clout, spur fund-raising, and otherwise ensure the success of their campaigns simply because they lack confidence in their skills or capacity. Where this is the case, such groups must view hiring someone with new-media skills as a necessity, not a luxury. When activist organizations doing vital work are off the information superhighway, the progressive movement loses. In an age of Facebook, Twitter, and other do-it-yourself media, activists have no excuse for not using these tools for promoting issues and mobilizing campaigns.

BUILDING GRASSROOTS CAMPAIGNS: THE NETROOTS

In addition to exposing issues and campaigns, a vast network of activist websites mobilizes progressive support on the major political issues of our time. Often described collectively as the "Netroots," these sites enable activists to bypass corporate media gatekeepers both to expose social and economic injustices and to build public support for solutions. The Netroots revives a role once played by 1960s-era antiwar alternative weeklies by publicizing activist events, recruiting participants, and then providing coverage. New-media tools allow photographs or videos of the protest or rally to be posted even as they occur, enabling even those thousands of miles away to feel part of the experience.

The Netroots helps validate engaging in progressive activism. This applies to the value both of individual participation in social change activities, and of the event itself. When an anti–Keystone Pipeline activist protesting in rural Minnesota or a worker in Los Angeles challenging Walmart's employment policies reads online accounts about similar protests in other states, it reaffirms the importance of their individual role in a broader movement and encourages them to continue participating in the struggle. In contrast, when such protests were ignored in the old-media world, some participants likely concluded that the event was not important or that they had wasted their time; the lack of traditional-media coverage deterred future activism. The Netroots has forever altered this dynamic.

The Netroots also includes membership groups like MoveOn.org that use new-media tools to mobilize grassroots activism and help build national campaigns. MoveOn has an unusual history. It started in 1998 when its founders, software entrepreneurs Joan Blades and Wes Boyd, created an email petition asking Congress to "censure President Clinton and move on," as opposed to impeaching him. The petition was an early application of new-media tools to activist campaigns, and MoveOn's ability to get more than 500,000 signatures was viewed as extraordinary. MoveOn then became an early pioneer in online fund-raising for progressive causes, and it still plays this role. Reversing the normal trajectory of activist groups, MoveOn grew from being a strictly online activist group to one that now primarily uses new-media tools to mobilize support for traditional offline rallies, protests, and other events.

A key factor in the group's transition was the enormous electoral outreach operation that MoveOn and short-lived groups like America Coming Together built for Democratic candidate John Kerry's November 2004 presidential campaign. This was the first U.S. national election campaign in which email proved a powerful mobilizing tool. It was also the first national campaign in which thousands of activists responded to email appeals to travel to other states to work for a national candidate. (I spent the ten days before the 2004 election coordinating ACORN's "Project Vote" campaign in Cincinnati.) The hastily assembled electoral outreach operation in 2004 showed activists what new-media tools combined with traditional electoral organizing could accomplish, paving the way for Barack Obama's 2008 fall campaign, which was a model for such efforts.

MoveOn learned after the election that its members enjoyed the human interaction of the campaign and wanted to pursue offline actions. Its leadership had the vision to change course, shifting toward using online tools to boost traditional forms of activism. As with Netroots websites like Daily Kos, MoveOn enlists and mobilizes activists who often lack other organizational vehicles. The Netroots and membership groups like MoveOn and Democracy for America have greatly increased progressive civic engagement. Their actions refute critics who falsely portray "email activists" as ranting in front of their computers while ignoring traditional activist events.

The Netroots provides vital entry points for activist engagement. As increasing numbers of Americans are "bowling alone" and not affiliated with organizations—a trend accompanied by a sharp decline in labor union membership—sites like Daily Kos and Firedoglake provide organizational vehicles that spur activism. Their importance in this regard cannot be underestimated. Many interested in working for social change need direction and a sense of common struggle. As I discuss in my book *Beyond the Fields,* in the 1960s and 1970s the United Farm Workers became a vital activist incubator for many young people who went on to dedicate their lives to working for social and economic justice. Activists need entry points to get involved, and the lack of such vehicles is a major obstacle to movement building. Activist-oriented sites, which annually convene in a Daily Kos–initiated Netroots Nation conference, provide these essential ingredients. The Netroots creates real personal connections between activists that have greatly enhanced online and traditional activism.

NEW-MEDIA ELECTORAL ACTIVISM

New media have also played a major role in perhaps the biggest shift in activism since the original publication of *The Activist's Handbook*: the dramatic increase in electoral activism. I never heard of activists flying to another state at their own expense to work on Bill Clinton's 1992 or 1996 presidential campaigns or Al Gore's in 2000. But in 2004 it seemed every California activist I knew was in a swing state trying to elect John Kerry. It is now customary for out-of-state activists to help election campaigns across the nation, from a gay marriage ballot measure in Maine to the recall of Wisconsin's Governor Scott Walker.

To be sure, the rise of the Netroots was not the sole reason for increased electoral activism among progressives; rightward shifts by the Republican Party also raised the stakes in state and national elections. But new-media tools have greatly fostered progressive electoral activism by facilitating grassroots participation and raising money for progressive campaigns.

The turning point for Netroots electoral activism was Howard Dean's 2004 campaign to be the Democratic Party nominee for president. Dean was a Vermont governor known best for supporting civil unions, opposing the Iraq War, and implementing progressive health care policies. He often introduced himself as being from the "Democratic wing of the Democratic Party," a phrase borrowed from the late Minnesota senator Paul Wellstone. Dean was given little chance to win the nomination when he announced his candidacy. He began his campaign with fewer than 500 known supporters and only $100,000 in donations. Yet by the start of 2004, he had over 600,000 identified backers and had raised more than $50 million. Incredibly, Dean had raised more money than any Democratic primary candidate in history, with the vast majority of donations in amounts of $100 or less. How did Dean accomplish this? By being the first presidential candidate to harness the power of the Internet.

Dean initially used new-media tools to attract people to campaign events. The campaign used Meetup.com to announce where the candidate would be appearing, and supporters signed up to attend. (Dean did not invent the term *meetup*, but his campaign did much to popularize it among activists.) Dean soon made it a practice to state during every speech that "if you want to do something, go to Meetup.com." His campaign had no idea of Meetup's potential until it scheduled a March 5, 2003, gathering in New York City. Dean was little known outside Vermont at the time, and his campaign initially selected a venue that could fit twenty people. As Meetup.com showed more and more people signing up to attend, the campaign moved the event to a 100-person venue. But two days before the event, more than 300 people had signed up, and to be safe, the campaign chose a room that could hold 550.

But even that venue proved far too small. Dean arrived to a packed room, with lines of people three and four abreast going out the door and down the block. If there is a single moment that highlighted the potential of new-media activism, this is it. Many had long believed that young people in particular were eager to get politically involved, but that the traditional system of politics gave them no entry point. Dean's campaign tapped into this hunger for activism, and it provided a road map for Barack Obama's successful mix of online and traditional mobilizing of young people in 2008. As Dean consultant Joe Trippi later put it, "Until something like the Dean for America campaign actively went online, these young people who wanted to do something were not being mobilized and didn't feel empowered."[5]

Although Dean's use of the Internet propelled him to the front-runner's spot, his campaign's inability to execute the traditional grass-roots organizing strategies necessary for the Iowa caucuses led quickly to its implosion. John Kerry, whose personal wealth and long donor list from prior Senate races did not require online fund-raising, won the nomination. But the Dean campaign forever reshaped how progressive activists use new-media tools in national politics, and it was where many future leaders in Netroots activism would hone their skills.

NATIONALIZING CAMPAIGNS

New media have also boosted electoral activism by *nationalizing* progressive campaigns. In the pre-Internet days, a progressive Democrat running in a House or Senate primary would attract little support outside her or his district or state. These races could be nationally publicized through direct-mail fund-raising appeals or by a story in a progressive publication like *The Nation*. But these offline vehicles gave readers no ability to instantly send a campaign donation or to quickly type in a link to learn how to volunteer for the candidate.

Today, all winnable races involving progressive candidates for the House or Senate are on the national activist radar screen. Candidate websites and emails connect activists to daily happenings on the campaign trail and offer diverse opportunities for involvement. Daily Kos and other sites play crucial roles in introducing progressive candidates to a national audience and in raising essential early money online for these campaigns. Netroots publicity and support are especially important during the critical primary races that determine whether a progressive is elected in a strong Democratic district. Corporate interests have long invested in candidates in all parts of the nation; new-media tools enable progressive activists to support candidates across the nation as well.

Contrary to misconceptions about "email activists" never leaving their computers, new-media tools have greatly bolstered traditional organizing. The 2008 Obama campaign's massive voter contact effort would have been inconceivable absent new-media tools. As far back as the California elections of 1968, 1972, and 1976, Cesar Chavez's United Farm Workers of America (UFW) knocked on doors to reach voters and recruit activists, but new-media tools made it possible to use such people-driven electoral outreach strategies on a national scale in 2008. Email greatly facilitated recruiting volunteers and targeting them where they were most needed. YouTube videos gave every

Obama speech and campaign rally a national audience, boosting volunteers' sense that they were part of a broader movement. Facebook, too, became a critical activist tool, as thousands of young campaign volunteers posted photos of their events and used the site to chronicle their activism. The Obama campaign trained an entire generation in combining new-media tools with traditional organizing strategies. That made the Obama campaign's refusal to invest in keeping this activist organization together after Election Day 2008 particularly regrettable. (Realizing this error, the president's campaign team created Organizing for Action to mobilize Obama's campaign base after the 2012 election.)

Traditional outreach methods face increasing challenges reaching voters. Door-to-door visits are ideal, but do not easily work for large apartment buildings that restrict access. Working couples and busy children's schedules mean voters are less often home and, when home, are less available to talk to campaign workers. Phoning voters is still valuable, but many screen their calls or exclusively use cellphones, whose numbers are not widely available to campaigns. Campaign mailers and television ads are primarily the terrain of big-money interests, and progressives can rarely match opponents in these areas. Even reaching out at transit stops and other public spaces is less effective than it used to be, as voters there may too busy texting or talking on their cellphones to spend time hearing about your candidate or cause.

It's no wonder that activists increasingly rely on YouTube videos, email, websites, Facebook, and the rest of the online world to reach voters. A YouTube video that goes viral provides far more bang for the buck than any television ad, and is more likely to be seen by the age eighteen-to-thirty-four voting group that activists seek to energize behind progressive campaigns. New-media tools also have a hipness factor that few television, radio, or print ads can replicate, increasing their effectiveness among the target audience.

NEW MEDIA'S LIMITS

The use of new media to nationalize progressive campaigns does have its limits. First, a candidate's strong presence in the Netroots can obscure the reality that they have little chance of winning; one-sided defeats can then discourage others from making future out-of-state donations. Second, it is harder to hold a candidate elected through strong national

Netroots support politically accountable. As chapter 2 discusses, activists must hold politicians to their commitments, but doing so is even more challenging when the politician has greatly benefited from online resources obtained outside his or her home state.

A prime example of this phenomenon involved the 2006 U.S. Senate race in Montana. Daily Kos founder Markos Moulitsas played a pivotal role in helping an obscure rancher named Jon Tester win the 2006 Democratic primary. Moulitsas then helped make the Montana Senate race a top national progressive priority. Tester narrowly defeated incumbent Republican Conrad Burns, and would not have won absent the progressive resources Moulitsas brought to the campaign. Yet once in office Tester proved a disappointment. After he and a handful of Democrats voted against the DREAM Act in December 2010 (and also voted to extend the Bush tax cuts for the wealthy), Moulitsas responded on the Daily Kos site:

> There are Democrats I expect to be assholes. I never thought Jon Tester would be among them.
>
> Anybody who votes to punish innocent kids is an asshole. Plain and simple. And while I expect it from Democrats like Ben Nelson and C-Street denizen Mark Pryor, I honestly thought Jon Tester was different. I was wrong. I am now embarrassed that I worked so hard to help get him elected in 2006. I feel personally betrayed.
>
> Not only will I do absolutely nothing to help his reelection bid, but I will take every opportunity I get to remind people that he is so morally bankrupt that he'll try to score political points off the backs of innocent kids who want to go to college or serve their country in the military.
>
> To me, he is the Blanche Lincoln of 2012—the Democrat I will most be happy to see go down in defeat. And he will. Nothing guarantees a Republican victory more than trying to pretend to be one of them.

Moulitsas knows as well as anyone how to hold politicians accountable. But Tester's performance shows that using online tools to attract out-of-state resources can leave activists with little leverage should the politician betray their commitments.[6]

STATE AND LOCAL NEW-MEDIA ACTIVISM

The Netroots has yet to match its tremendous fund-raising and mobilizing success for progressive federal candidates in local or state campaigns. These races are harder to nationalize because they typically lack the broader political implications of House or Senate races. Furthermore, fewer activists focus on state politics. This may be attributable to the distance many state capitals are from activist-filled population centers (Madison, Wisconsin, being a rare exception) and to less media coverage of state politics. In addition, state politics may not impact issues that activists care most about. When *BeyondChron*, the website I edit, runs a lead story involving California politics, it invariably gets fewer readers than for local or national topics.

The Netroots' lesser state impact weakens the progressive agenda. When young people—the demographic most reliant on new-media tools—are not connected to these electoral outreach vehicles, they are far less likely to vote. Low voter turnout among young people in 2010 brought several right-wing governors to power, including Wisconsin's Scott Walker. The 2010 elections reaffirm that when the Netroots is not mobilizing activists for state campaigns, there is little to counterbalance big-money interests or the power of conservative messaging. While lower proportions of younger voters have historically turned out in nonpresidential elections, the Netroots could change this dynamic.

California demonstrates that greater state-based Netroots activism is vital even in the bluest of states. Democrats have controlled the California legislature for most of the past four decades. In 2012, Democrats held every state office and both U.S. Senate seats. Republicans have maintained power through ballot measures limiting legislative power and through the state constitution's unusual two-thirds majority requirement for legislated tax increases. (Democrats won a two-thirds majority in both houses of the state legislature in the 2012 elections.) Despite little Republican opposition, California has a shortage of activists mobilizing for progressive state policies. The Netroots does a terrific job mobilizing California activists for national campaigns—which is why so many worked in swing states during the November 2004 and 2008 elections— but little Netroots activism is targeted at state politics. This absence has prevented progressives from reversing the sharp decline in funding for education and public services produced by past ballot measures like Prop 13. A state that Republicans do not even bother contesting in presidential elections has low levels of public service funding rivaling those of Mississippi and other red states. Yet outside of organized labor, public employee unions, and statewide community organizations like the Alliance of Californians for Community Empowerment (ACCE), there is surprisingly little state-based grassroots activism.

The Courage Campaign is a California group trying to change this. Founded by Rick Jacobs, who headed Howard Dean's California campaign in 2004, the Courage Campaign operates much like a statewide version of MoveOn (which has many California members). It uses new-media tools to mobilize both online activism and traditional organizing, and had 750,000 members in 2012. The Courage Campaign has influenced state struggles on issues ranging from gay marriage, to taxing the wealthy, to labor rights and has provided desperately needed resources to progressive forces in California not controlled by the state Democratic Party.

The Courage Campaign is less well known among the state's activists than MoveOn, but its efforts to harness the Netroots as an effective mobilizing vehicle for state politics offer a road map for activists in other states. State governments make far too many critical decisions for the Netroots to stay on the sidelines, and activists seeking to make a difference should consider filling this void.

NEW MEDIA CREATIVITY

New-media tools do not change the activist rule that "media coverage alone is not enough." These tools are a means to an end, which means that activists should not squander time perfecting a YouTube video that few swing voters will see, or creating a website that fails as a communication and mobilizing vehicle. For all their novelty, new-media tools can prove most effective in concert with "old school" campaign tactics.

I saw this lesson borne out during a campaign for the San Francisco Board of Supervisors in 2010. San Francisco is a tech-savvy city, and all leading campaigns use Facebook, email alerts, tweets (Twitter is headquartered in the city), YouTube videos, and the like. This particular race covered the South of Market district that hosts many high-tech companies and houses many voters employed by high-tech firms. Candidate Jane Kim's campaign came up with an idea whose roots were not in tech, but rather in the Charlie Brown comic strip of the 1960s. It built a "Jane Kim for Mayor Listening Booth" designed to resemble Lucy's "Psychiatric Help 5 Cents" structure. The booth offered voters a chance to give advice to the candidate. Each day the booth moved to different street corners, with the location of Kim's "Listening Tour" tweeted the day before. Photos of Kim in her listening booth appeared on Facebook and in a YouTube video and were used in traditional mailers and cable television ads. This retro, pre-new-media idea was a huge hit, and did more to convey the candidate's interest in hearing from district residents than any other strategy. And, yes, Kim won the election.

THE BACKLASH

Some prominent critics downplay the role of new-media tools in bringing social change. Malcolm Gladwell argued in a widely discussed October 4, 2010, *New Yorker* article that "the revolution will not be tweeted." He claimed, "We seem to have forgotten what activism is." Gladwell argued that unlike the powerful personal relationships formed by civil rights protesters in the 1960s, "the platforms of social media are built around weak ties. The evangelists of social media don't understand this distinction; they seem to believe that a Facebook friend is the same as a real friend and that signing up for a donor registry in Silicon Valley today is activism in the same sense as sitting at a segregated lunch counter in Greensboro in 1960."[7]

Gladwell is not an activist. His criticisms likely resonated with those also skeptical of traditional activism, the type of people who claim protesters attend marches due to the nice weather, rather than out of a commitment to social justice. I have never met any activist who confuses Facebook friends with real friends, or equates joining a donor registry with risking one's personal safety at a segregated lunch counter. Do some inflate social media's role in securing social change? Of course. Are there "email activists" who rail at injustice without ever leaving their computers? Absolutely. But exaggerated claims for new-media tools should not lead to the equivalent mistake of wrongly downplaying their impact. Take for example the mass uprisings in the Middle East in 2011. While some described this as the "Facebook Revolution," others countered that, as one Egyptian teacher put it, "this wasn't a Facebook revolution; it was a workers' revolution." The truth is that the revolution was spurred by both forces: social media tools facilitated and enhanced the longtime community and labor organizing that ultimately forced Egyptian dictator Hosni Mubarak from power.[8]

By recognizing that new-media tools are only a means to an end, and by joining these efforts with traditional media and grassroots organizing, activists maximize their chances for success. Overall, new media have unquestionably facilitated progressive change.

7

Direct Action

Acting Up, Sitting In, Taking
to the Streets

Since the original publication of this book, activists' participation in direct action has increased tremendously. This is chiefly attributable to activists having less faith in the ability of the political process to achieve their goals, as well to the growing power of corporations largely immune from democratic control. Although the term *direct action* is often used to describe marches, rallies, or other public protest tactics, it usually refers to events that immediately confront specific individuals, corporations, or other entities with a set of demands. Direct actions are distinct from protest activities such as bridge blockades that are designed to send a political message to the broader public. These protest activities are particularly valuable as spontaneous responses to sudden events and, like annual "solidarity day" marches, build social bonds, reduce feelings of political isolation, and demonstrate the constituency's strength to the public and media.

Public protests are important, but they are no substitute for developing a proactive program for social change. And direct actions are often critical to this purpose. Confronting an adversary on his or her own turf creates a rush of excitement not often found during legislative lobbying, and activists tend to remember such incidents fondly, even if the tactic brought only mixed success. The thrill of taking direct action, however, is distinct from achieving specific goals. For example, picketing and chanting in front of your adversary's corporate headquarters may create community spirit, but if the activity is not connected to specific demands, the action may not advance the organization's agenda. Engaging in unfocused direct actions drains organizational and volunteer energy and creates a false sense of progress toward social change.

Direct action is the one area of activism in which past success can be an unreliable guide to future results. The reason is that some targets of direct action quickly adapt, eliminating past vulnerabilities. For example, the incredibly successful "Battle in Seattle" WTO protests in 1999 led activists to try similar disruption strategies at subsequent global trade meetings. But those host cities erected massive barriers to prevent activists from getting anywhere near the meetings, thereby precluding Seattle-type disruptions. This strategy was then taken even further by President Obama in May 2012 when he shifted a planned G-8 Summit (a forum for the governments of eight of the world's largest economies) scheduled for Chicago to Camp David; this assured that protesters could not disrupt the event.

This means that effective direct action not only must choose the right targets and tactics but also must value innovation and surprise. This chapter begins with two movements that embodied this approach. The AIDS Coalition to Unleash Power (ACT UP) and the disability rights movement utilized innovative and strategic direct action to achieve remarkable success in politically challenging eras. Both movements show the potential power as well as the limitations of direct action as a proactive strategy for achieving social change. The chapter then discusses how the immigrants' rights movement effectively used unexpected direct actions in 2006, creating a national movement for comprehensive immigration reform. The chapter concludes by analyzing the Tea Party's storming of congressional town hall meetings in the summer of 2009, a tactic that shifted the public debate about health care reform and showed how conservative activists are borrowing from the progressive playbook.

"SILENCE EQUALS DEATH"

ACT UP was created in March 1987 for the express purpose of using direct action to ensure an adequate government response to the AIDS crisis. An aggressive, confrontational approach to the AIDS epidemic was long overdue for several reasons. First, AIDS emerged during a decade of great progress for gay and lesbian rights in the United States. This progress triggered a reaction from conservative religious figures and their political allies. Homophobia became a centerpiece of Republican political campaigns, and anti-gay forces overwhelmingly supported Ronald Reagan in his victorious 1980 and 1984 campaigns. Although

Reagan's political handlers claimed that his Hollywood years had made him personally tolerant of gays, his chief political base was prone to view AIDS as God's punishment for immoral behavior. The Reagan administration ignored the mounting evidence of a burgeoning AIDS crisis; Reagan himself refused to use the term *AIDS* until his friend movie star Rock Hudson died of the disease in 1985.[1]

AIDS emerged during a presidency that was committed to slashing spending for domestic programs and that saw political value in government hostility to gay rights. This circumstance alone could have necessitated reliance on direct action. AIDS activists, however, faced obstacles even greater than presidential opposition to their cause. The nation's medical and scientific establishment was also delaying AIDS research. Activists wanted people with AIDS to have access to experimental drugs that could treat the disease, whereas the interlocking empire of private drug companies, the scientists they funded, and government research agencies instead viewed AIDS as an opportunity for huge profits, Nobel Prizes, and dramatic funding increases.

The medical and research establishment's hostility to the goals of AIDS activists meant that success in the political arena did not necessarily translate into better medical options for people with AIDS. Although grassroots and legislative political advocacy eventually forced the Reagan administration to increase AIDS funding to the National Institute of Allergies and Infectious Diseases (NIAID) from $297,000 in 1982 to $63 million in 1986 and $146 million in 1987, few people with AIDS ever benefited from the additional research funds. NIAID was thrilled to receive such significant budget increases but seemed more concerned with bureaucratic empire building than with offering treatment to gay men facing premature death.

NIAID received a major funding increase in 1986 but did nothing with the funds for nine months. When confronted with his failure to use $20 million appropriated to set up a network of testing facilities for AIDS drugs, NIAID director Dr. Anthony Fauci claimed that he needed additional money for staff to write the necessary protocols. When AIDS activists convinced Congress to provide the additional funds, still no action resulted. Fauci explained that he had not had the time to interview for the new positions and lacked funds for office space and desks. Soon after this admission, AIDS activists concluded that a strategy focusing on direct action was essential.[2]

Direct action was also necessary to overcome another major hurdle: corporate greed. The Burroughs Wellcome Company used its financial control over scientists in and out of government to ensure that its own drug, AZT, would be the centerpiece of federally funded clinical AIDS tests. This was true even though other drugs appeared to provide better results. The government's limiting experimentation to a single drug whose chief merit appeared to be the financial clout of its corporate sponsor infuriated AIDS activists. Their anger intensified when, after AZT became the only drug legally available to treat AIDS, Burroughs Wellcome announced on February 13, 1987, that the cost of AZT would be $10,000 per person per year. Thus did the tortuous battle to ensure access to treatment for AIDS come to parallel the fight against the disease itself.

An additional factor, internal to the gay community, led to the creation of an AIDS organization dedicated to direct action. In 1982 Larry Kramer, a New York City–based playwright, joined with other people in establishing an organization named Gay Men's Health Crisis (GMHC). At this time the term *AIDS* had yet to be commonly used to describe the mysterious illnesses suddenly afflicting gay men. Many gay activists and organizations ardently supported bathhouses and viewed criticism of gay promiscuity from gay figures such as Kramer as evidence of self-hatred. GMHC became the largest AIDS service organization in the country. Its approach, however, reflected the upscale, professional backgrounds of its founders, some of whom were still in the closet. GMHC sought to become part of city health care systems rather than openly criticize public health care policies.

Kramer was more confrontational than other GMHC founders, and he failed to get the organization to politically oppose government inaction on AIDS. In the mid-1980s Kramer and others publicly attacked GMHC for its unwillingness to engage in an all-out war against the medical-scientific establishment and argued for establishing a more militant advocacy group. In a speech on March 10, 1987, Kramer labeled GMHC a "sad organization of sissies" and called on "lobbying, advocacy, public relations people to get the word out, and [engage in] increased political activities." He asked his audience, "Do we want to start a new organization devoted solely to political action?" The crowd answered with a resounding "Yes!" Two days later more than three hundred people met to form ACT UP.[3]

ACT UP's creation reflected a growing consensus in the gay community that politely accepting government, scientific, and corporate inaction was equivalent to accepting death sentences for thousands of people potentially infected with or already suffering from AIDS. The consequences of continuing to work patiently through "the system" could not be starker. People were dying, and the health care delivery system was unconcerned about their fate. Six gay men created the motto "Silence = Death," put it on a pink triangle against a black background, and printed and posted the message at their own expense. The men, who were members of the Silence = Death Project, were present at the founding of ACT UP and lent the organization the design it became identified with. The motto spawned direct action in two ways. First, people who themselves faced death from AIDS were motivated to wage any type of battle that might save their lives. Second, ACT UP was able to attract activists motivated not by the personal fear of contracting AIDS but by the absolute gravity of the issue. This second factor contributed to ACT UP's unparalleled success in attracting young people to its cause.[4]

ACT UP in Action

ACT UP sent a powerful message about its commitment to a direct action agenda when it held its first event less than two weeks after forming. On March 24, 1987, more than 250 ACT UP members invaded Wall Street to protest the Food and Drug Administration's decision five days before to license Burroughs Wellcome's AZT as the only government-approved therapy for AIDS patients. The granting of monopoly status to a drug whose $10,000-per-patient annual cost made it the most expensive treatment in history created a theme that would remain central to ACT UP events: big business was making unconscionable profits off terminally ill patients. ACT UP snarled traffic for several hours and hung an effigy of FDA chief Frank Young in front of Trinity Church. Seventeen people were arrested for civil disobedience. Kramer had written an op-ed piece in the *New York Times* the previous day laying out the basis for ACT UP's anger at the FDA; thousands of copies were handed out on Wall Street, along with a fact sheet detailing "Why We Are Angry." The demonstration made national news, and ACT UP was publicly credited for having forced Young's subsequent promise to broaden drug testing.[5]

This national attention spawned ACT UP chapters throughout the nation. Such a tactically and technically sophisticated direct action was likely unprecedented for a newly formed group. The event was effective for three key reasons. First, both the action and the accompanying handouts clearly conveyed the message of the event: an AIDS protest on Wall Street automatically linked a growing medical problem to big-business practices. Second, the direct action occurred only five days after the FDA announcement on AZT, enabling the media to easily connect the two events and to accept ACT UP's framing of its action as a response to the FDA's. Media-savvy ACT UP members no doubt understood that delaying the action for even a few weeks could jeopardize media understanding of the context of the protest.[6]

The third reason the event succeeded was that it used local activists to nationalize ACT UP's demands. Clearly, gaining national news coverage is easier when network television news departments are headquartered in the city of the event, but ACT UP's focus on national targets such as the FDA, the National Institutes of Health (NIH), and the president made the group's protest a national issue. ACT UP consistently proved that local activists can use direct action to influence national politics to a far greater extent than many realize.

ACT UP's second demonstration occurred on the night of April 15, 1987, at New York City's main post office. Post offices are always mobbed on April 15 with taxpayers filing last-minute returns. The setting was perfect for ACT UP's argument that taxpayer money for AIDS was both inadequate and misspent. Attracting media to the event was easier than usual; local television broadcasts regularly covered the frantic scene of last-minute filers. Even stations uninterested in the protest could not avoid showing a crowd holding "Silence = Death" placards.

ACT UP's first two direct actions proved so successful that support for its confrontational approach grew. The group's participation in the October 1987 March on Washington for Lesbian and Gay Rights served as a recruiting tool, as ACT UP members were distinguished among the 500,000 marchers by their "Silence = Death" T-shirts. Attendance doubled at the next ACT UP meeting, clearly demonstrating that the group's direct action strategy had filled a void in the community. Social change organizations strategizing over how to attract new participants should note the ability of successful direct action tactics to create a sense of excitement.

ACT UP continued its successful strategy of staging direct actions at sites connected to its demands. The group held a vigil July 21–24, 1987, at New York's Memorial Sloan-Kettering Hospital to protest the fact that the hospital was receiving $1.2 million from the NIH to treat only thirty-one patients, a statistic that proved how few people with AIDS were actually benefiting from increased government funding. Similarly, on January 19, 1988, ACT UP went to the Hearst Magazine Building in New York City, the headquarters of *Cosmopolitan*. *Cosmo*'s January

1988 issue had printed an article claiming that heterosexual women had little risk of contracting AIDS and that condom use was generally unnecessary. The article prompted the creation of an ACT UP Women's Committee, whose demonstration in front of *Cosmo*'s offices protested the misinformation the magazine had conveyed to its readers. The action brought national attention and countered the prevailing media dogma that the AIDS crisis affected only gay men. ACT UP's poster to support its Women's Committee's campaign, titled "AIDS: 1 in 61," was based on studies showing that one out of sixty-one babies in New York City was born with AIDS or HIV.

One year after its first action, ACT UP returned to Wall Street. As noted earlier, returning to the scene of a successful direct action includes both risks and rewards. For example, if the follow-up event falls short of the original, the media might frame its coverage around this "decline." And authorities unexpectedly burned by direct action may take precautions to prevent an anniversary repeat. But anniversary protests can be an excellent way to remind the public how little progress has been made on a group's demands. ACT UP had a spectacularly successful first year from a strategic and tactical standpoint, but this very success could have led the public into confusing the group's obtaining publicity with actual progress on its demands. It was therefore essential that ACT UP return to Wall Street on March 24, 1988, to remind the public how little had been done to alleviate the AIDS epidemic. Its members were better this time at tying up traffic, and the number of those arrested for civil disobedience increased from 17 to 111. The event highlighted that one year had passed without any new drug approvals by the FDA, without significant new funding for AIDS research or treatment, without the promised national AIDS education campaign, and without any new emphasis on AIDS by the president. ACT UP activists added a colorful new twist to its anniversary action, scattering thousands of photocopies of $10, $50, and $100 bills bearing slogans critical of Wall Street.

ACT UP's first-year offensive primarily involved white, middle-class gay men. As the number of drug-related AIDS cases rose among both male and female African Americans and Latinos, most of whom were straight, low-income individuals, ACT UP recognized the need to focus on these groups' unmet needs. For example, the Women's Committee organized several events highlighting measures to educate and protect women from the sexual transmission of AIDS. In a particularly creative action, ACT UP members went to a New York Mets game and unfurled banners bearing such slogans as "No Glove, No Love," and "Don't

Balk at Safe Sex." They also handed out information and condoms to the overwhelmingly male crowd.

ACT UP undertook actions against health care facilities such as University Hospital in Newark and Cook County Hospital in Chicago for failing to offer necessary services to women with AIDS. Although 5 percent of babies in University Hospital were born HIV positive, the facility was conducting no clinical trials for people with AIDS. Cook County Hospital, the main public hospital in Chicago, had established an AIDS clinic, but women were not allowed to use it. ACT UP responded to this discriminatory policy by placing mattresses along the street in front of the hospital's administrative offices. The instant the mattresses hit the ground, Chicago's Finest swooped down and arrested more than one hundred people. The predominantly female ACT UP members were charged with "mob action" and treated with the brutality and intolerance associated with the Chicago police. The action achieved its goal, however, as Cook County Hospital reversed its exclusionary policy a week after ACT UP's protest.[7]

ACT UP sought the Reverend Jesse Jackson's support of its efforts to enhance AIDS education in New York's minority communities. Jackson endorsed ACT UP's work with New York's African American and Latino churches to fight AIDS. ACT UP distributed a flyer emphasizing the disproportionate impact of AIDS on both of these minority groups and offered to plan AIDS awareness and outreach programs for church members. ACT UP's willingness to expand its base to politically unpopular intravenous-drug users exposed to HIV would have been unheard of in a less principled organization; its eagerness to work with women and minorities, many of whom were straight, and its focus on substance abusers and people with AIDS in prisons showed that ACT UP was not only interested in gay white men. The group's outreach efforts also demonstrated its strong political commitment to social and economic justice. This combination of direct action and progressive ideology was crucial to ACT UP's success in attracting volunteers and broadening its political support.

On October 11, 1988, ACT UP undertook its most ambitious direct action yet. More than one thousand ACT UP members from around the country staged a mass "die-in" at FDA headquarters in Rockville, Maryland. The action brought massive publicity and an exaggerated police response. The protesters attacked the FDA for its refusal to legalize experimental drugs, its failure to conduct sufficient drug trials, and its insistence on trials that gave half of the participants placebos rather than medication. The die-in participants lay down in the street holding paper tombstones blaming the FDA for their "death." Chalk outlines on the street represented people who had died of AIDS. The die-in was met by a force of some 360 police officers, many of whom wore riot gear.

The primary impact of this massive police response was to elevate the significance of the event. The police tried to keep arrests low to minimize media attention; people who blocked buses holding the 176 protesters who *had been* arrested or who tried to enter the headquarters were dragged off the street rather than arrested themselves. This effort to reduce publicity clearly failed, as the constant street theater and the presence of ACT UP banners covering the building's exterior gave television cameras everything they needed for a great story. The FDA was not a frequent target of mass protests, which further contributed to the media's interest in the event. Further, police officers wore rubber gloves when making arrests at this and other ACT UP events, bolstering ACT UP's contention that the government, the American Medical Association, and the scientific community had utterly failed to provide even the most basic education about AIDS transmission. Newspaper and television coverage of the gloves no doubt caused some people to inquire about AIDS, so the tactic of arrest may also have served an educational purpose.[8]

Direct action always carries the risk that some participants will "go too far." This risk increases when a series of carefully strategized events bring widespread media coverage yet fail to produce tangible policy results. Just as the frustration of 1960s activists led to the formation of the tactically suspect Weather Underground, so did anger at the lack of progress lead some AIDS activists to engage in high-profile but strategically suspect protest activities. Three such highly controversial events occurred in 1989.

On January 31, 1989, fifty-five protesters stepped into traffic at the height of the morning commute on the Bay Area's world-renowned Golden Gate Bridge. The group, using the Silence = Death slogan and focusing its protest on demands associated with ACT UP, identified itself as "Stop AIDS Now or Else" (SANOE). The protesters blocked traffic in both directions, causing a standstill that lasted almost an hour. It was the first time ever that demonstrators had closed the bridge, then fifty-two years old. To ensure that their message was conveyed, the protesters strung a banner across the span reading "AIDS = Genocide / Silence = Death / Fight Back." They also distributed leaflets calling on drivers to demand more government funding for AIDS and to end mandatory testing for the HIV virus.

Was interfering with people's morning commute a wise or effective tactic for accomplishing the protesters' goals? Most of the affected commuters who were quoted in news stories did not think so. Nor did San Francisco's mayor, newspaper columnists, or Pat Christen, director of policy for the region's largest AIDS organization, the San Francisco AIDS Foundation. Christen told the press that the protest could hurt support for AIDS patients; already, people were threatening to withhold donations to AIDS support groups.[9]

The common complaint was that the protesters had picked the wrong target. Many noted that the commuters affected were likely supportive of the protesters' concerns. Nor were the drivers in a position to alter federal AIDS policy. One columnist argued, "If they want Washington to do more about AIDS, they should block the 14th Street Bridge over the Potomac." At a press conference after the demonstration, the protesters defended their actions on the grounds that they had forced people to spend time "thinking about AIDS." Their spokesperson noted that they sought to be as disruptive as possible because "AIDS is disrupting our lives, and until people's lives are disrupted, they don't pay attention."[10]

On September 8, 1989, SANOE struck again. At the opening night performance of the San Francisco Opera, about seventy-five protesters rushed through the crowd shouting, "We're here! We're queer! Stop AIDS now!" SANOE's spokesperson argued that no progress had been made since the group's Golden Gate Bridge blockade and that members of the politically and economically powerful crowd could "use their influence to do something about AIDS."[11]

The third action in 1989 involved ACT UP's confrontation with New York's Cardinal John Joseph O'Connor at St. Patrick's Cathedral on December 10, likely the most famous and most controversial action in ACT UP's history. Cardinal O'Connor had been a staunch opponent of the gay and lesbian movement ever since his appointment as archbishop of New York in 1984. He banned the gay Catholic group Dignity from Catholic churches, led opposition to New York City's 1986 Gay Rights Bill and, most important, advanced an agenda hostile to that of AIDS activists. O'Connor opposed safe-sex education in schools and the use of condoms to prevent HIV transmission, and he attacked assertions that condoms and clean needles could lower the risk of infection as "lies" perpetuated by public health officials. Graphic artists affiliated with ACT UP created a subway poster and placard picturing O'Connor next to a condom under the boldly printed words, "Know Your Scumbags." The caption under the condom read, "This one prevents AIDS."

Despite widespread belief among ACT UP members that O'Connor constituted a menace to people with AIDS, many group activists questioned the value of an action against the cardinal. People felt that ACT UP would not influence the church's anti-gay posture and that it could be assumed that the media would portray an attack on the cardinal as an attack on the Catholic Church or all Catholics. Nevertheless, a consensus was reached that O'Connor had to be publicly confronted over his anti-gay stance. His open support of the anti-abortion group Operation Rescue, known for its harassment of women visiting family planning clinics, also angered ACT UP, and so ACT UP joined with the New York Women's Health Action and Mobilization (WHAM!) on December 10, 1989, in a demonstration to "Stop the Church." The plan called for a legal picketing protest to turn into a mass die-in around St. Patrick's Cathedral. ACT UP affinity groups would engage in secretly planned civil disobedience inside the church while O'Connor said Mass. More than forty-five hundred people attended the picketing, carrying signs and chanting slogans attacking O'Connor's anti-gay, anti-abortion agenda. Those inside disrupted the Mass and forced O'Connor to abandon his sermon. People lay down in the aisles, threw condoms, chained themselves to pews, and verbally attacked the man the placards outside identified as a "public health menace." One participant, a former altar boy, threw a communion wafer on the church floor. The police, who knew of the event in advance, converged on the activists with a brutality that reflected their own pro-Catholic, anti-gay fervor. They arrested 131 people and beat at least one demonstrator repeatedly.[12]

Media coverage was overwhelmingly critical of ACT UP. Cardinal O'Connor was portrayed as a martyr, and ACT UP was accused of violating Catholics' freedom of religion by interfering with the Mass and the distribution of the sacrament. The coverage most prominently featured the person who threw the wafer; this act became transformed into "homosexual activists desecrating the host." Randy Shilts, author of the national best seller on the AIDS epidemic, *And the Band Played On*, viewed the "Stop the Church" event as so "strategically stupid" that the activists must have been "paid by some diabolical reactionary group dedicated to discrediting the gay community."[13]

In their post-action meeting, ACT UP members agreed they should more rigorously analyze their choice of targets in the future. The group concluded, however, that the O'Connor attack was a success. The event had forged a coalition with women's health and reproductive rights groups and had shown the country that there was no barrier that ACT

UP would not cross to save lives. It also served as a clear reminder that gay activists continued to be targets for police-sanctioned violence.

The bridge blockade, opera protest, and "Stop the Church" actions all drew heavy criticism. However, the strategic underpinnings of the first two actions clearly differed from those of the last. The first two events were public protests rather than direct actions in that neither involved a confrontation with the target of their demands. Even assuming that powerful people attended the opera's opening night, nobody among the crowd was identified specifically as having a role in federal AIDS policy. The SANOE protests were similar to other disruptions demanding that there be "no business as usual" while the AIDS crisis grew. Such events are rarely as counterproductive as their critics fear, but they should not be confused with direct actions designed to force a target to change its policy.

The Cardinal O'Connor action requires more careful scrutiny. ACT UP knew going in that the event would be unlikely to influence its target; the same argument could have been made about attacks against the Reagan administration. Yet unlike the bridge drivers and operagoers, Cardinal O'Connor had injected himself and the church he controlled into a political dispute in opposition to ACT UP's agenda. National media coverage of the action ignored O'Connor's actual role in fomenting anti-gay, anti-abortion, and anti–ACT UP political advocacy. Because the media used the vandalized communion wafer to create the dominant spin on the event, the action came to be perceived as an attack on a religious ceremony rather than on a political advocate. However, the "Stop the Church" protest differed from actions by gay activists seeking to prevent conservative ministers from preaching that homosexuality is evil; it was a political, not a religious, attack.

ACT UP knew in advance that the media would side with O'Connor. Should it have proceeded with an event likely to create a media backlash against the organization and having no prospect of influencing its target's policy? Prominent ACT UP members were divided on the question. However, two factors seem to support ACT UP's decision to proceed with the confrontation. First, progressive activists cannot allow themselves to remain on the defensive because of the identity or power of their adversary. Cardinal O'Connor's claim that he "wished he could join Operation Rescue" was an overt effort to encourage people to harass women seeking to exercise their legal right to an abortion. His vocal opposition to any education about safe sex, AIDS, or condoms in schools increased public health risks. These were political rather than religious stances. Having assumed the role of a politician, the cardinal became fair game for direct political action. ACT UP could not allow a political opponent to avoid confrontation by disguising his political message as religious teaching.[14]

The second and perhaps more important factor justifying the "Stop the Church" action relates to ACT UP's organizational culture and identity. The acronym ACT UP was so frequently used that people may have forgotten the organization's full name: the AIDS Coalition to Unleash Power. ACT UP was supposed to harness the rage, fury, and passion of AIDS activists committed to achieving their goals "by all means necessary." Group founder Kramer even wore a shirt bearing this slogan, above Malcolm X's picture, during his video address to the Sixth International AIDS Conference. Given this organizational culture, ACT UP could hardly forsake actions against certain enemies for fear of a media backlash. ACT UP's formation became necessary precisely because nonconfrontational measures had failed. Placing Cardinal O'Connor off-limits to confrontational attack would have reflected this failed approach and imposed artificial limits on ACT UP's power. Activists must sometimes use tactics that may not produce direct results but that are necessary for organizational growth, morale, and development. The "Stop the Church" action had to be done; it should be seen as just one in a continual stream of actions that ACT UP staged in pursuit of its agenda.[15]

During the same year in which the tactics of AIDS activists became the subject of national controversy, ACT UP finally achieved a political breakthrough. At the Fifth International Conference on AIDS in Montreal in June 1989, more than 250 AIDS activists stormed the convention center just prior to the opening ceremonies. Carrying placards and charts as they mounted the stage, the activists announced their twelve-point plan for government AIDS efforts, urging the scientist-dominated audience to "read the manifesto." The audience initially applauded the activist takeover but grew restive as what had started as a well-orchestrated direct action broke down into isolated yelling and disruption. After refusing for ninety minutes to leave the meeting hall, the protesters were permitted to remain following extensive negotiations with conference organizers. For the balance of the conference, the protesters did not hesitate to heckle speakers and engage in street theater–type activities. Scientists attending the conference resented this intrusion of "patients" into a scientific meeting and argued against holding future meetings unless a "more productive format" was arranged.

Most news coverage of the conference emphasized the open warfare between scientists and AIDS activists. Randy Shilts, in his speech at the closing ceremony, articulated the prevailing sentiment when he criticized the application of anger unconnected to "intelligence about its best tactical timing and best strategic targets." Despite the consensus that what had begun as a strategic direct action was transformed into "tantrums" by an "irresponsible few," ACT UP's initial action in Montreal represented a watershed in the history of its struggle; its presentation ultimately reversed the government and scientific establishment's longtime unwillingness to take the group seriously.[16]

The group's unveiling of its comprehensive model for change no doubt contributed to NIAID director Anthony Fauci's acceptance, a few months after the event, of ACT UP's demands for greater input from people with AIDS in policy setting, greater access to treatment and experimental drugs, and more cost-effective use of government funds. Fauci's conversion validated activists' reliance on direct action to achieve their goals. The positive developments following the conference also demonstrate that even actions that "go too far" do not necessarily damage the fundamental message. Despite tactics that were sophomoric rather than strategic, ACT UP's opening presentation clearly made a powerful impression on Fauci and other influential figures. Activists who fear that a few thoughtless participants have undermined an otherwise successful action should keep this dynamic in mind.

ACT UP and Elected Officials

As befits an organization willing to confront New York's most powerful Catholic official, ACT UP established the necessary fear-and-loathing relationship with elected officials. The group often attacked politicians by crashing events and obtaining a public dialogue. For example, on AIDS Awareness Day at Georgetown University Medical Center in November 1993, ACT UP hecklers forced a nationally televised, person-to-person "debate" with President Clinton. During a speech designed to showcase Clinton's "unprecedented commitment" to AIDS and gay and lesbian rights, a member of ACT UP courageously stood up and challenged the president's record on these issues, yelling, "You promised during your campaign that you would establish a 'Manhattan Project' for AIDS, and all we got was another task force." That sentence distilled the fundamental reality of Clinton's approach to AIDS. Although Clinton responded by talking about how much he had done, how much was still left to do, and how he understood the speaker's frustration and impatience, the powerful impact of the heckler's true, succinct statement already had set in.

Everyone familiar with Clinton's AIDS record knew that although he was more committed to the issue than his Republican predecessors, he had not attempted to maximize government resources used in the fight against AIDS. Clinton had indeed promised during his campaign, "When it comes to AIDS, there should be a Manhattan Project." A "Manhattan Project" would entail more than increased funding; like the effort to split the atom, it would bring together experts from multiple disciplines to work in an environment that favored cooperation and innovation over competition and secrecy. Such a project would facilitate the testing of treatments lacking industry financial backing and investigate possibilities rejected by corporate interests. Clinton no doubt recognized that the activist had raised an uncomfortable fact during what was supposed to be a back-patting affair; although his administration began doing more on the AIDS issue shortly after the event, Clinton made no effort to encourage passage of the bill introduced to create an AIDS Manhattan Project.[17]

The tactical advantage of directly confronting the president becomes evident when we evaluate the alternatives. ACT UP could have held a press conference attacking Clinton for substituting a task force for his promised AIDS Manhattan Project, but in that pre-Internet era there was no assurance of media coverage. Picketing the White House would be unlikely to spark national press interest. Marches, rallies, or die-ins might attract national media attention, but whether the coverage conveyed the desired message would depend on the whim of news editors. In light of ACT UP's mixed record in winning positive mainstream press coverage, the protests' message would likely be ignored.

Direct confrontation was the best strategy for enabling ACT UP to express its position to the president exactly as desired. Further, no other strategy would have forced Clinton to respond immediately. Other types of events probably would only have produced responses from White House spokespersons or cabinet officials; if the protest were so successful that the national media asked Clinton to comment, he would have had time to anticipate the questions and to fudge the issue. ACT UP's willingness to hold its supposed ally accountable for his Manhattan Project commitment was essential. Unlike many other organizations, ACT UP refused to accept the oft-repeated argument that progressive groups should not pressure a Democratic president for fear of turning government over to Republicans in the next election. The group sent a clear message during Clinton's first year that it would not cut him any slack until he delivered on his commitment to gay rights and the fight against AIDS.

ACT UP recognized that many problems facing people with AIDS were products of local government policies. Its New York City chapter, the largest in the country, faced a particularly intractable nemesis in Mayor Ed Koch. Koch consistently blamed the state and federal governments for their failed response to AIDS while allowing his city's health care system virtually to collapse. On March 28, 1989, more than five thousand ACT UP members launched a "Target City Hall" action in front of Koch's office. The action emphasized that the city funds requested by community-based AIDS groups were only one-sixth the amount of the city's typical tax rebates to private corporations; that city cutbacks in drug treatment programs resulted in far more costly acute care treatment after drug users contracted AIDS; and that increased funding for education and prevention efforts would save the city hundreds of millions of dollars in hospital costs. The action tied up traffic and City Hall for several hours and resulted in more than two hundred arrests. A large media contingent was present at the event, and ACT UP took no chances that its message would be misconstrued: a four-page supplement, "The New York Crimes," was surreptitiously inserted into that morning's *New York Times* to ensure that the nation's paper of record would finally tell the truth about the city's dismal record on AIDS.

ACT UP's Success

ACT UP's media image as a no-holds-barred direct action organization conceals a truth central to its success: ACT UP knew what it was talking about. Mere opposition to drugs and testing procedures could not have succeeded if ACT UP had not provided accompanying alternative strategies credible to the government, the medical establishment, and more mainstream gay organizations. In fact, ACT UP and associated AIDS activists have so convinced the government of their expertise that they came to be viewed as having veto power over government AIDS policy. This astonishing ascension to power and influence in only a few years was largely attributable to ACT UP's credibility as an organization that effectively mobilizes facts as well as bodies. The group's composition facilitated its ability to obtain power through knowledge. There may never have been another social change movement that included such a high percentage of participants with media, public relations, advertising, and, most important, graphic arts and computer expertise. ACT UP members created the AIDS treatment registry and developed software for people with AIDS. Because the disease knows no class boundaries, ACT UP included people who ran successful businesses, had office and secretarial support, and knew how to get things done. It is difficult to see how a movement lacking people so well versed in information technology could have successfully tackled the government's multibillion-dollar, scientist-dominated health system.[18]

Although ACT UP in the 1980s could not match the medical establishment's professional credentials, it could argue that it was equally well informed, because none of the leaders of government AIDS efforts had learned about the disease in medical school. The knowledge critical to AIDS policy was derived from the time-consuming and nonmedical effort of obtaining and interpreting data. Other key information, such as whether people with AIDS would be willing to enroll in particular types of testing, was best obtained at the street or local clinic level. In retrospect, it seems obvious that AIDS activists eventually would have a major voice in setting government AIDS policy, but it is equally obvious that they would never have gained this voice without direct action.

By the early 1990s ACT UP had become accepted as an indispensable party to government AIDS policymaking. ACT UP's changing role at the annual International Conference on AIDS provides a significant measure of the group's rise in status. In 1989 ACT UP protesters had to storm the fifth annual conference to announce their twelve-point AIDS plan; five years later, at the tenth conference, ACT UP and people with AIDS were invited guests. Articles about AIDS policy even described AIDS activists as part of an "interlocking triumvirate" with their former opponents, as a group once forced to shout to be heard had now gained a seat at the table of power.[19]

ACT UP's success in giving AIDS patients a major role in determining the government's approach to potential treatments or cures was a historic achievement. Federal spending on AIDS rose from $234 million in 1986 to nearly $2 billion in 1992, a nearly tenfold increase in only six years. ACT UP's astonishing effectiveness and success, however, also resulted in the group's decline. ACT UP was always more an alliance of independent local chapters than a national organization, and by 1994 most of the chapters outside New York City were seldom involved in the type of direct actions that had once typified ACT UP. In a *New York Times* article titled "Larry Kramer's Roar Turns to Contented Purr,"

Kramer's own turn inward became a metaphor for ACT UP's declining reliance on boisterous confrontations to achieve its goals. Although Kramer's status as a gay man forestalled his receiving his just due as an innovative, historically significant political strategist, the *Times*'s willingness to praise its longtime adversary reflects the respect ACT UP has earned for its accomplishments.[20]

ACT UP's technically proficient, strategically sound direct action confrontations against powerful corporate and government opponents were unprecedented in recent U.S. history. A generation born in the 1960s that was often portrayed as spoiled by prosperity and uninterested in, if not opposed to, social change activism (in contrast to generations that survived the Depression, won World War II, and marched for civil rights) proved its mettle through AIDS activism. And while ACT UP's nationwide success in enlisting and mobilizing young people during the regressive 1980s and early 1990s was not unique—Central American support groups like the Committee in Solidarity with the People of El Salvador (CISPES) and Neighbor to Neighbor also attracted young activist energy during the ACT UP years, as did the People for Ethical Treatment of Animals (PETA)—ACT UP's legacy is arguably the most powerful today. It infused a "by all means necessary" mind-set into a lesbian and gay civil rights movement previously dominated by those promoting less confrontational tactics. Many factors contributed to the movement's steadily increasing power over the past two decades, but none may be greater than the strategic savvy bequeathed by ACT UP.

"STOP STEALING OUR CIVIL RIGHTS": DIRECT ACTION FOR DISABILITY RIGHTS

AIDS activists adopted a direct action strategy after their less confrontational tactics brought no response. The disability rights movement stands as another striking example of how government can fuel direct action opposition by leaving social change activists no alternative. Although less well known than other social change movements, the disability rights movement engaged in one of the most impressive acts of civil disobedience in the United States over the past four decades. Its use of direct action not only humiliated a newly elected president and his administration but also sent a message across the country that people with disabilities were a powerful political force.[21]

The struggle that eventually involved the longest occupation of a federal building in U.S. history began quietly. In 1973 Congress enacted a comprehensive Rehabilitation Act. Section 504 of the act prohibited discrimination against disabled persons by any institution or agency receiving federal funds. As the *New York Times* consistently reminded readers during the occupation, Section 504 was enacted "without hearings or formal debate." One reason for this lack of debate may have been that the law would not take effect until implementing regulations had been drafted. Universities, hospitals, and other institutions hostile to Section 504 could avoid the bad publicity associated with opposing civil rights for disabled persons by quietly derailing the Rehabilitation Act through the regulatory process. So it was not surprising when the federal government put the process for developing implementing regulations for the one-sentence Section 504 in the deep freeze.[22]

The lead agency for developing the Section 504 regulations was the Department of Health, Education, and Welfare (HEW, which became the Department of Health and Human Services after Jimmy Carter made Education a separate department). After it became apparent that HEW was making no progress, disability rights groups filed a federal lawsuit to force the agency to act. In July 1976 the federal district court ruled that there had been unusual delay and ordered HEW to issue final regulations immediately. After extensive discussions with both proponents and opponents of Section 504, final regulations were sent to President Gerald Ford's HEW secretary, F. David Mathews, eight days prior to his replacement by the incoming Carter appointee. All Mathews had to do was sign the regulations, and legal discrimination against people with disabilities would come to an end in federally funded employment, health, and social services and educational institutions.

But Mathews did not sign the regulations. In response, disability rights groups returned to federal court, and on January 18, 1977, the court agreed with activists' claims that Mathews had unreasonably delayed the final regulations and ordered HEW to issue the rulings immediately. HEW appealed, however, and Mathews left office with the regulations unsigned.

When the Carter administration took over on January 20, 1977, the court was still considering the appeal, and incoming HEW secretary Joseph Califano pleaded for time to review the rules. As far as the disability rights activists were concerned, the fix was clearly in: at the last minute, opponents of the 504 regulations had obtained a reprieve. The new secretary may have thought that disability rights activists would hesitate to protest in the hoopla of a new, Democratic administration. If so, he was wrong.

Organizations working for the Section 504 regulations had created an umbrella group called the American Coalition of Citizens with Disabilities (ACCD). ACCD learned soon after Califano's refusal to sign the regulations that he had created a task force to study the rules and make recommendations. No people with disabilities were included on the task force, nor were there any representatives from the organizations making up ACCD. Word soon filtered out that a major watering-down of Section 504 was under way. The entire thrust of the regulations, which mandated integration of disabled persons into mainstream institutions, was being shifted toward a "separate but equal" approach. Upon hearing these reports, ACCD indirectly contacted President Carter, who in a highly publicized campaign speech at the federal rehabilitation center in Warm Springs, Georgia, had promised to sign the regulations. Carter refused to intervene, however, leaving ACCD to battle with Secretary Califano.

Rather than waiting for the task force's recommendations to become public, ACCD proactively announced that if the regulations were not signed by April 4, 1977, it would launch nationwide demonstrations. ACCD thus regained control of the agenda, forcing Califano to either accept its timetable or face protests. The April 4 deadline was soon enough to maintain the pressure on Califano but still gave ACCD enough time to plan nationwide protests. Organizing for the events began in March under the motto "Sign 504 Unchanged." ACCD planned protests at HEW headquarters in Washington, D.C., and at regional offices in New York City, Boston, Seattle, Dallas, Denver, Chicago, Philadelphia, and San Francisco. Califano would soon learn that the disability rights movement did not fit the erroneous stereotype of a constituency dependent on public sympathy or handouts. Disabled activists were demanding their civil rights, which included an end to separate-but-equal accommodations for disabled persons, particularly when the separate facilities were no more "equal" than schools for African Americans had been in the pre–*Brown v. Board of Education* era. Many disability rights activists were veterans of the civil rights and antiwar movements and understood how the tactics of those struggles could apply to their own. Their strong identification with the political movements of the 1960s fueled their response to Califano's tactics and was a major factor in their ultimate success.

Judy Heumann, a disabled person who later became an undersecretary of education in the Clinton administration, served in 1977 as a board member of ACCD and as deputy director of the Center for Independent

Living (CIL) in Berkeley. She took responsibility for planning the San Francisco component of the nationwide April 5 protest. Heumann and fellow CIL staffer and wheelchair-user Kitty Cone, both of whom had spent most of their adult lives as political organizers, focused on expanding political support for the protest to include other civil rights organizations, the religious community, labor unions, and progressive activists and officials. The disability rights movement had traditionally operated apart from other movements for social change, and Heumann and Cone's strategic approach gave the San Francisco protest a power lacking in the other events around the nation.

The ACCD activists made another critical strategic decision to advance the disability rights agenda. A one-day nationwide protest would focus national attention on the Section 504 regulations, but the public's interest in the issue would likely then evaporate. No follow-up protests had been planned, so Califano would have only to weather one day of negative press before continuing his efforts to weaken the regulations. Further, getting disabled persons to demonstrations on short notice was no simple matter. For the ACCD to maximize its pressure on Califano, a tactic had to be utilized that did not require additional events with their accompanying logistical complexities. The solution was to hold sit-ins in HEW's offices until the regulations were signed. Heumann was charged with organizing the San Francisco protest. She did not want the press or Califano to know about the planned sit-ins. If HEW had advance knowledge, it would ensure that the protesters did not gain access to its offices. The organizers thus quietly took people aside and told them to bring sleeping bags or blankets to the rallies across the country.

As the San Francisco demonstration began on April 5, 1977, the sit-in remained under wraps. A crowd of more than five hundred people listened to a series of speeches; then Heumann took the stage. She urged the audience to "go and tell Mr. Maldonado [the HEW regional secretary] that the federal government cannot steal our civil rights." Most of the crowd followed Heumann's direction and entered the floor of the federal building containing HEW's offices. The unexpectedness of this relatively harmless tactic increased its value. Secretary Maldonado was in his office when the protesters entered. His presence made for the type of confrontation that ensures good coverage on the evening news. Taken by surprise, Maldonado did not appear even to know about the existence of Section 504. As cameras rolled, the regional secretary's inability to justify Califano's position, and the sense he conveyed of being overwhelmed by the protesters, fueled a sense of empowerment throughout the group. When the San Francisco protesters had matters well in hand, they used HEW's phones to call other cities to check on the progress of other events.

Having flooded HEW's San Francisco office with protesters, the organizers announced they would not be leaving. More than two hundred people, most of them disabled, slept in HEW's offices, hallways, and meeting rooms. There were no showers, bathtubs, or cooking facilities, and there was only one accessible toilet for men and women. While the protesters could get by without maintaining normal standards of cleanliness, they had to eat. In Washington, D.C., more than seventy-five disabled demonstrators were effectively starved out of their sit-in after twenty-six hours. A sit-in by six disabled protesters at HEW's New York City office also ended because of the lack of food.

But Cone and company had established a network of volunteers from groups like the Delancey Street Foundation and Black Panthers who would have risked arrest to bring food to the sit-in. Once the sit-in became established, even Safeway and McDonald's contributed food. The organizers of the San Francisco sit-in had laid the groundwork to support a long siege.

Despite the high-profile San Francisco sit-in, Califano was continuing to take a hard line. He had dramatically stood on his office coffee table during the Washington, D.C., sit-in to announce that he would not sign the regulations until he could study them and understand their implications. HEW's general counsel was even more confrontational, stating that the regulations would "have to be changed" before Califano signed them. Such statements only further incited the disability rights community.[23]

To Heumann, Cone, and the other strategists, HEW's obstinacy meant that ACCD had to flex additional political muscles. Two weeks into the sit-in, with virtually every politician and progressive political group in the region now ardently supporting the protest, two San Francisco Bay Area congressmen held a special hearing in the occupied HEW offices. San Francisco's legendary Representative Phil Burton, a burly bear of a man, presided over the hearing and was brought to tears by the testimony of disabled activists. Ed Roberts, who used an iron lung and was serving as head of California's Department of Rehabilitation, captured the prevailing mood, claiming, "We are not even second-class citizens, we're third-class citizens." An HEW bureaucrat sent to the hearing to explain why the Section 504 regulations had to be changed made the terrible mistake of using the phrase "separate but equal," thus confirming everybody's suspicions about HEW's retrograde agenda. After completing his testimony, the official left the hearing, went into an office, and locked the door. Burton, wanting Califano's emissary to continue to hear from the protesters, ran to the office and began kicking on the door, demanding that the official return. A social change organization rarely gets a powerful political leader so emotionally involved in its cause.

As the local and national media continued regular coverage of the San Francisco sit-in, millions of Americans became exposed to the life experiences of persons with disabilities. The media broadcast individual profiles of many sit-in participants, increasing the public's understanding of why discrimination against disabled persons must end. People who were deaf or blind or used wheelchairs were now seen not as wanting special help but as simply seeking equal access to employment, schools, housing, medical care, and public transportation. The positive press, however, did not change a critical fact: the sit-in could not last forever. Although morale was strong and people had been willing to experience serious pain in order to continue, the protest strategists recognized that Califano had to be forced to act sooner rather than later. Heumann, Cone, and several other leaders thus flew to Washington, D.C., after the sit-in had lasted two weeks. They realized that Califano needed more to worry about than an embarrassing protest three thousand miles away.

Upon arriving in the capital, the disabled activists took to the streets. Califano's luxurious house was picketed day and night. His neighbors must have wondered what he had done to provoke twenty-five people in wheelchairs to hold candles outside his home while singing "We want 504" to the tune of "We Shall Overcome." The activists also sat in front of President Carter's church on Sunday morning, only to have him exit through a rear door.

After a White House meeting between activists and Stuart Eizenstat, Carter's top domestic adviser, Califano surrendered. On April 28, 1977, he signed the Section 504 regulations virtually unchanged and ended the struggle prior to his own May deadline. Califano claimed the regulations would "usher in a new era of civil rights" and would be implemented with "flexibility" and "common sense." The San Francisco sit-in ended two days later. After twenty-five days of sleeping on floors, eschewing baths or showers, and eating mostly fast food, the 150 remaining protesters were exhausted. Most were filthy, and many had lice. Two sign-language interpreters had stayed throughout, as did a handful of attendants. The protesters had become like family to one another, with HEW's offices as their home. A determined group of people traditionally portrayed as weak and helpless had engaged in the longest occupation of a federal office building in U.S. history and had forced a newly elected political administration and the bureaucracy it controlled to meet their demands. As Kitty Cone told the media, "Nobody gave us anything. We showed we could wage a struggle at the highest level of government and win."[24]

The successful Section 504 campaign used a number of strategies recommended throughout this book. First, the disability rights movement did not allow the election of a Democratic president to sidetrack its agenda; instead it maintained a proper fear-and-loathing attitude. Second, disability activists were proactive. They consistently took the offensive and forced HEW to operate on ACCD's timetable, not vice versa. Largely because of the movement's proactive approach, the media consistently framed the dispute in the civil rights terms set by the protesters. Third, a lengthy sit-in by disabled protesters took its opponents by surprise. Finally, as with many of ACT UP's actions, the sit-in demonstrated activists' "by all means necessary" approach. This approach fueled the moral power of their activism and sent a message to Califano that disability rights activists would outlast him.

PUBLIC ATTITUDES AND DIRECT ACTION

It is important to contrast the public's response to direct actions by disability rights with the response to AIDS activists. Activists using wheelchairs generated far more sympathy and did not have to contend with widespread homophobia and right-wing assertions that AIDS was God's vengeance on gay people. Also, disability rights activists did not inconvenience people going about their everyday business, as ACT UP and its affiliates sometimes did. Local and federal police forces treated disability rights protesters with none of the brutality that typified their response to ACT UP sit-ins. Behavior viewed negatively when carried out by ACT UP activists was identified with courage and commitment in the Section 504 protest. Politicians kept their distance from ACT UP, but San Francisco mayor George Moscone showed his support for the disability rights sit-in by bringing a shower attachment to help make up for the lack of bathing facilities at HEW's San Francisco office.

These contrasts show that activists considering direct action tactics must analyze how public attitudes toward their constituency impact the response to their conduct. For example, ACT UP would never have been allowed to take over a federal office for nearly a month. Conversely, fifteen thousand Hasidic Jews could halt traffic on the Brooklyn Bridge for a march to protest an incinerator without being accused of wrongly targeting commuters. Would the same march by welfare recipients demanding cost-of-living increases have met with similar acceptance? Of course not. The public and media would demand to know why the welfare recipients were not out looking for jobs rather than marching to increase their public support.

Social change organizations are often unable to alter the media's double standard and unfair bias against their exercise of direct action. The group Earth First! was founded in April 1980 by environmentalists opposed to what they perceived as weak compromises by major environmental groups over the future of roadless national forest lands. Earth First! prided itself on its deliberate disorganization, which allowed different chapters to remain formally unconnected to illegal direct action activities undertaken by various members. The group blockaded logging roads to save old-growth forests and protect habitat for the spotted owl in the Pacific Northwest. It also temporarily prevented campers at Yellowstone National Park from reaching a campground that interfered with a bear habitat.

Earth First! members were amazingly courageous. They climbed giant trees to protect them from being cut and put themselves at risk of being run over by trucks. The organization's use of direct action to stop clear-cutting and preserve ancient redwoods would seem to represent the type of good deeds that would garner mainstream media support. However, as former Earth First! activist Mitch Friedman recalled, "Earth First! was never portrayed as Robin Hood, it was portrayed as terrorists. Society doesn't want a crisis dealt with through crisis tactics." Society also doesn't want activists promoting the "radical" view that humans have no greater claim on natural resources than do other species. Media coverage of Earth First!'s civil disobedience against the timber industry came almost exclusively to dwell on its most controversial tactics, such as tree spiking. When two prominent Earth First! activists, Judy Bari and Daryl Cheney, were injured by a bomb explosion in their car, police and the media falsely alleged that the nonviolent victims had built the bomb themselves to fulfill their "terrorist" agenda.[25]

Sometimes activists can choose whether to try to overcome or accommodate built-in biases that impact public attitudes toward direct action. Such decisions involve thinking about what type of participant can best convey the event's message. For example, a squatters' organization planning a public squat of a vacant flat can attempt to house a single working mother with two kids, or it can try the same thing with three young male adults with long hair. Public support for squatting will be greater if it results in housing for the mother and children, even though the three men also need homes. In fact, some would argue that the latter trio would better establish the real value of squatting, because public sympathy for the children would obscure the action's underlying rationale. My own view is that it is difficult enough to prevail on an issue like squatting without using unsympathetic people as public examples. The most militant direct action tactics, or those that blatantly seek to defy public attitudes, are not always the best. If the family succeeds in winning public acceptance for squatting, less sympathetic individuals will benefit from greater opportunities for private occupation. Given the wide-ranging obstacles to achieving social change, activists should utilize tactics that build, rather than impede, public support for their cause.

As with ACT UP's protests, the Section 504 sit-in infused the disability rights movement with a "We will not be stopped" spirit that permeated its future activism. The victory inspired activists to push for more sweeping civil rights legislation, which occurred with passage of the Americans with Disabilities Act (ADA) in 1990. The American Disabled for Attendant Programs Today (ADAPT) has become a permanent direct action and civil disobedience wing of the disability rights movement, winning its own share of victories.

IMMIGRANT RIGHTS PROTESTS OF 2006

In the spring of 2006, immigrant rights activists engaged in arguably the most politically significant use of nationwide direct action in U.S. history. The millions that took to the streets for immigrant rights reflected coordinated mass protests in both small rural towns and major cities, and many protest turnouts were the largest ever seen in these areas. As with the ACT UP and Section 504 protests, the direct action for immigrant rights involved people not typically seen as "usual suspects" in political protests—in this case, Latino immigrants. The scenes of Latino parents marching down public streets with kids by their side left an indelible impression on both the participants and the broader public.

And while the direct actions did not achieve their immediate goal of enacting comprehensive immigration reform, the events set this result in motion, helped boost Latino voting, and transformed American politics.

The 2006 marches were sparked when U.S. Representative F. James Sensenbrenner, a Republican from Wisconsin, introduced legislation in early December 2005 to make it a federal crime to live in the United States illegally. Not content to criminalize 10 to 12 million hardworking immigrants, Sensenbrenner's HR 4437 also made it a felony to assist or offer services to undocumented immigrants. Health care workers, teachers, and priests would, if the law passed, risk five-year prison terms and seizure of their assets. The House of Representatives passed the measure on December 16, 2005, only ten days after it was introduced. Sensenbrenner stated during the floor debate that he was making "unlawful presence" in the country a felony "at the administration's request." Accordingly, President George W. Bush issued a statement that day to "applaud" what he described as a "strong immigration reform bill." He also urged the Senate to take action on immigration reform so that he could sign a "good bill" into law.[26]

In response, immigrant rights activists' scheduled three mass protests. The first would be on or around March 25, the date on which many cities in the Southwest celebrate Cesar Chavez's birthday. The second would be held on Monday, April 10, a workday; and the third was slated for May 1, International Workers Day. The activists also had a legislative strategy: the direct action protests in the streets would be used to pressure senators, representatives, and the president to enact legislation creating a path to citizenship for the nation's 10 to 12 million undocumented immigrants.

Before any immigrants took to the streets, Los Angeles cardinal Roger Mahony sent a powerful message that foreshadowed the massive protests to come. On Ash Wednesday, March 1, 2006, Mahony directed parishioners to spend the forty days of Lent in prayer and reflection on the need for humane immigration laws. He also announced that if the Sensenbrenner bill were enacted and the act of providing assistance to undocumented immigrants became a felony, he would instruct both priests and lay Catholics to break the law. Mahony's declaration made it clear to millions of Catholics that all the services the church was providing to undocumented Catholic immigrants—job training, child care, counseling, emergency shelter, and much more—were now at risk. Mahony's solidarity with undocumented immigrants inspired action among the nation's Catholic clergy and laity, and sent a pointed message to Latino immigrants of that faith that the church supported their taking to the streets.[27]

March 2006: Mass Protests Begin

The Illinois Coalition for Immigrant and Refugee Rights got a jumpstart on the protests by organizing a March 10 demonstration in Chicago that brought out a previously inconceivable 500,000 persons. On March 23 in Milwaukee, a city that had not seen mass protests in years, a crowd of 30,000 rallied for immigrant rights under the theme "A Day without Latinos." Crowd estimates ranged from 10,000 to 30,000 in Phoenix on March 24 for perhaps the city's largest protest event ever. An estimated 80,000 Latinos skipped work in Atlanta to protest passage of anti-immigrant legislation by the Georgia House of Representatives. In Detroit on March 27, a crowd of more than 50,000 protesters chanting "Sí, se puede!" wended its way from Holy Redeemer Catholic Church to the McNamara Federal Building in yet another event, which many described as the city's largest political rally in years. In Denver, a March 25 rally brought between 50,000 and 75,000 protesters to the state capital. Also on March 25 there were between 5,000 and 10,000 protesters, primarily students, in Houston; in Charlotte, North Carolina, there were about 7,000; and large rallies were held in areas as diverse as Boise, Idaho, and Knoxville, Tennessee.[28]

The March 25 protests in Los Angeles included between 200,000 and 500,000 people marching in one of the largest demonstrations in L.A. history. Organized labor and the Catholic Church played important roles in generating this turnout, but when an event that was predicted to draw 20,000 protesters mushrooms to 500,000, a new element is likely in play. That element was the Spanish-language media, specifically Los Angeles's leading Spanish-language radio personalities, who went all out to mobilize their listeners. Eddie Sotelo, known to listeners of his highly rated morning talk show as "El Piolín," or Tweety Bird, said he felt personally obligated to fight on this issue, because he had entered this country illegally in 1986 and had gained legal status as a result of the 1986 Immigration Control and Reform Act. Sotelo arranged for a March 20 summit on the steps of City Hall that included such rival deejays as Ricardo Sanchez ("El Mandril," the Baboon) and Renán Almendárez Coehlo ("El Cucuy," the Bogeyman), often described as the Latino version of Howard Stern. After these leading Spanish radio personalities joined forces to promote the March 25 protest, momentum "just blew up."

The March protests conveyed themes not usually emphasized in mass direct action events. First, the peaceful nature of the marches—with few arrests and virtually no acts of violence—sent a clear message that America's immigrants were law abiding. In this respect, the tone projected by these marches differed from that of the "Battle in Seattle" protests against the World Trade Organization in 1999, the huge nationwide marches opposing the Iraq War in 2003, or the demonstrations at the Republican National Convention in New York City in 2004. Although those marches were primarily peaceful, media footage typically portrayed some protesters battling police or engaging in conduct that detracted from their message. Activists often criticize the media for promoting such images, arguing that random acts are inevitable in mass events and cannot be controlled by event organizers. But such acts were absent from the immigrant rights marches of 2006. This was attributable in large part to the labor movement's leadership and the clergy—reflecting the alliance that had helped organize the mass events.

Second, the immigrant rights marches were overtly patriotic. Backers of the massive Los Angeles protest urged immigrants to wave American flags, and these flags became a potent and highly visible symbol in events across the country. Deejay Eddie Sotelo, who played a major role in boosting turnout at all the Los Angeles marches, explained: "We wanted them to show that we love this country. Bringing the U.S. flag, that was important. There are so many people who say 'I'm glad my parents came here and sacrificed like they did for us.'" Susan Meehan, a veteran antiwar protester who attended the April national rally in Washington, D.C., noted, "I've been to a zillion marches and this is the first one with people shouting 'USA! USA!' and with so many American flags." Reflecting this conscious attempt to send a patriotic message, Jaime Contreras, president of the National Capital Immigration Coalition, a leading organizer of the national events, ended his speech by leading the crowd in chanting "U.S.A.! U.S.A.! U.S.A.!"[29]

The marchers use of the symbolic potency of American flags harkened back to the marches and rallies by the primarily Latino United Farm Workers of America (UFW) in the 1960s and '70s. During the 1970 Salinas lettuce strike, the union's red flags with a black Aztec eagle were hung along a hundred-mile stretch of highway from Watsonville to King City. After the Teamsters and other UFW opponents charged that these "red" flags represented communism, UFW leader Cesar

Chavez told his staff to buy up every American flag they could get their hands on. Soon the UFW strikers were seen waving these flags as well, and Chavez himself was captured waving a huge American flag. The many U.S. flags at the immigrant rights events of 2006 were designed to show immigrants' allegiance to their newfound home.

Not surprisingly, anti-immigrant activists ignored the preponderance of American flags and instead focused on the Mexican flags in the crowds. They claimed that marchers put allegiance to Mexico first. While Mexican flags never outnumbered American flags, activists encouraged protesters to leave their Mexican flags at home. Rafael Tabares, a senior at Los Angeles's Marshall High School who helped plan that school's March 24 walkout, "ordered classmates to put away Mexican flags they had brought to the demonstration—predicting, correctly, that the flags would be shown on the news and that the demonstrators would be criticized as nationalists for other countries, not residents seeking rights at home." Although Mexican flags were not often seen in future marches, groups like the anti-immigrant Minuteman Civil Defense Corps, based in Phoenix, continued to insist that the sight of "people marching on the streets and waving Mexican flags" was resulting in "a quiet rage building."[30]

Patriotic spirit was also reflected in the rallies' support for veterans and current members of the military. Latinos accounted for 16.5 percent of marine recruits at the time of the marches, reflecting a steady increase in the past decade. Uniformed soldiers were sometimes singled out for applause, and military personnel were a "popular presence" at the immigrant rights rallies. Eliseo Medina of the Service Employees International Union (SEIU) noted that at the April rally in Houston, which was attended by more than 50,000, "speakers repeatedly pointed to people in uniform at a nearby bridge, and they received roaring applause." He added, "'When [demonstrators] see people in uniform, it gives them tremendous pride and validates that we are contributing to this country." At San Diego's huge April 9 rally, Latino veterans carried signs that read WE FOUGHT IN YOUR WARS. Jorge Mariscal, a Vietnam veteran who went on to become director of the Chicano Studies Department at the University of California, San Diego, observed that "after serving our country, to see our relatives now criminalized through this legislation [HR 4437] is provoking a lot of people."[31]

Not since the heyday of the farmworkers' movement had Latinos predominated in mass protests—and never before had Latino immigrants so powerfully conveyed a moral message about the function of immigrant workers in the U.S. economy. The undocumented immigrant marchers left the shadows to publicly proclaim that the U.S. economy depended on them. They announced without apology that it was undocumented immigrants who worked in America's restaurants, cleaned America's buildings, cared for America's sick, and made much of the nation's food industry possible. The very sight of hundreds of thousands of Latino immigrants marching made a statement more powerful than any slogan on a banner.

April 2006: National Day of Action

While the immigrant rights movement was doing its own "negotiating" by demonstrating support for legalization through mass marches across America, key leaders struck a deal in the Senate to pass a compromise legalization measure said to have Bush's support. Under its terms, undocumented immigrants who had been in the country for at least five years would get a path to citizenship, but those who had lived here between two and five years would benefit little, and recent arrivals (those with less than two years' residence) would get nothing. The proposed compromise legislation fell short of many advocates' expectations, with many arguing that the plan to bar millions of immigrants from access to citizenship was unacceptable. Yet even this weakened bill failed to get the sixty Senate votes necessary to cut off debate, and it subsequently died. This spurred activists to send an even more powerful legalization message to Washington, D.C., in the rallies planned for Monday, April 10.

The weekend events leading up to the National Day of Action signaled that anger about HR 4437 had not abated. A march in San Diego on Sunday, April 9, included crowds of between 50,000 (the *San Diego Union-Tribune*'s estimate) and 150,000 (the Spanish-language media estimates). All agreed that it was the largest demonstration in the city's history. Again, many marchers carried American flags to show their desire to become citizens. In Dallas, police estimated that more than 350,000 marched, with many waving U.S. flags, in the city's largest protest event ever. Detroit's event drew an estimated 50,000 protesters. More than a dozen cities that had historically lacked large Latino populations—including Birmingham; Boise; Lexington, Kentucky; Salt Lake City; and St. Paul, Minnesota—had crowds that numbered in the thousands. The St. Paul march had 30,000 participants.[32]

On April 10, more than a million protesters in over one hundred cities marched during the National Day of Action for Immigration Justice.

Cardinal Theodore McCarrick gave the opening prayer at a rally of an estimated 200,000 protesters in the nation's capital, a short distance from where senators were still struggling to reach consensus on legislation. Crowd estimates numbered 80,000 in Atlanta, 50,000 in Houston, more than 100,000 in New York City, 10,000 in Boston, and between 100,000 and 200,000 in Phoenix. There were over thirty marches in the South alone. Fort Myers, Florida, not known for its immigrant rights activism, had 75,000 protesters; the Atlanta march was two miles long. In Omaha, Nebraska, also not viewed as an activist hotbed, 8,000 people marched.

In Fresno, located in California's Central Valley, 10,000 people marched in what police described as "by far the largest event we ever had in our city." Portland, Oregon, another city not known for a large Latino immigrant population, had several thousand marchers, and 25,000 to 50,000 protesters marched in Seattle. Immigrant advocacy groups based in Nashville decided to forgo another rally in that city (they had had a successful event on March 19) and instead held protests in Memphis, Knoxville, and Jonesborough, in upper east Tennessee. In the little-known farming town of Garden City, Kansas, 3,000 people—10 percent of the town's population—took to the streets.

The size of the marches, and the huge number of Latino immigrant families participating, dominated the strongly favorable media coverage. Even President Bush said the April 10 rallies were "a sign that this is an important issue that people feel strongly about." Congress was in recess for two weeks, and immigrant advocacy groups hoped that members would get feedback from their districts prior to the third planned nationwide event, the May 1 "Day Without Immigrants."[33]

May 1, 2006: A Day without Immigrants

The May 1 marches sought to show America that undocumented immigrants were so indispensable to the economy that if they did not show up to work for a day, business would grind to a halt. It was hard to imagine, however, that the immigrant rights movement could top its two prior events. But the turnout of Latino immigrants on Monday, May 1, exceeded all expectations, as at least a million people walked through more than two hundred American cities in a truly dramatic display of "people power." Once again, Los Angeles led the way, with more than 650,000 marchers. The city's usually active port was almost completely closed. Cardinal Mahony had urged immigrants not to risk losing their jobs by skipping work and had asked children not to miss school; the Los Angeles march was held in the early evening to address these concerns. Crowd estimates in Chicago ranged from 450,000 to 700,000, with more than 75,000 in San Francisco and a similar number in Denver, where the event was described as the largest protest in the city's history.

More impressive than the large turnouts in major urban strongholds was the extraordinary geographical breadth of the marches, which covered nearly all states and many small rural towns where national protest actions were rare. The thousands marching in places such as Omaha, Nebraska; Salem, Oregon; and Lumberton, North Carolina, sent a powerful message that Latino immigrants now lived in and were inextricably linked with local economies well beyond the traditional areas of concentration in California, Florida, and the Southwest.[34]

The Marches' Historic Legacy

The May 1 Day Without Immigrants was like a social earthquake rumbling across the American landscape, leaving all to wonder what it really meant. In the short run, hopes that the mass turnouts would make it politically untenable for Republicans to continue opposing comprehensive immigration reform proved unrealistic. The Republican Party shifted away from supporting a path to legalization when the House passed HR 4437, and the GOP soon became even more unified against measures that as recently as 2007 had bipartisan support. But the marches' failure to quickly achieve this key legislative goal does not detract from the historic transformation of Latino and national politics triggered by these protests. This transformation took three forms.

First, Latino voting increased exponentially. A striking feature of the May Day rallies was the thousands of signs that read TODAY WE MARCH, TOMORROW WE VOTE. Immigrant advocacy groups in Arizona, Colorado, California, Illinois, and many other states followed the protests by launching voter registration and citizenship drives to boost Latino voting in November. Voting became a central issue for the movement. Historically large Latino voter turnouts in the November 2006 elections defeated anti-immigrant Republicans in Colorado and Arizona, and increased Latino voting in 2006 and 2008 helped Democrats retake control of the U.S. House in 2008 and played a central role in Barack Obama's 2008 presidential victory. The 2008 election saw Latino voting swing four states won by Bush in 2004—Nevada, Colorado, New

Mexico, and Florida—into Obama's column, and Latino votes also helped the Democrat win in the former red state of Virginia.

When Arizona enacted Senate Bill 1070 in April 2010, the Support Our Law Enforcement and Safe Neighborhoods Act, the law's strong anti-immigrant provisions further galvanized Latino voters. In Nevada, Senate Majority Leader Harry Reid won a tough reelection fight by securing 90 percent of the Latino vote, with Latinos making up a record 15 percent of the electorate. California Democratic senator Barbara Boxer won 86 percent of the Latino vote in a race in which 18 percent of voters were Latino, and Democrat Michael Bennett survived a fierce battle in Colorado by winning 81 percent of the Latino vote, with Latinos comprising 10 percent of all voters. Not only did the marches permanently awaken the sleeping giant of Latino voters, but a constituency that Bush strategist Karl Rove thought in 2004 was up for grabs is now solidly in the Democrats' camp.

Second, in addition to greatly advancing Latino political empowerment, the marches also spawned a new generation of young Latino activists willing to take a "by all means necessary" approach to asserting their rights. The campaign for the DREAM Act (see chapter 9), which would grant a path to citizenship for young immigrants who arrived in the United States as children and who have graduated from U.S. high schools, effectively used marches, protests, sit-ins, fasts, and other direct action tactics that effectively put the issue on the national map. DREAM Activists represent the next generation of Latino political activism, and many were politicized while marching as children in the 2006 protests.

Finally, while the 2006 protests did not quickly lead to the enactment of comprehensive immigration reform, they put the issue on the national political radar. President Obama's support for reform helped win him 72 percent of the Latino vote in the 2012 presidential election, while Republican opposition to creating a path to citizenship for the 8 to 12 million undocumented immigrants drove Latino voters to overwhelmingly back Democrats in national and state races. The inevitable passage of this critical legislation has its roots in the 2006 protests.

DIRECT ACTION ON THE RIGHT: THE TEA PARTY

While some conservatives condemn community organizing and the use of direct action, others on the right recognize their power. A great example occurred on February 19, 2009—less than one month into

President Obama's term—when CNBC commentator Rick Santelli called for "Tea Party" protests against the new administration. Santelli's call for rebellion so early in the new president's term caused controversy, but quickly echoed through the conservative media. It particularly resonated at Fox News, which provided extensive coverage of Tea Party protests on February 27, 2009, and April 15, Tax Day.

Strategically, conservative activists were testing Obama to see how he would react to their attacking him during what is traditionally a presidential "honeymoon" period. And they became even more aggressive when their attacks got little blowback. By the time the activists emerged under the "revolutionary," grassroots name Tea Party, they were a rising force. These activists soon launched the savviest political strategy of 2009: the Tea Party takeover of congressional town hall summer meetings, which changed the political dynamics and framing of the health care struggle.

Tea Party activists portrayed themselves as akin to grassroots peasants with their pitchforks, battling against powerful forces of injustice. Here's how *Politico* described the Tea Party actions on July 31, 2009, "Screaming constituents, protesters dragged out by the cops, congressmen fearful for their safety—welcome to the new town-hall-style meeting, the once-staid forum that is rapidly turning into a house of horrors for members of Congress. On the eve of the August recess, members are reporting meetings that have gone terribly awry, marked by angry, sign-carrying mobs and disruptive behavior. In at least one case, a congressman has stopped holding town hall events because the situation has spiraled so far out of control."[35]

The first reported Tea Party "riot" occurred in Setauket, New York, whose Democratic U.S. representative, Tim Bishop, had previously held more than a hundred town meetings without problems. "Boiling anger and rising incivility" were also seen in early July at a health care town hall event in nearby Syracuse. Close to one hundred sign-carrying protesters greeted Democratic representative Allen Boyd at a late-June community college small-business development forum in Panama City, Florida.[36]

What made the Tea Party strategy particularly clever was the elitist backing for these "populist" protests. As an August 16 *Washington Post* article on the Tea Party explained, "One of the most prominent organizers is FreedomWorks, a Washington-based advocacy group headed by former House majority leader Richard Armey (R-Tex.) that is also pushing to defeat Democratic climate-change legislation. FreedomWorks's major financial backers have included MetLife, Philip Morris and foundations controlled by the archconservative Scaife family." Other visible Tea Party backers were Americans for Prosperity, the funding engine for the right-wing Koch brothers. Despite the clear corporate and elite backing for the town hall protests, the dominant media spin accepted Armey's description of the efforts as "a real grass-roots uprising."[37]

Some elements of the media could not get enough of the Tea Party. According to Mark Jurkowitz of the Pew Research Center, from August 3 to 9 "health care accounted for only 5% of the newshole [the universe of news] in newspapers, online and network news. But it dominated cable news (37%) and radio (33%)," with the thirteen leading cable and radio talk shows devoting 59 percent of their airtime that week to the health care debate. More than three-quarters of all the coverage was focused on the politics of the legislative battle and the newest and most incendiary angle to the story—the town hall confrontations.[38]

Right-wing efforts to use the Tea Party mantle soon endangered the once-certain prospects for health care reform. An August 3 *Los Angeles Times* story ("Health Measure Will Be Tough Sell") addressed the challenges many Democrats faced as they encountered vocal opposition to health care legislation. "Republicans and other critics portray Obama's plan as a federal takeover of medicine, making it a much riskier issue for Democrats in more conservative districts," the story said. "That includes the many Democrats elected in Republican-leaning districts in the 2006 and 2008 elections and the Blue Dog coalition of fiscal conservatives." Other media echoed these thoughts. "Voices are being heard all over the country, voices of protest, and they're growing louder," noted CBS anchor Katie Couric on August 3. And much of the town hall narrative, particularly on the talk shows, was an argument over whether those protests represented broad grassroots sentiment or an orchestrated effort by conservative interest groups.

CBS correspondent Wyatt Andrews's August 3 report—which included scenes of protesters shouting down Senator Arlen Specter and Health and Human Services secretary Kathleen Sebelius in Philadelphia—ended up somewhere in the middle. "The crowds are partly the result of conservative web sites asking for turnout, . . . but the turnouts also reflect real fear over the increased taxes and government controls," Andrews said, adding that opponents are "trying to kill what they call Obama-care with a show of August heat."[39]

Many attributed the success of the Tea Party "riots" to their massive coverage and promotion by Fox News, whose reports then echoed throughout the conservative media and into traditional coverage. But the Tea Party's strategy also worked for other reasons.

First, it was unexpected. Activists had not stormed congressional town halls in recent memory, so the Tea Party's direct action offered the media something new. That's why progressive complaints about the media's failure to provide similar coverage of their even larger pro–health reform rallies missed the point; the traditional media are accustomed to such events, but they saw direct action by predominantly older, conservative-looking white people as involving the *un*usual suspects. This same media logic contributed to the significant media coverage of Latino families marching down city streets during the immigrant rights protests in 2006.

Second, organizers of the Tea Party town hall campaign understood that angry confrontations between politicians and "average citizens" are newsworthy. A strategy memo distributed by one Tea Party activist urged town hall attendees to "rock-the-boat early in the Rep's presentation . . . to yell out and challenge the Rep's statements early. . . . to rattle him, get him off his prepared script and agenda . . . stand up and shout and sit right back down." Our world of sound bites and YouTube videos is tailor-made for scenes of older white people shaking fists at their member of Congress. And while the media typically condemn over-the-top vitriol and aggressive actions by young protesters, it would respond differently to Tea Partiers in a state of public rage; the traditional media portrayed such behavior as reflecting an authentic groundswell building against health care reform.[40]

Third, Tea Party organizers recognized that the town hall protests were particularly likely to garner coverage during the slow summer news season. One reason cable news and radio talk shows kept talking about the protests is that, with Congress out of session, there was not much else to report. Absent a national political convention, July and August have historically been slow political news months because so many Americans are on vacation. But the new media leave people connected to news events while traveling or lying on the beach. By filling the summer news vacuum, the town hall protests got far greater attention than if they had occurred while Congress was in session. (This pattern was confirmed by the Tea Party's September 12 "Taxpayer's March on Washington," whose lesser media impact led Fox News to publicly criticize other major networks for not providing wall-to-wall coverage.)[41]

Finally, the town hall protests worked because President Obama and Democratic leaders failed to call out the corporate and elite backers of the actions. Whether they were caught by surprise, were uncertain how to respond, did not anticipate the political fallout, or forgot that July and August are not months to put politics aside, Obama and Democratic leaders failed to reframe and then delegitimize Tea Party activism. President Obama held some health insurance town halls of his own and urged supporters to challenge opponents, but he did not respond with the aggressiveness that typified his fall campaign retorts to John McCain's mistruths. This weak response to the town hall protests was a key factor in the strategy's success.

The Tea Party's successful use of direct action tactics is a vivid reminder that progressives do not have a monopoly on the successful tactics and strategies of grassroots activism.

8

Lawyers

Allies or Obstacles to Social Change?

Many activists go to law school so that they can use the legal system to promote social justice and progressive change. I count myself in this category. I started law school in 1979, at the tail end of over a decade of expansion in the number of federally funded Legal Services Corporation (LSC) jobs as well as public interest jobs in government and the private nonprofit sector. This period also saw Supreme Court decisions that advanced progressive values. Our highest court's willingness to recognize and expand constitutional and, specifically, minority rights filtered down to lower courts, fostering the view that the legal system could be an ally of, rather than obstacle to, social change.

Today, we confront a vastly different legal environment. The legal rulings that inspired many activists to become attorneys generated a conservative backlash that has returned the courts to their historic role of reinforcing social and economic unfairness. Federal funding for legal services began a steep decline with President Reagan's 1981 budget and has never recovered even under sympathetic presidential administrations. Although Reagan's eight-year campaign to kill federal funds for legal services failed, his administration significantly reduced employment prospects in legal aid and forced cutbacks in existing staff. Attacks on legal services became part of a broader strategy of "defunding the left." In the 1990s, congressional Republicans barred attorneys from using LSC funds from filing class action lawsuits, from collecting attorneys' fees after winning cases (a source of funds that once helped compensate for declining federal support), and from representing undocumented immigrants—a major client base in Los Angeles and other cities. Today, few go to law school expecting a legal services job upon graduation, and despite unmet demands for attorneys to represent low-income people, restoring legal services to past levels is off the political radar.

President Reagan also began a forty-year process of returning the Supreme Court to its historic role as an opponent of progressive social change. Reagan's appointees opposed expanding constitutional or statutory protections to benefit women, minorities, and the poor and rolled back many Warren Court rulings. President George W. Bush moved the Supreme Court even further to the right, leaving little doubt that social change movements had far more to lose than to gain by challenging government policies in the federal courts. The High Court's ruling in the *Citizens United* case, overturning decades of legal restrictions on campaign contributions, was perhaps its most politically influential decision in decades, and showed the extent to which right-wing judicial activism is achieving its goals.

Despite the less hospitable judicial climate, social change activists and organizations can still benefit from legal resources in seeking to fulfill their goals. Activists must recognize how best to use attorneys and the courts and how to avoid the tensions and conflicts that often mar activist-attorney relationships. As both a practicing attorney and an activist, I have experienced these sources of friction firsthand. By understanding the areas of potential conflict, activists and attorneys can establish the positive relationships necessary to achieving progressive change.

PREVENTING ATTORNEYS FROM ENCROACHING UPON STRATEGIC DECISION MAKING

During the summer of 1980, while still a law student, I worked both at the Tenderloin Housing Clinic and as a law clerk for a legal-aid agency serving senior citizens. The summer began with the announcement (discussed in chapter 1) of the proposed luxury high-rise hotels in the Tenderloin. I soon also became involved in an unrelated fight, helping tenants of the residential Glenburn Hotel, who were threatened with eviction from their homes by a new owner. That owner, a British physician, wanted to turn the Glenburn into an English-style bed-and-breakfast for tourists. Although the hotel had numerous vacancies, the owner did not want his tourists to share living space with the hotel's long-term elderly and disabled residents.

The owner started a two-pronged strategy to get rid of the tenants, whom he disparagingly described as "squatters." First, he engaged in psychological warfare against the vulnerable residents, telling them they were not wanted at the hotel and should move. He bolstered this illegal strategy by issuing eviction notices to all of the tenants, stating that they must vacate for upgrading of the property. Little did I know when I met with the tenants to discuss the landlord's efforts to displace them that the Tenderloin Housing Clinic would spend the next fourteen years in court fighting this hotel owner.

Many similar hotel conversions had already occurred in San Francisco during the 1970s, resulting in the loss of more than five thousand low-rent residential hotel rooms. To prevent further losses, the city enacted the Residential Hotel Ordinance in 1979, which restricted the conversion or demolition of residential hotel rooms. Legal-aid attorneys representing elderly tenants had been involved in drafting the new law. Because the Glenburn Hotel tenants were facing formal evictions in addition to psychological threats to force them to move, a legal-aid agency for seniors and the federally funded San Francisco Neighborhood Legal Assistance Foundation (SFNLAF) both agreed to represent the tenants. I was involved both as a law clerk for the legal-aid agency for seniors and as staff for the Tenderloin Housing Clinic.

The British physician displayed open contempt for the Glenburn tenants, describing them as "vagrants" and creating an atmosphere designed to make them feel so unwelcome that they would "voluntarily" vacate their homes. Many of the tenants were under great stress from their landlord's psychological assault, but the attorneys opposing him kept looking for signs that he would be "reasonable." This focus on reasonableness is ingrained during law school and even influences progressive attorneys. Nonlawyers seeking social change are far less likely to expect adversaries to act reasonably. The attorneys did not want to contest the issue in court, seeking instead to negotiate an agreement under which the landlord would end his eviction actions. Reaching such an agreement was difficult, however, because the hotel owner was slow and contradictory in setting forth his positions—in other words, he was not acting reasonably.

Further, settling the formal eviction actions was less important than deterring the landlord's abusive conduct; a jury would never have voted to evict the tenants, but the abuse might compel them to leave before any settlement could be reached. As the owner continued to delay an agreement, the strain on tenants began to tell. Some began drinking heavily, and others experienced stress-caused medical problems. The tenants, the attorneys, and I agreed that we needed to pressure the owner to end his eviction attempts. We decided that a good way to get the owner's attention was to schedule a demonstration in front of his medical office. Because the Tenderloin Housing Clinic did not yet have lawyers and thus was not the legal counsel for the tenants, I was charged with organizing the event. This would insulate the tenants' attorneys from being implicated in such "unreasonable" conduct.

As the demonstration approached, I observed a renewed sense of vigor and excitement among the hotel tenants. After months of being on the receiving end of the landlord's abuse, they were now going to get the chance to fight back. We all liked the idea of going after him at his medical office, where his patients and employees would learn of his conduct. Our press release, titled "Landlord Malpractice," connected the doctor-landlord's mistreatment of tenants to his treatment of patients; we felt that people reading about the former would not feel comfortable getting medical care from this physician.

After sending out the press releases, I learned that the attorneys had called a tenants' meeting for the night before the demonstration. Apparently, the hotel owner was once again appearing reasonable and was now interested in negotiating. The attorneys, who had kept their distance from the proposed demonstration, felt that holding the event would jeopardize the possibility for a negotiated settlement. Of course, the attorneys would leave the decision about whether to proceed with the protest up to the tenants; the nighttime meeting would allow the attorneys to explain their position so that the tenants could make an informed decision.

I knew as soon as the meeting was scheduled what the result would be; the scene has likely been repeated thousands of times, explaining why so many organizers have come to distrust and even despise their attorney "allies." The lawyers set forth the facts so as to guarantee that the tenants would cancel the demonstration. The tenants' position in any future legal action, the lawyers said, had suddenly become precarious, making it essential to reach a negotiated settlement; the landlord was exhibiting a new openness to compromise, but this window of opportunity could quickly close if the protest angered him. The attorneys did not emphasize that the landlord had so far agreed to nothing; nor did they focus on the landlord's pattern of promising compromise, only to renege. Those facts were not stressed, because they undermined the attorneys' position. I was permitted to give a dissenting view, but there was no way tenants were going to trust a law student over their own lawyers. The tenants accepted their attorneys' recommendation and canceled the protest.

In my opinion, the legal-aid attorneys had wrongly interfered with the tenants' decision-making process. Rather than objectively laying out all the options, the attorneys treated the tenants as if they were a jury, rather than clients. A lawyer must persuade a jury to accept his or her perspective on the case, but an attorney should not treat a client in the same fashion. I would not have objected had the attorneys laid out the facts fairly and expressed their own strategic preference. There is a difference, however, between expressing a viewpoint and falsely implying that any other perspective could spell disaster.

The attorneys' chief failure was misunderstanding the tenants' needs. Lawyers, including those who support social change, look for solutions in the law. In the Glenburn Hotel case, this outlook led the tenants' attorneys to focus on resolving the specific legal problem confronting their clients: the eviction notice. They were unable or unwilling to understand the greater risk that tenants would be displaced by the landlord's psychological attacks, which would not end with the resolution of the eviction issue but would cease only when the tenants made it clear that they could not be pushed around.

Although the tenants had voted to cancel the protest, most of them deeply regretted the decision. They had been excited about going after the doctor on his own turf, and now they were again reduced to passive participation in the ongoing drama affecting their lives. The tenants had lost a sense of personal empowerment and, more critically, a sense of unity. The legal-aid attorneys ultimately obtained the withdrawal of the eviction notices, but the settlement merely confirmed the legal reality that a San Francisco jury would never have allowed the landlord to evict the Glenburn tenants. More significant, the number of tenants benefiting from this legal "victory" steadily declined as tenants moved anyway, convinced the landlord would ultimately be able to evict them and not wanting to postpone the inevitable. That the tenants incorrectly assessed their legal position was irrelevant; few low-income people are willing to trust the legal system to protect them. What the tenants needed was a sense of control based on their own perceived power. By carrying out the protest, the tenants would in effect have said to the landlord: "Our power over you is based on our strength, not simply our attorneys." Had the attorneys understood and been willing to accommodate the tenants' psychological and emotional needs, they would have advocated the demonstration and actively encouraged future actions.

The story of the Glenburn Hotel tenants illustrates some of the reasons community organizers distrust attorneys. Activists typically criticize attorneys for relying on the legal system instead of direct actions designed to strengthen the constituency's sense of empowerment. But the Glenburn story has a deeper lesson: tenant activists made a fundamental error in granting the legal-aid attorneys too large a role in the decision-making process. Although organizers from the local Gray Panthers chapter and other community groups were centrally involved in the fight against hotel conversions, the issuance of eviction notices at the Glenburn suddenly transformed the tenants from autonomous members of the community into "clients" represented by attorneys. The informal relationship between a social change organization and its constituency was supplanted by a powerful and legally recognized *attorney-client* relationship. The decision about whether to proceed with the protest at the landlord's clinic was made in an attorney-client setting rather than in a strategic meeting between nonattorney organizers and tenants.

This transfer of influence to attorneys and away from the social change organizers and the affected constituency itself is at the heart of the problem. Unfortunately, overcoming attorneys' undue influence in tactical and strategic decision making is not easy. Attorneys can't be eliminated from the social change process, because legal issues and the need for technical legal skills emerge constantly. But the very creation of an attorney-client relationship necessitates formalized legal and ethical procedures, including confidentiality of communications, and gives most low-income "clients" a sense of obligation to their attorney that outweighs their informal ties to their constituency group.

Fortunately, strategies exist to prevent the creation of an attorney-client relationship from eroding constituents' strategic power.

First, attorneys who are not actively involved in a social change organization should be brought in for technical assistance only. Attorneys defending those arrested in civil disobedience protests are not authorized to influence the group's broader strategic agenda, and this model should equally apply in cases like the Glenburn Hotel eviction battle involving low-income clients, who typically lack a college education and are not political activists. Tactical activists working with low-income groups must ensure that attorneys do not encroach on their clients' strategic decision-making power.

Second, tactical activists must ensure that all decisions about nonlegal tactics are made in the presence of community organizers and acknowledged resident leaders. Such individuals have the ability to equal if not exceed the influence of attorneys when all are in attendance. To facilitate nonattorney input, activists should hold meetings at a social change organization's office or another familiar setting rather than in a law office conference room; even longtime activists can be intimidated in unfamiliar and formal surroundings. Attorneys may try to discourage the selection of a familiar site by raising the fear of compromising attorney-client confidentiality. In truth, the substance of strategic meetings held on the eve of planned protests such as the Glenburn Hotel tenants' rarely if ever reveals useful legal information not otherwise obtainable by your adversary in a lawsuit.

A third tactic to keep attorneys from becoming too involved in decision making is to work only with those who understand the limits of their role. Most legal-aid organizations have more than one attorney in each subject area, and the lawyers eagerly seek cases that have a broad impact. Social change activists should select the attorneys with whom their organization can best work and avoid those who view "impact" litigation as a personal power trip. Legal-aid attorneys need access to exciting cases, and this need gives activists the upper hand; too many activists err in focusing only on the organization's need for an attorney and forget that, in the legal-aid context, it is often the attorney who needs the client.

The problems that can arise after the creation of an attorney-client relationship, however, are not eliminated by limiting attorneys' involvement in strategic decisions. Additional attorney-organization friction may arise. Most participants in community-based social change organizations—and nearly all individuals or groups eligible for free legal services—have less education, income, self-esteem, and self-confidence than the average attorney. When tenants who have come to me for legal advice start asking me whether they should move, where they should move, or what they should do about nonlegal matters, my response is always that they can answer these questions themselves better than I can. Yet despite widespread public distrust and even dislike of attorneys, people of all income levels tend to defer to them even on issues of common sense or personal preference.

Let's assume that the Glenburn Hotel meeting between attorneys and clients had taken place at a community center with community organizers and neighborhood leaders present. Let's further assume that the attorneys had had no desire to steer the tenants toward a certain outcome and had objectively laid out the pros and cons of holding the scheduled protest. Also assume that, when asked for their opinion, the attorneys had expressed a preference for canceling the demonstration. Based on my long experience working with low-income, elderly, and disabled people such as those who lived at the Glenburn Hotel, I think the residents would probably have sided with their attorneys. They would have done so even if the attorneys involved had exhibited no understanding of the political environment; the social, psychological, and emotional value of the protest; or the social change organization's broader strategy. Such unwarranted deference to attorneys incenses community activists and often motivates organizations to forgo potentially effective strategies by refusing to work with lawyers.

How, then, can a social change organization reach decisions untainted by attorney influence? Returning to the modified Glenburn Hotel example, assume that, when asked for their opinion, the attorneys had stated that the group was in the best position to determine whether the protest should be held. The attorneys might have emphasized that it was the landlord's intimidating behavior, rather than his issuance of eviction notices, that posed the greatest risk to the tenants' future in their homes. They could have added that they were involved for their legal skills only and would stand behind whatever decision was made. By expressly renouncing the opportunity to sway the outcome, the attorneys would have encouraged the group to make its own decision. This process not only best serves the group but also increases the attorneys' credibility and trust within the organization.

A successful model thus exists by which social change organizations can obtain legal assistance without sacrificing control over their agenda to outsiders. The model clearly presupposes organizational discussion and agreement about the proper scope of the attorneys' role. As in other areas of tactical activism, the absence of such internal discussions can cause unfortunate results, as in the Glenburn Hotel example. It is easy to blame attorneys for overstepping their bounds, but activists also bear responsibility for not taking the steps necessary to forestall this result.

WHEN ATTORNEY CONTROL IS UNAVOIDABLE

Activists' concern with attorney influence over community decision making is heightened when such influence is unavoidable. This circumstance typically arises when a social change organization seeks a legislative response to a problem. Although a basic legislative framework can be developed through a community-, neighborhood-, or constituency-based process, attorneys are left to draft the actual language. This unavoidable reliance on attorneys raises two issues. First, deciding how to word legislation involves substantive, not simply procedural issues. The person doing the actual writing must make decisions that relate to the political effect of the legislation. Second, the attorney is often the only person who can assess the substantive impact of changes made to the original legislation as it travels through the political process. Such changes are often negotiated literally at the last minute. Because the timing of such decisions does not allow for open decision making, the group's attorney typically makes the call.

Social change activists frequently complain about attorneys' influence over drafting decisions. I have heard numerous organizers complain that their attorneys "sold out" the community organization as victory approached. This suspicion arises when the organization's involvement in the redrafting process becomes so attenuated that its members do not witness the true cause of the unsatisfactory result. A last-minute lobbying blitz by the opposition may weaken legislation on the eve of enactment; unless activists are present to see the process, they may blame their attorneys and not their opposition.

An excellent example of how community organizations and attorneys can avoid ill feelings during the drafting and legislative processes arose during the Tenderloin Housing Clinic's yearlong campaign to strengthen San Francisco's Residential Hotel Ordinance (RHO). Enacted in 1979, the ordinance was so riddled with loopholes that it failed to serve its goal of preventing the conversion of residential hotels to tourist lodgings. In 1989 the Clinic joined neighborhood groups throughout the city in redrafting the ordinance to facilitate and ensure vigorous enforcement. The Clinic participated both in organizing around the issue and in drafting the proposed legislation. The campaign began with community meetings in the Tenderloin neighborhood, whose residents proposed the necessary reforms. Subsequent meetings yielded a consensus on how to proceed, and the community's proposal was introduced to the city's Board of Supervisors.

In August 1989 hundreds of low-income residents turned out for a committee hearing on the proposed legislation. Our hopes for quick legislative approval were dashed, however, when the "progressive" committee chair stated at the outset that the issue was "too complex" to be voted on that day. The issue seemed to have increased in complexity after one of her financial supporters privately requested that she delay the matter until he could resolve the concerns of his wealthy, hotel-owning clients. This initial delay kicked off a series of additional hearings and postponements that continued until the measure was finally enacted into law in April 1990. The various delays were designed to give our opposition a full opportunity to weaken the legislation.[1]

These delays put the community-based organizations supporting the legislation in a difficult position, because few of their members could attend hearing after hearing over a period of several months. To prevent members from feeling alienated from the process, backers of the legislation established a small network of residents and organizers to keep each other informed. The network's small size served three functions. First, it enabled residents to continue their psychological investment in the campaign without feeling guilty about missing some hearings. Second, it ensured that the political base behind the legislation remained at the ready should a larger mobilization become necessary. Third, the smaller network allowed me, the attorney responsible for drafting the amendments, to receive quick feedback on changes to the legislation proposed during the lengthy campaign.

As frequently happens when legislation approaches a final vote, the opponents offered a continual stream of revisions and technical amendments to the ordinance. It was my job as attorney to understand the substantive impact of the proposed changes, but the network retained the authority to decide whether to accept or reject them. We were thus able to avoid the scenario in which attorneys make a deal on statutory language without receiving the constituency's prior assent.

Because some community residents and their organizational representatives were always present during hearings and legislative votes, we also avoided the more common scenario of a group having to rely exclusively on information provided to its attorneys by elected officials. In such cases, the politician tells the attorney what language is politically acceptable; the attorney then tells the group that unless it agrees to this language the bill will fail. Constituency members have no time to meet with other officials to verify this assessment, nor can they be certain that their attorney has not already promised that the group will accept the change. With the constituency group removed from the sources of primary information, the attorney's knowledge becomes power—and this power can be used to influence decision makers. That's why tactical activists should insist on hearing directly from the source of any information material to a decision. They should also rely on strategies that force elected officials to deal with the constituency directly rather than through their attorney. Unfortunately, even well-intentioned attorneys can become so vested in reaching a "reasonable" agreement on legislative language that they fail to consider whether a compromise might upset their constituency group. And when attorneys agree to language unacceptable to the community, it provokes anger.

Attorneys should recognize that their own self-interest demands that the constituency group makes critical decisions about legislation. An attorney jeopardizes his or her future credibility with both the constituency group and the legislators by usurping decision-making authority, which belongs with the people actually affected by the outcome. Legislators may be attracted to an attorney willing to compromise constituency interests but will soon learn that their ally has lost the group's confidence. Also, ongoing grassroots support for laws is critical to their enforcement and, potentially, their continued existence. Because community residents shared in the victory of the strengthened Residential Hotel Ordinance, they were ready to lend support when the law was subjected to a lengthy federal court challenge. That low-income tenants filled the courtroom may not have affected the appellate judges' decision to uphold the ordinance, but their attendance certainly gave a psychological boost to me and the other attorneys who were defending the law. When constituencies affected by laws retain decision-making power throughout the legislative process, their attorneys retain the backing necessary to ensure the measure's continued potency.

WHEN SOCIAL CHANGE ADVOCATES SHOULD USE THE COURTS

As noted above, I started law school in 1979, and my three years of legal training coincided with a rightward shift of the courts that has continued to this day. Yet despite decades of conservative High Court rulings, many people still see the courts as a vehicle for progressive change. Under the right circumstances, courts can bring such change. But activists and their attorneys must better understand the grave risks to progressive goals from potentially adverse court rulings, which makes even seemingly promising lawsuits the wrong strategic choice. Following are two prominent examples.

Welfare Wrongs

California's counties have long tried to save money by cutting welfare payments to single indigent adults. In response, legal-aid attorneys won appellate court rulings requiring grants to at least appear to reflect the cost of living. In January 1991 legal advocates for the poor thought they had hit the jackpot. In a suit brought by private attorneys, a state court of appeal ruled that Alameda County must raise welfare levels to reflect the true cost of housing. The judges rejected county arguments that state mandates for grant levels should be ignored because of their alleged steep fiscal impact. After several years of inadequate grant levels, which forced many welfare recipients into homelessness, justice for the poor apparently was at hand. My organization, the Tenderloin Housing Clinic, conducted a housing survey that found the court ruling would require San Francisco to raise its monthly grant by at least $25. This would increase the city's annual welfare costs by an estimated $3 million. Because the ruling was based on the plain language of a state statute, chances for reversal even by the California Supreme Court seemed slim.[2]

County governments, however, responded to the ruling by quickly winning state legislation abolishing the state mandate linking aid levels to the cost of necessities. The new regulation established minimum dollar amounts for aid with no provision for increases in the cost of living. A new state agency was given the authority to lower grant levels even further. The legislation left welfare recipients in their worst position in two decades and eliminated the prospect of grant increases for the foreseeable future.

I relate this story not to castigate the winning attorneys. On the contrary, their legal strategy brought, albeit very temporarily, a prospect of economic justice for welfare recipients that could never have been achieved through the political process. But this episode illustrates that although legal advocates for the poor were already operating in a dangerous legal and political climate by the early 1990s, they nevertheless advanced a litigation strategy that ignored the risks.

Today's legal environment for advancing the rights of the poor or challenging corporate power is even worse. This makes it imperative that attorneys go through a checklist of factors prior to filing such lawsuits. These include the potential negative consequences of losing at the trial or appellate level, or both; the prospect of a court victory being overturned by legislators or by the voters; the ability to achieve a comparable result without litigation; the court's capacity to provide the specific relief sought; the value of expending resources on litigation as opposed to some other strategy; the potential that a resort to the courts will reduce participation in grassroots political action; and the length of time necessary for a final victory to be achieved. Initiating a lawsuit to achieve progressive social change without carefully evaluating these factors can place a constituency's security and future at risk.

Walmart: Too Big to Hold Accountable

An even more striking example of the risks of litigating for social justice in today's judicial climate involves the landmark case of *Wal-Mart Stores v. Dukes*. The case began in 2000, when Betty Dukes, a female Walmart worker, filed a sex discrimination class action lawsuit on the grounds that the nation's biggest retailer had denied her promotions on the basis of her sex. Plaintiffs' legal team filed the case as a nationwide class action because their research found that women were systematically denied promotions at Walmart and that the company's discriminatory promotion policies were consistent throughout its stores.

Betty Dukes worked in California, and the plaintiffs' attorneys had the option of limiting the class action to Walmart workers in that state. This approach would have reduced the size of the class and the impact of the case outside California, but had the advantage of coming entirely under the Ninth Circuit Court of Appeals precedent that allowed compensatory damages (including back pay) for class action discrimination cases brought under Title VII. Title VII is the federal statute prohibiting discrimination on the basis of race, gender, or national origin. While the Second Circuit Court of Appeals had given tacit support for allowing such damages, the other circuit courts disagreed. Some believed this conflict between the circuits made the issue of compensatory damages in Title VII class actions ripe for Supreme Court review, but Dukes filed her case in the Ninth Circuit, so this issue did not appear significant.

The trial began in June 2001 in federal district court in San Francisco. The plaintiffs sought class certification for 1.5 million women, including current employees and those who had worked at Walmart since December 26, 1998. After the first of the many lengthy delays that would typify this case, in June 2004 Judge Martin Jenkins ruled in favor of class certification. Not surprisingly, Walmart appealed the decision, which, if upheld, would have authorized the largest sex discrimination class action lawsuit in United States history.

On February 6, 2007, a three-judge panel of the Ninth Circuit Court of Appeals affirmed the district court's class certification. Walmart filed for a rehearing and a rehearing en banc, and on December 11, 2007, the same Ninth Circuit panel issued a new opinion that altered some of its prior legal findings but still granted class certification. Walmart again filed for a rehearing en banc, and on February 13, 2009, the Ninth Circuit granted Walmart's petition. A panel of eleven Ninth Circuit judges heard the appeal on March 24, 2009, and on April 26, 2010, the en banc court affirmed the district court's class certification on a 6–5 vote. On December 6, 2010, the Supreme Court agreed to hear Walmart's appeal.

I knew some of the plaintiffs' attorneys in the case and closely followed its decade-long procedural path. While they always seemed optimistic that justice would ultimately prevail, I had my doubts. Would the nation's legal system allow its biggest employer to take a $1 billion–plus financial hit because it discriminated against women in promotions? An employer whose low-paid workers and anti-union sentiments made it a role model for the corporate interests that greatly influenced the Supreme Court?

It was clear from the oral arguments in the case that a majority of the justices would rule for Walmart. They sounded offended that the case could have proceeded so far against such a great company. On June 20, 2011, the Supreme Court issued a ruling that killed not only the underlying class action case, but also the Ninth Circuit's allowance of compensatory damages in class action discrimination cases filed under Title VII. In other words, a lawsuit brought to address sex discrimination on a massive and unprecedented scale resulted in a Supreme Court ruling that effectively prevents victims of such mass discrimination from using class actions to get money compensation.

It is hard to fault attorneys who sought relief for all of Walmart's victims, rather than limiting the class and the stakes of the case by confining the class action to California. But the latter strategy would have been more prudent, and non-California victims could have been assisted through separate statewide class actions. Plaintiffs' counsel issued a press release when they filed their Supreme Court brief, stating, "Wal-Mart is attempting to dismantle the Supreme Court's employment discrimination class action jurisprudence. Such far-reaching changes to the law would require the Court to overrule 45 years of civil rights and class action precedent. This would rule out certification of all but the smallest employment discrimination cases—and that's not what Congress intended." But the attorneys had to know that this Supreme Court would have no qualms about throwing out forty-five years of precedent, and would not be deterred by Congress's intent. After all, the conservative majority had followed a similar course in its *Citizens United* ruling on campaign financing. The *Dukes* case offers a cautionary lesson, reaffirming that attorneys turning to the courts to rectify social injustice need to broaden their assessments of worst-case scenarios.[3]

When Litigation Is Unavoidable

There remain instances when filing a lawsuit is the only option for activists to achieve their goals. This is particularly true in the areas of voting rights, civil rights, and land use.

Voting and Civil Rights. Voting rights lawsuits address three strategies that deny racial minorities political representation: at-large voting systems and runoff elections that virtually guarantee all-white local representation; gerrymandered legislative districts drawn to reduce minority representation; and gerrymandering that funnels racial minorities into a small number of concentrated districts in order to reduce the constituency's overall voting clout. In such lawsuits, the status quo is the worst-case scenario, and legal action runs little risk of an unexpected downside.

The most prominent recent example of such use of the courts occurred in Texas after Republicans drew lines after the 2010 census to minimize the impact of a growing Latino electorate. After Latino civil rights groups sued, a circuit court of appeals redrew the proposed new legislative districts to more fairly apportion Latino voters. Texas appealed, and on January 20, 2012, the Supreme Court again rescued Republicans by ruling that the district court should "take guidance" from the state's recently enacted (though clearly discriminatory) plan. Due to pressure to get the new districts in place in time for party primaries, a federal three-judge panel in San Antonio approved "compromise" interim maps on February 28, 2012. The interim maps were better than the original Republican version, but black and Latino groups continued litigating. On August 28, 2012, they won a ruling from a federal three-judge panel in the District of Columbia that Texas's maps discriminated against minority voters in violation of the Voting Rights Act of 1965.

The plaintiffs had no choice but to file these voting rights lawsuits, and won much better results for minority voters in 2012 and the opportunity for far better voting maps for 2014 and beyond—unless the Supreme Court again intervenes.[4]

Litigation is also unavoidable when voters overturn civil or constitutional rights, as occurred in 2008 when Prop 8 repealed California's constitutional right to marriage equality. Prop 8 was put on the ballot after the California Supreme Court ruled in May 2008, that statutes and a prior ballot measure barring gay marriage violated the equal protection clause of the California constitution.[5] In passing Prop 8, voters changed the state constitution to eliminate this constitutional right.

The Prop 8 lawsuit involves multiple legal issues that go to the heart of our democratic system. Can voters revoke a constitutional right? If so, can they repeal other such rights that lack federal protections? And if laws must have a rational relationship to a legitimate government interest, can Prop 8 meet this test when its proponents' beliefs about gay marriage are unsupported by empirical data? Or does the electorate's passage of Prop 8 make it per se rational?

The legal challenge to Prop 8 won in the federal district court and the Ninth Circuit Court of Appeals, and will ultimately be decided in the Supreme Court. In light of gay marriage winning on four state ballots in November 2012 and the Republican Party no longer promoting its opposition to gay marriage, the politics of the Court's ruling have changed, and the Prop 8 lawsuit could become a historic example of using the legal system to achieve progressive change.

Land Use Lawsuits. Activists most commonly find litigation unavoidable on land use matters. Lawsuits are commonly the only activist strategy to stop poorly conceived development projects. This is particularly true in cities like New York that prevent activists from using ballot initiatives to stop destructive land use plans. Activists usually sue on the grounds that the environmental impacts caused by the proposed project were insufficiently explored in the planning review process. The threat of such lawsuits is often the only way activists can rein in ardently pro-development government bodies. In the 1980s environmental impact litigation focused on the effects of intensive high-rise office construction in our nation's major cities. Other suits addressed urban sprawl, as new housing developments encroached on agricultural land and open space, increasing traffic, creating problems with sewage disposal, and so on. The rise of Walmart and large-scale suburban malls in the 1990s expanded the scope of environmental impact litigation to smaller towns desperate for the employment opportunities the stores offer. Rural and suburban communities continue to be split over the benefits of such projects, and potential litigation over defective environmental analysis is an important strategy for preventing them.

Actual or threatened litigation over development is particularly effective because activists can succeed simply by delaying the project. When a court rules that a development project has a defective environmental impact statement, the developer must create a new, legally sufficient report. The project cannot commence until the new report is approved by the local planning agency. This new report also can be challenged in court, and because few developers are willing to risk resuming construction until the final challenge is resolved, there is further delay. In a well-publicized case in Hawaii in the 1980s, a developer completed a condominium tower while the local residents' court challenge to the project's height was still pending. Presumably, the developer assumed that he would either win the case or, if he lost, simply have to pay a fine for exceeding the height limit. The court instead ordered the developer to remove the illegally erected eight stories. Most developers are unwilling to risk such a costly result and choose to delay construction until lawsuits are resolved.

Delay can kill a development project for several reasons. Financing can disappear, the business purpose of the development can change, or a corporate merger, reorganization, or bankruptcy can render the project moot. During delays, project opponents can elect officials opposed to the venture, the overall business climate can change, interest rates can rise, and new problems with the project can be discovered. There is also what I have called the "aggravation factor" caused by the filing of a lawsuit. After going through the time-consuming process of planning the project and hiring expensive lobbyists to remove political hurdles, some developers simply get fed up and abandon their plans once the new roadblock of a lawsuit emerges.

Lawsuits challenging environmental impact reports are increasingly used by opponents of socially beneficial land use projects like affordable housing and bike lanes. It's hard to believe, but in June 2006 a San Francisco Superior Court judge granted a preliminary injunction preventing San Francisco's implementation of its bicycle plan until the city completed a costly and time-consuming environmental impact report. Although the bike plan was designed to encourage people to give up cars for cycling—an obvious plus for the environment—the court barred the city from also moving forward on such bike-related physical streetscape changes as removing parking spots and traffic lanes for use as bike paths. It took the city four years to comply with the court's requirements, and the court did not fully approve the plan until August 2010.

And it is not only in San Francisco where opponents of bike lanes use the courts as their last strategy to stop bike lanes. In 2011, neighbors unhappy with bike lanes on Prospect Park West in Brooklyn's Park Slope community sued to stop the environmentally friendly project. The prominent and expensive national firm Gibson, Dunn and Crutcher represented the plaintiffs in the case, which drew widespread publicity due to outspoken opposition to the bike lanes from Iris Weinshall, wife of New York senator Charles Schumer. A court dismissed the lawsuit on August 16, 2011, and the bike lanes went forward as the ruling was appealed.

Anti-development lawsuits are also unavoidable when challenging the legal basis of the project's approval process. These cases typically charge that a local planning commission or other approval agency has ignored or violated the law or ignored the evidence in order to fulfill a political agenda. A lawsuit exposing such administrative abuses can achieve two goals. First, it can keep the project under a cloud of uncertainty despite its victory in the political process. Second, such lawsuits tell the approval agency and developers that social change organizations will not tolerate circumvention of the law. Neighborhood residents can yell and scream about agency wrongdoing at a public hearing, but filing a lawsuit really gets their attention.

AVOIDING CONFLICT WITH ATTORNEYS

When progressive political movements or social change organizations are forced to turn to the courts to achieve a central goal, conflict between organizers and lawyers can emerge. This conflict differs from that described in the Glenburn Hotel example, in that the tension is not based on attorneys' improper intervention into a fundamentally nonlegal struggle. Nor is there competition between organizers and attorneys over who speaks for the client or over how decisions at meetings with clients are made. The conflict that can emerge once a litigation strategy takes center stage is far deeper and potentially even more divisive. It frequently arises when activists skeptical of participating with government bodies are forced to work with attorneys who are seeking social change within the government's courts. This chasm between people organizing for change at the grassroots and those advocating from inside the legal system is best bridged when the two groups have an ongoing and equal relationship. Otherwise, serious conflict can emerge.

For example, in his Pulitzer Prize–winning history, *Parting the Waters: America in the King Years, 1954–63*, Taylor Branch details the rancor in the 1950s and 1960s between Roy Wilkins and Thurgood Marshall, respectively executive director and chief counsel of the NAACP, and Martin Luther King, Jr. Whereas the NAACP was intent on pursuing a legal strategy to achieve civil rights for African Americans by way of Supreme Court rulings, King and his allies preferred the direct action tactics of sit-ins, bus boycotts, and Freedom Rides. Wilkins-Marshall and King not only saw little value in each other's tactical approach but also believed the other was interfering with his own camp's strategy and reducing the potential for its success.[6]

It is easy to understand how even two of the leading civil rights advocates of their time could fail to create a unified approach. The differences revolved around issues of power between ministers and lawyers, between people who suffered under Jim Crow laws on a daily basis and those living outside the South, and between people of different ages, educational backgrounds, and economic classes. King's strategy was based on the willful violation of state laws, whereas Marshall and the NAACP assumed the legitimacy of the legal system. The conflict between the activist and legal factions of the civil rights movement typifies the tensions underlying many social change movements. The media have often created a false impression of a unified and harmonious civil rights movement; for example, media coverage of Thurgood Marshall's death in 1994 included almost no focus on the split between legal and activist forces. Instead, journalists and broadcasters commenting on Marshall's life acted as if the NAACP and King's Southern Christian Leadership Conference had worked hand-in-hand for civil rights.[7]

Social change activists cannot afford to idealize the past this way. Those who naively expect that everyone supporting their agenda will unite in one big happy family may abandon political involvement when reality sets in. To avoid such disillusionment, activists and attorneys must recognize the need to reach agreement on their respective roles. Such an accord may not emerge, but the dialogue will at least reduce the tension and enhance prospects for success.

Social change organizations can avoid conflict with legal organizations working for similar goals either by hiring their own legal staff or by relying exclusively on a small circle of attorneys they trust. The great model for the former approach is the United Farm Workers of the 1960s and 1970s. UFW founder Cesar Chavez built a movement for social and economic justice that attracted some of the best young legal minds of that generation. With low-paid but high-quality in-house legal talent on hand, Chavez retained complete control of the UFW's litigation strategy. The organization's top-notch legal staff and hard work enabled the organization to overcome the greater resources of its agribusiness adversaries. Although few contemporary causes can match the commitment given by

UFW lawyers to the farmworkers' movement of the 1960s and 1970s, social change organizations can at least approximate the UFW's strategy simply by hiring a staff person with a law degree. Many top-quality, committed activists cannot obtain progressive legal jobs after becoming attorneys, and if they have other useful skills, they can bring an extra dimension to social change organizations. As litigation has increasingly become part of many environmental disputes, even grassroots organizations hostile to the legal system should try to hire staff with legal training. This staff can at the very least monitor environmental litigation so that grassroots activists can get crucial information from someone they trust.

In-house staff with legal training can also preclude unnecessary disputes between activists and attorneys over litigation. For example, lawsuits filed amid great publicity and optimism for success can hit unanticipated snags. The attorneys may recognize these problems and realize that a compromise settlement is necessary. Activists who have stayed out of discussions of the litigation since the press conference announcing its filing may not understand why the attorneys now seem unwilling to take the case to trial. Discussions of complex legal issues or case precedents may seem little more than a cover-up for a sellout. If an organization's own staff understands the legal issues, there may be agreement on the need to accept a disappointing result. Conversely, the activist group may have the analytical ammunition needed to counter the attorney's claims and avert a bad settlement. In either case, having a staff member with legal training can help bridge the chasm between the two forces.

LAWSUITS AS PART OF A BROAD STRATEGY

Lawsuits are particularly effective when used as part of a broader social change campaign. For example, in the Tenderloin Housing Clinic's battle against slumlord Guenter Kaussen (discussed in chapter 5) we filed a class action suit challenging Kaussen's policy of failing to refund tenants' security deposits. The lawsuit increased public interest in our Kaussen campaign for two reasons. First, both of our plaintiffs were refugees—one from Cambodia, the other from Ethiopia—who had sought the Clinic's assistance. They and their families had fled terror and starvation in their native lands to come to the United States. One could not have invented more sympathetic plaintiffs, and Kaussen's mistreatment of them bolstered his image as an unscrupulous profiteer. Second, by filing the tenants' case as a class action suit, the Clinic greatly magnified the scope of Kaussen's wrongdoing. Evidence existed that hundreds, if not thousands, of San Francisco tenants had been cheated out of their deposits, so that a huge sum of money was potentially at stake. The media would want Kaussen's former tenants to know of the suit, thus increasing the likelihood of widespread press coverage.

The local NBC affiliate, whose contract with the Center for Investigative Reporting had led it to produce dozens of Kaussen stories, led off its evening news with a piece on the class action suit. It described the suit as yet another Kaussen-related scandal and reiterated the string of abuses connected to the mysterious slumlord. The story primarily focused on the fate of the refugee-plaintiffs, who had fled oppression abroad only to be cheated in the United States. The fact that people so distrustful of legal systems would nevertheless turn to the courts for justice highlighted the degree of Kaussen's wrongdoing. The lawsuit helped reconnect human faces to Kaussen's abuses and gave an always-hungry media the additional fuel necessary to justify their continued investigation into his practices. The refugee plaintiffs ended up recovering all of their deposits plus additional compensation, so the lawsuit achieved its specific and more comprehensive objectives.

Deterring Wrongful Conduct

Activists should also consider litigation for its deterrent effects. A lawsuit can help activists achieve their goals even if the suit itself is ultimately lost. For example, lawsuits have long been filed challenging race discrimination by local police. Although U.S. Supreme Court rulings have made it difficult for such suits to prevail, initiating litigation places a spotlight on the issue. This attention puts the police on notice that future claims of abuse are less likely to be ignored. It also gives media covering such suits a basis for follow-up stories. Police misconduct cases also give attorneys for the city and the police department an opportunity to give greater input on department practices that could reduce the likelihood of future misconduct. If the defense lawyer does not believe a jury will find an ongoing police practice "reasonable," the department will have the necessary motivation to change the policy.

Suits charging a city's police department with race-based misconduct are hard to win, but there have been successes. In 2012 a federal judge in California threatened to place Oakland's police department in receivership under his control if its long-standing misconduct was not corrected. Such lawsuits are often the only option available for addressing misconduct, as few politicians want to publicly battle police over this issue. Voters once willing to create civilian oversight commissions for the police are increasingly likely to oppose such measures on the grounds that they "tie the hands" of the officers. Some minority neighborhoods once critical of police tactics now see the police as valuable allies in the war against drugs and gang violence. Litigation has therefore become the leading strategy for changing unfair or unconstitutional police practices. Federal court judges, whose life tenure insulates them from anti-crime political pressure, are best positioned to afford relief to victims of illegal police activity.

Lawsuits are also the leading deterrent to police who would otherwise violate the civil rights of homeless persons. Since the 1980s brought widespread visible homelessness to cities across the United States, lawsuits have been filed by social change organizations to deter police enforcement of local laws prohibiting loitering, blocking the sidewalk, and panhandling. Municipalities throughout the country have sought to deter the entry of poor and homeless persons by criminalizing such conduct as sitting on a bench next to a bedroll or pack, resting with one's back leaning against a building, or even carrying possessions in a shopping cart. Critics have understandably viewed these laws as unconstitutional anti-loitering measures disguised under a different name. Such measures also have been challenged for violating poor people's constitutional right to travel and for illegally transforming homelessness and poverty into crimes. The real tragedy is that after three decades of widespread public homelessness in the United States, there is no way to legally compel Congress and the president to provide the affordable-housing funding necessary to make lawsuits over the right to panhandle or sleep on a park bench unnecessary.

Disputes over the Merits

Activists and attorneys can differ on what constitutes a meritorious claim requiring a lawsuit, and serious conflict can result. Early in my career, I was involved in a campaign to ensure that the police responded properly to calls from tenants who were illegally locked out of their homes. Lockouts were commonly used to oust without due process tenants who were behind in their rent. Some police consistently sided with the landlord; others erroneously told tenants that lockouts were "a civil matter." Our campaign was quite successful and featured a picket of a police station and the arrest and handcuffing—in front of cameras—of a prominent landlord with a history of utilizing illegal lockouts.

In a situation that occurred during the anti-lockout campaign, a person moved into a nonprofit-owned residential hotel primarily serving seniors. During his first month of residency, he was seen walking around the lobby carrying a gun. Tenants expressed alarm at this behavior and reported the conduct to management. Management confronted the man, an argument ensued, and the hotel handed him a refund and ordered him to leave. He proceeded to seek assistance from a neighborhood community organizer, who urged me to file a lawsuit against the hotel for perpetrating an illegal lockout. I refused to initiate such action on the grounds that the hotel had seemed to act reasonably in response to a gun-waving resident who had only recently arrived.

I saw no value in suing the most publicly acclaimed hotel in the neighborhood for conduct that might technically violate the law but that most people would agree was proper. The hotel's tenants supported the management's action, indicating that a lawsuit on behalf of this short-term resident would be opposed by the constituency my office represented. The organizer's position was that the law was the same for everyone and that attorneys could not pick and choose when to enforce it. He felt I was betraying my obligation to the community, and we did not speak for several months as a result of the dispute.

My decision not to file the lockout case was not difficult, as the case was legally questionable and would have undermined tenant and neighborhood support for the Clinic's anti-lockout campaign. A lawsuit would also have focused on an incident that was atypical of the problem, confusing the message. Although my conflict with the organizer was in part a tactical disagreement, another aspect of it was that he, like some other activists, had little conception of what constitutes a meritorious case. Unfortunately, this lack of knowledge may not impede activists' zeal for filing legally doubtful cases in an attempt to achieve their goals.

In the mid-1980s, a small group met to discuss possible legal challenges to San Francisco's homeless program. The one nonlawyer at the meeting, the newly hired executive director of a shelter, insisted that there had to be grounds for a lawsuit. A few of us carefully explained that, as much as we disagreed with city homeless policy, we saw no basis for a suit; yet the shelter director thought we were in effect "letting down the cause" by not proceeding to court. We later heard that the director had concluded from our comments that we "were not interested in dealing with the problem"; he equated our failure to sue with political indifference.

That is not the only time I have heard a lay activist equate an attorney's refusal to file an unmeritorious lawsuit with a lack of commitment to the cause. These disputes are frustrating and can prevent future working relationships. Progressive attorneys often see themselves as activists, and resent having their credibility challenged by someone with little understanding of the law who won't be the person having to file papers and appear in court in what the attorney believes is a frivolous case.

To reduce this all too common source of friction, tactical activists should learn the basic legal issues applicable to their work. Activists who insist that they do not need to read about laws or the legal system make two key errors. First, they limit their understanding of possible strategies to achieve their goals, because many strategies relate to legislation or legal interpretation. Second, they cede power to the very attorneys of whom they are so suspicious. When grassroots activists meet with their lawyers to discuss potential litigation, they should be directed to the online citation of the cases on which the attorneys are relying to reach their conclusions. This request does not imply any distrust of the attorneys; it is no different from activists asking for a line-by-line itemization of the budget during a fight over spending cuts. For those lacking computer access, the attorneys can hand out photocopies of the key cases. After reading and discussing them, activists will have a better sense of their attorneys' legal position.

More commonly, activists dissatisfied with their attorney's tactical approach ignore legal issues and try to find an attorney who agrees with them. This process wastes time and maintains the activist in a subordinate role. In contrast, by becoming informed about legal issues affecting their agenda, activists can deal with attorneys on a more equal footing. Differences of opinion on the strategic value of filing a lawsuit may still emerge, but the dispute will not arise out of distrust based on misinformation.

COMMUNITY BENEFITS AGREEMENTS

One area that intersects many of the issues in this chapter—the attorney's role in fostering social change, community lawyering, and using legal skills as part of a broader strategy—involves the still-underutilized strategy of community benefits agreements (CBAs). CBAs are designed to ensure that major development projects provide *community benefits,* which typically include a living wage requirement for workers employed in the development, local hiring agreements, and funding for parks or recreational facilities, affordable housing, and similar mitigations. Negotiating CBAs is among the most important ways attorneys can assist community organizations in land use matters. The agreement achieved in 1981 by Tenderloin residents concerning the three luxury hotels was a precursor to formal CBAs. Labor and community coalitions in many cities have pressed for, and obtained, some or all of the benefits listed above.

Among the most prominent CBAs is that reached by the Figueroa Corridor Coalition for Economic Justice in Los Angeles in May 2001 for the development of a project adjacent to the Staples Center, best known as the home of the Los Angeles Lakers and Clippers. The same company that built the Staples Center sought to build an adjacent hotel, a seven-thousand-seat theater, a housing complex, an expansion of the convention center, and plazas including restaurants and entertainment and retail businesses. Considerably more ambitious and massive than the typical development projects that community and labor organizations confront, this plan posed a tough challenge for activists: convincing developers to offer benefits to the community in order to win political support for a project that some would see as too big for politicians to reject regardless of community opposition.

But Los Angeles is among the growing number of cities where community and labor groups recognize that development projects can do as much to help as to ruin working-class neighborhoods. And in the absence of adequate federal funding to address inner-city problems, leveraging private development projects for community needs has become a critical activist strategy. To this end, more than thirty labor and community groups led by the Strategic Actions for a Just Economy, the Los Angeles Alliance for a New Economy (LAANE), and Coalition L.A. built a large coalition that demanded and won community benefits from what was known as the Staples Center project.

The Staples CBA brought unprecedented benefits. According to its provisions, the developer would fund an assessment of the community's park and recreation needs and pay $1 million toward those needs; would guarantee the city's living wage for 70 percent of the jobs the project would generate; agreed to a first-source hiring program for community residents; would build more affordable housing; and would consult the community on the selection of commercial tenants. In addition, the developer would contribute funding to housing, parks, the arts, and other programs required under city laws.

Julian Gross, the former director of the Community Benefits Law Center who now operates a solo law practice, was the lead attorney negotiating the Staples CBA. Skilled attorneys like Gross are essential because CBAs are enforceable contracts, and groups signing a CBA can sue the developer—independently of city legal actions—if it does not fulfill its commitments. This independent right to sue for enforcement can prove pivotal when community benefits are to be received over time, since subsequent elections may put politicians and city attorneys in office who allow developers to "renegotiate" the city's development agreements—or to ignore them altogether.

Of course, a community group's capacity to enforce a CBA depends on whether its attorneys drafted the agreement correctly. Sometimes they do not. Consider one prominent, poorly written CBA, the controversial Atlantic Yards project in Brooklyn. The developer agreed to provide high levels of affordable housing in exchange for political backing from the community groups party to the CBA for a huge project encompassing a sports arena, condominium and office towers, and retail and entertainment space. Nothing in the CBA, however, required the developer to contribute funds for affordable housing off-site in the event that funding problems delayed or prevented on-site construction—which is what occurred. Nor was there any provision requiring the affordable housing to be built prior to or simultaneous with the arena and non-housing projects. The result: Atlantic Yards opened as a sports and entertainment complex, with its affordable housing "community benefits" far off in the future—if they are ever built.

Julian Gross has negotiated more CBAs than any other attorney, and his manual *Community Benefits Agreements: Making Development Projects Accountable* is required reading for those interested in this area of the law. He has seen a number of CBAs that give the process "a bad name." For this reason, attorneys interested in helping community groups on land use issues should become skilled in contract law, though it is not often described as part of a "public interest" law curriculum.[8]

Why would a major developer sign a CBA? The main reason is that they believe the city will not approve the project without it. CBAs help persuade community and labor groups to advocate for projects that they would oppose absent such benefits, expediting the approval process. And CBAs can subtly smooth passage of projects that politicians feel uncomfortable voting on either way. A politician torn between wanting to support the project's construction jobs and not wanting to alienate community supporters can use a CBA to justify endorsing the project on the grounds that all relevant interest groups are now happy. The community and labor groups creating the CBA have essentially done the politician a favor, which can help in future dealings.

One challenge for attorneys who get involved in the CBA process lies in compliance with professional responsibility laws relating to representation of multiple parties. These laws require a retainer agreement clearly acknowledging the attorney's multiple representations, and obligate the attorney to make sure clients understand the implications. In the typical CBA process, groups signing as clients with the same attorney have a sufficiently close relationship that conflicts over bargaining strategy do not emerge. To avoid ethical conflicts, however, attorneys must be aware of the interests of the groups seeking their representation. In Gross's experience, disputes over bargaining strategy that can threaten to splinter a coalition usually involve groups not represented by counsel. Some community lawyers often work with groups without formal representation agreements, but in the CBA context such retainers are essential.

Many successful CBAs have been concluded in Los Angeles and San Francisco, where community and labor groups have strong influence over local governments. But they are increasingly found in other cities as well. In 2006, community groups in Seattle formed the Dearborn Street Coalition and—along with Puget Sound Sage, a coalition of labor, faith, and community groups—sought to ensure that a $300 million retail and housing complex planned for the city's Little Saigon and neighboring areas would meet the needs of the local community. The groups reached agreement on Seattle's first CBA on August 29, 2008, and the project was approved. Regrettably, in April 2009 the project was canceled due to the economic downturn. Puget Sound Sage executive director David West noted that despite the cancellation, "for the first time in the Puget Sound region, community stakeholders, including neighborhood councils, Vietnamese small businesses, community organizations and labor unions negotiated and won a legally binding commitment from a developer to provide community benefits." These benefits included funds for low-cost housing, traffic mitigations, and Little Saigon small businesses, as well as guarantees of local and living-wage jobs. Gross and Columbia Legal Services Seattle attorney Andrew Kashyap assisted the community coalitions in negotiating and drafting the CBA.[9]

In some cases community groups are unable to obtain a CBA, but their advocacy results in the inclusion of many of their desired community benefits in the development agreement with the public entity. This is what happened in Denver after a redevelopment project was proposed for a fifty-acre brownfield in downtown owned by the Gates Rubber Company. A coalition of community and labor groups organized by the Front Range Economic Strategy Center (FRESC) spent more than three years trying to negotiate a CBA, but could not get the developer to the table for a direct deal. But the agreement reached in 2006 between the developer and the Denver redevelopment agency brought substantial community benefits, which in addition to provisions for affordable housing, living-wage jobs, and local hiring also included a ban on big-box stores. Denver's first example of what some call a public CBA (which, unlike true CBAs, are public agreements that cannot be privately enforced) also fell victim to the economic downturn, and the project was pulled in September 2009. Nevertheless, Denver activists showed once again that pushing for a CBA is an indispensable strategy for ensuring that major urban development projects benefit those living and working where they are built.

At a time when many attorneys are frustrated by the lack of opportunities to help community organizations, CBAs provide a promising avenue for such involvement. And with funding of federal urban housing and jobs programs steadily declining, CBAs should become even more widespread as local politicians join community groups in seeking new ways to secure resources. This means that attorneys with the legal skills to negotiate and draft enforceable CBAs on behalf of community and labor groups will be more in demand than ever. Those looking to become community lawyers or to devote some portion of their work to land use matters should read Julian Gross's manual on CBAs and consider whether this opportunity to further economic justice could work in their community.

9

Student Activists Lead the Way

When the original edition of this book came out in the 1990s, the term *student activism* was associated with the antiwar and civil rights protests of the 1960s and 1970s. Students were active in later social justice struggles, but campus activism was deemed a relic of the past. Today, the situation has dramatically changed. From DREAM Activists, to students battling sweatshops, to campus protesters against rising education costs, student activists are making a difference. Students are not only leading winning campaigns but are also galvanizing the larger progressive community.

To be sure, student activism will never attract the national media attention it got in the 1960s—when campus protests were new and were heavily covered—but students continue to prevail against powerful interests. These interests know all too well that student activism is not a relic of the past, which is why in recent years they have waged a war on campus activism. Attacks on programs and student groups that encourage activism are widespread and have even occurred at such historically progressive institutions as the University of Oregon, the University of California, Santa Cruz, and Santa Monica College. As public colleges and universities become increasingly dependent on private donors, suppressing student activism has become a troubling by-product of the schools' "private-public partnership."

BATTLING NIKE SWEATSHOPS

Since the late 1990s, college students have been the leading force for ending sweatshop labor in the foreign factories that make most of the nation's clothes. The group United Students Against Sweatshops (USAS) has exposed and curtailed labor abuses in these global manufacturing plants, improving the lives of countless low-wage, primarily female workers. Students were well positioned to impact sweatshops because most universities had contracts with companies like Nike to provide clothing bearing the school's logo or name. These lucrative deals gave students bargaining leverage, as they could pressure college administrators not to identify the school with sweatshop labor. Since the wearing of such apparel implicated students in corporate profiteering from sweatshops, campus activists were able to personalize the issue; activists built broad student support demanding that colleges ensure that their branded clothing was not made by sweatshop labor.

Student anti-sweatshop activism began in the fall of 1997 when groups targeted the more than two hundred contracts Nike had with college and university athletic programs. Nike's "partnerships" with schools to produce sweatshirts, T-shirts, hats, and other logoed clothing was a multimillion-dollar venture, and all of these goods were being made in sweatshops primarily based in Indonesia and Vietnam. In October 1997, students from more than twenty campuses participated in international anti-Nike protests. Students called for an end to universities' contractual relationships with Nike unless wages and working conditions for the company's overseas workers improved. More than fifty students at the University of Michigan handed out flyers and unfurled a huge banner at the school's football game that day. Students at the University of New Mexico passed out anti-Nike leaflets at two shopping centers in Albuquerque and had people sign letters to Nike president Phil Knight. The University of North Carolina at Chapel Hill had a campus "speak-out" on November 7 to coincide with a school football game. And more than sixty students protested at the University of Illinois at Urbana-Champaign.[1]

Pressure from "Students Against Sweatshops" at Duke University led the school's president, Nan Keohane, to insert a clause in Duke's contract with the Collegiate Licensing Company that opposed labor abuses by licensees. The students subsequently met with administrators to develop a more detailed code of conduct requiring manufacturers of items bearing the institution's logo to disclose the working conditions of their employees. Duke adopted the tougher code, which included independent monitoring, on March 6, 1998. Bruce Siegal, general counsel for the Collegiate Licensing Company, observed that "when top schools such as Duke pay attention to this issue, I wouldn't be surprised if other colleges don't jump on the bandwagon."[2]

Students soon learned that convincing college administrators to give up Nike's royalties would not be easy. Students organized a Nike Awareness Campaign at the University of North Carolina at Chapel Hill, a key target because it was the alma mater of Nike's top advertising icon, basketball superstar Michael Jordan (after whom Air Jordans were named). The school had agreed in July 1997 to a five-year, $7.1 million cash-and-clothes deal with Nike covering all its athletic teams. Although student protests against Nike at UNC received national media coverage, university officials were not persuaded. When the students met with the school's former basketball coach, Dean Smith, he adopted Nike's perspective and said he "didn't understand why we were questioning what they were doing in Asia."[3]

To forestall threats to its lucrative college endorsement deals and ensure continued loyalty among students exposed to information about its labor abuses, Nike sent public relations staff to campuses around the country in October 1997. The corporation hosted a conference call with college newspaper editors, took out full-page ads in college newspapers, and visited several campuses. But its efforts to blunt student concern about its labor practices failed.

In July 1998 student anti-sweatshop activists from dozens of universities formed the United Students Against Sweatshops (USAS) to ensure enforcement of codes of conduct and to push for a living wage. USAS then joined with university administrators and international labor rights experts to found the Workers Rights Consortium (WRC) in April 2000. The WRC was created to assist universities with the enforcement of their labor rights codes of conduct, which were adopted to protect the rights of workers producing apparel and other goods bearing university names and logos. Beginning with the support of 44 universities, the WRC had 180 affiliated schools by 2012.

INSTITUTIONALIZING VICTORIES

As stable institutions, USAS and the WRC enable campus anti-sweatshop activism to overcome the problem of ongoing student turnover. Most students attend college for four or five years, and many go abroad for a semester or a year. With the personal, health, financial, and academic factors that can deter student activism, many campus struggles are pushed by key leaders whose graduation can bring even once-flourishing campaigns to a halt.

When I met with student anti-sweatshop activists in the late 1990s, I asked them how they planned to keep the campus movement going after they graduated. Most expected that if new students were interested, they would keep it going, a sort of Field of Dreams, "If you build it, they will come" approach that overlooks the importance of aggressively recruiting students to a cause. The resulting lack of recruitment caused student anti-sweatshop activism to decline after its initial successes. Campus anti-sweatshop groups needed a vehicle for institutionalizing their movement, and the WRC filled this need.

Since its founding, the WRC's achievements have been nothing short of remarkable. On April 4, 2003, the *New York Times* told the inspiring story that the BJ&B cap factory in the Dominican Republic had a union and "recently negotiated a labor contract that provides raises, scholarships and other benefits that are unheard of among the country's 500 foreign-owned plants." United Students Against Sweatshops had sent thousands of letters to the factory and assigned a student volunteer to help the union organize. Ignacio Hernández, the general secretary of the Federation of Free Trade Zone Unions, told the *Times* that the students clearly made the difference: "I never thought a group of students, thousands of them, could put so much pressure on these brands." Molly McGrath, USAS development director, explained the source of the students' power: "We are the target market of a lot of these brands and they want a positive image on campus because they want consumers for life. We also have the moral and ethical argument being on the side of a university, so we can pressure the university to use their leverage in society to change the policies of the brands."[4]

In November 2009, the WRC reached a historic agreement with Russell Athletic (whose parent company is Fruit of the Loom, Inc.) to reopen a unionized Honduran garment factory the company had closed in October 2008. Student pressure over the closures and Russell's labor practices had "prompted nearly 100 colleges and universities to drop licensing deals with the company that allowed it to print clothing with colleges' names, logos and mascots." WRC director Scott Nova called Russell's reversal a "gigantic breakthrough for labor rights in the region," and USAS organizer Jack Mahoney noted that "this is the first time we know of that somebody has reversed a company's decision."[5]

In 2010, USAS achieved an even greater victory. Recognizing the limits of monitoring overseas factories, USAS arranged with Knights Apparel to produce T-shirts and sweatshirts for bookstores at four hundred American universities—while also paying workers a living wage. Knights Apparel's shirts sell for the same price as those made by Nike and Adidas, whose goods are typically made in places like Bangladesh (where the minimum wage is 15 cents per hour) or China (85 cents). In contrast, workers at Knights's Alta Gracia factory in the Dominican Republic (whose national minimum wage is 85 cents) are paid $2.83 per hour. USAS's direct intervention in the marketplace quickly made Knights the leading provider of college apparel, as campus groups arranged for their schools to partner with the new supplier. USAS has shown what's possible when you avoid dealing with corporate chiefs like Nike's Phil Knight who make tens of millions of dollars annually off the poverty of third-world workers.

In addition to battling sweatshops abroad, USAS has become an ongoing support center for campus struggles by workers seeking to unionize or get a fair contract. While many still see campuses as ivory towers, USAS brings home to students the daily economic realities of those serving campus meals and cleaning dorms and lecture halls. Like other student activist campaigns discussed in this chapter, USAS is fighting real-world struggles for social and economic justice. It has become a valuable incubator for students seeking permanent organizing jobs in such struggles after graduation, and a powerful refutation to stereotypes about today's students as lacking the idealism of past generations.

DREAM ACTIVISM

In 2001, legislation was introduced in Congress to legalize young undocumented immigrants who had come to the United States as children and were now in college or the military. The measure had bipartisan support and was viewed by immigrant rights activists as a step toward comprehensive immigration reform. Politically, the bill seemed set on an easy course for passage: many Republicans, including President George W. Bush, supported creating paths to citizenship for undocumented immigrants. The GOP could use passage of what became known as the DREAM Act to win future support from a growing Latino electorate.

But after 9/11, it became harder to pass any bill that appeared to reward undocumented immigrants. The Bush administration took a harder line in 2005 in backing the Sensenbrenner bill, legislation that made it a federal crime for undocumented immigrants to be living in the country, and also a crime for anyone to provide aid to such immigrants. When millions of Latino immigrants and their supporters took to the streets in mass protest of this bill and to demand immigrant rights in the spring of 2006 (see chapter 7), Congress still failed to positively respond. Republican opposition to any measure addressing the needs of the 8 to 12 million undocumented immigrants further hardened after the 2008 elections. Arizona senator John McCain, the GOP's 2008 presidential nominee and once a key sponsor of immigration reform, became an outright opponent. By 2010, prospects for comprehensive reform were nil. Passage of the less comprehensive but still vitally important DREAM Act became the central goal of the immigrant rights movement.

Students led the struggle to pass the DREAM Act, in a campaign that had two critical phases. The first occurred after Democrats lost control of the House in the November 2010 elections. DREAM Activists recognized that the bill would have no chance in the Republican-controlled House starting in 2011, so they launched an intensive campaign to win passage before the end of the year.

The DREAM Act campaign used nearly every possible activist strategy to prevail. Borrowing tactics first pioneered by Cesar Chavez and the farmworkers' movement, students used fasts and prayer vigils to bring attention to and build support for their cause. The students showed their value to affected communities by holding holiday food drives, and their desire to be Americans through Thanksgiving dinners with citizens. Student DREAM Activists built coalitions with labor unions, religious groups, and businesses and with the entire immigrant rights community. They also argued their case on economic grounds. A Congressional Budget Office report found that the DREAM Act would cut the federal deficit by $1.4 million, and a UCLA study that its passage would inject $3.6 billion into the economy in the next four decades. These findings helped refute arguments that undocumented immigrants take jobs from Americans, and showed that the entire nation would benefit from the legislation.

But the most powerful strategy used by DREAM Activists was unprecedented: students coming forward to publicly announce their undocumented status. These acts showed that students were so committed to the DREAM Act that they were willing to risk their own ability to stay in the country. This measure went beyond the activist tradition of "putting one's body on the line"; to risk deportation and separation from one's family and friends by publicly announcing one's undocumented status brought a human dimension that elevated the drive for the DREAM Act to a broader human rights struggle.

Stories were broadcast of students like Mario Lopez, who was brought to East Los Angeles by his mother when he was four years old. Lopez was scheduled to graduate with a political science degree from the University of California, Berkeley, in 2011, but without the DREAM Act he would still be undocumented and unable to obtain many jobs. Jose Luis Zelaya left Honduras as a child and immigrated to Texas, where he graduated as a middle school teacher from Texas A&M. The first undocumented student to run to be the school's student body president, he has a passion for teaching and working to positively change the lives of his students. Websites like UnitedWeDream.org enabled other students to provide their own personal testimonies, all of which demonstrated the extraordinary personal courage and commitment of DREAM Activists.

And DREAM Activists were savvy enough to show that the law was needed for reasons besides helping Latino students. At a Senate hearing on the DREAM Act, Ola Kaso, an eighteen-year-old Albanian American student facing deportation, described how she had just graduated from high school with a 4.4 GPA and had enrolled at the University of Michigan on a scholarship to study premed and pursue her dream of being a surgical oncologist. Undocumented Asian students like Joseph Kim and Frank Yang also spoke out at public events, as did others affiliated with Asian Students Promoting Immigrant Rights through Education (ASPIRE). It was estimated that 10 percent of students potentially impacted by the DREAM Act nationwide were Asian American, while at the University of California the proportion exceeded 40 percent.[6]

Many videos of testimonies by undocumented students were posted on YouTube. This further demonstrated DREAM Activists' willingness to go public, and further highlighted the absurdity of preventing so many young people who could have such a positive impact on society from either living in the United States or gaining employment in their chosen fields.

DREAM Activists combined the unprecedented strategy of announcing they were illegally in the country with tried-and-true activist strategies. On January 1, 2010, four immigrant students from Florida—Felipe Matos, Gaby Pacheco, Carlos Roa, and Juan Rodriguez—left Miami on a fifteen-hundred-mile journey to the nation's capital. Since three of the group were undocumented, they were risking deportation in a high-profile event that captured the attention of local media as the group passed through towns heading north to Washington, D.C. The students traveled through some of the nation's most conservative states and, in rural Georgia, were confronted by Ku Klux Klan members who called them "Mexican dogs" and "homeless prostitutes" and threatened to "eradicate" all Latinos from the United States.[7]

Named the Trail of Dreams, the march harkened back to Cesar Chavez's 1965 march from Delano to California's capital of Sacramento, an event that brought national attention for the UFW leader and the emerging farmworkers' movement. The students marched fifteen to eighteen miles a day, six days a week, before arriving at the White House on April 28, 2010. Their request for a meeting with President Obama was denied, and the marchers rejected an offer to meet with White House senior adviser Valerie Jarrett. The group then led the large immigrant rights march in D.C. on May 1, when DREAM Activists and their supporters took to the streets throughout the nation.

After Republicans took control of the House in the 2010 elections, activists were determined to get Congress to pass the DREAM Act prior to the Republicans taking power. Instead of becoming disillusioned by the election results, as did many older progressive activists, students became even more energized. They began a powerful campaign of fasts, marches, and other grassroots actions, winning assurances from Speaker Nancy Pelosi and Senate majority leader Harry Reid that they would do whatever they could to pass the measure. On December 7, grassroots groups from across the nation organized vigils to show support for passing the DREAM Act. Vigils were held in New York City, Chicago, and other large cities and even in such small towns as Marshalltown, Iowa, and Kennewick, Washington.

The campaign for the DREAM Act involved the most powerful grassroots effort to sway Congress since President Obama's health care reform measure in 2009–10. The DREAM Act passed the Democratic-controlled House, but needed sixty votes in the Senate to end a Republican filibuster. Students did everything possible to secure those sixty Senate votes, and won the support of three Republican senators. But five Democrats deserted the cause, leaving only fifty-five votes in support of allowing the Senate to vote on the bill.

No Defeat, No Surrender

Following the heartbreaking Senate vote, it would have been easy for DREAM Activists to give up on a struggle that now seemed unwinnable in the near future, due to Republican control of the House. But the student activists fought even harder. They understood that they could still achieve something close to the DREAM Act by appealing to someone who was depending on Latino votes to secure his reelection: President Obama.

As discussed in chapter 2, Obama greatly disappointed immigrant rights activists in his first term by setting records for deportations while doing nothing to create paths to legalization and citizenship. A February 2010 Latino Decisions poll found that 85 percent of registered Latino voters supported the DREAM Act and that, among Latinos who intended to vote for Obama in 2012, the proportion rose to 93 percent. After low voter turnout from base voters cost Democrats in 2010 (though Latino turnout bucked national trends), DREAM Activists and their supporters had leverage over a president who knew he could not win a second term without a strong and enthusiastic Latino vote.[8]

Immigrant rights activists began pressuring President Obama from the day of the losing Senate vote. This pressure paid off when the Obama administration announced in June 2011 that it would focus its deportation efforts on undocumented immigrants who posed a public safety threat rather than on those who did not, such as students. But it soon became clear that this vague new policy was having little impact; of the 300,000 deportation cases reviewed under the new approach, only 1.5 percent saw a reversal. With Obama in full reelection mode as 2012 began, he faced the challenge of energizing a Latino constituency that would not support his Republican opponent, but also might not go to the polls in the numbers that had swung four key swing states to Obama's side in 2008.

Obama faced another challenge in mobilizing Latino voters: student activists' willingness to adopt a "by all means necessary" approach. Unlike labor and community organizations that can feel restricted in challenging political allies due to personal connections or other factors, students typically have little to lose by establishing a fear-and-loathing relationship with politicians. In the case of DREAM Activists, this meant not keeping quiet about Obama's dismal immigration record out of fear it would help elect an even worse Republican; instead, they recognized that a victory for them would also provide the enthusiasm boost that Obama needed.

In June 2012, a year after Obama's failed deportation policy change, students took a bold and strategically brilliant action: they began sit-ins in Obama campaign offices in more than a dozen cities and in such swing states as Colorado, Nevada, and Florida, as well as in California. The sit-ins followed a May 28 letter delivered to the White House from ninety-five law professors asserting that the president had the legal authority to stop deportations of all young people who would be covered by the DREAM Act. In Denver, two activists sitting in at Obama's campaign office on June 5, 2012, Javier Hernandez and Veronica Gomez, acknowledged that they were undocumented and could face deportation if arrested for their protest. But, Hernandez insisted, "we decided it was time to escalate (the campaign) for an executive order that will end deportation for DREAMers. That's something (Obama) can do." Realizing there was no way the Obama campaign was going to be connected to the deportation of young DREAM Activists, the two continued their sit-in and fast in the Obama offices for six days, galvanizing support for similar actions across the nation.[9]

DREAM Activists accompanied the sit-ins with a walk, sponsored by the Campaign for an American DREAM, that began March 12 and went from Washington, D.C., to San Francisco. The combination of sit-ins, protests, and marches put more pressure on the president from his base than did any issue other than possibly gay marriage, and it could not have been lost on the students that Obama had recently come out in favor of gay marriage in response to similar pressure from his supporters.

A Historic Victory

On June 15, 2012, the Obama administration announced that it would implement much of the DREAM Act administratively. Those meeting the act's requirements would get both a two-year renewable right to stay in the country and a work permit. Also, states could grant these young people drivers' licenses, long a contentious political issue for all undocumented immigrants. While Obama lacked the administrative power to grant a path to permanent legalization and citizenship, the new policy allowed between 800,000 and 1.2 million young undocumented immigrants to live openly and work in their chosen fields.

Obama's action demonstrated the still-enormous power of grassroots activism to bring about progressive change. At a time when most political observers thought progress on immigration reform was stymied, a committed group of young people working from outside the system showed otherwise. They refused to accept prevailing political reality and never gave up their struggle. Lorella Praeli of the United We

Dream Network described students' response to Obama's action: "People are just breaking down and crying for joy when they find out what the president did." While angry Republicans accused Obama of "putting election year politics above responsible policies," those on all sides of the issue recognized the strategic brilliance of the DREAM Activists' taking advantage of Obama's need to win large Latino majorities in the fall election to secure critical benefits. And considering that the two-year plan would be revoked if Mitt Romney were elected, Obama's action gave even more incentive for Latino voters to get to the polls on his behalf.[10]

Having raised expectations with its announcement, the Obama administration worked round the clock to get the application process in place. On August 15, 2012, the new "Deferred Action for Childhood Arrivals" immigration program began accepting applications across the nation. First-day crowds exceeded all expectations, as 13,000 had lined up at the Navy Pier in Chicago by 11:00 A.M. The Illinois Coalition for Immigrant and Refugee Rights and other immigrant rights groups used the same organizing skills that built the immigrant rights movement to turn out large crowds in Los Angeles, New York City, and other areas with large immigrant populations.

The excitement and hope for the future seen in the August 15 events showed that despite the failure to secure comprehensive immigration reform following the 2008 elections, the Latino community had not lost hope. To the contrary, Latino voter enthusiasm for Obama soared after the Deferred Action program was implemented, as student activists recharged the broader immigrant rights movement. This new energy helped propel Latino voting to record levels in November 2012, leading President Obama both to credit Latino support for his reelection and to pledge to rededicate his efforts to pass comprehensive immigration reform. And since students could openly participate in political action without any fear of deportation, they brought their energy and experience to this critical struggle.

MOBILIZING FOR AFFORDABLE EDUCATION

While DREAM Activists fought to pursue the American Dream, students across California were mobilizing against steeply rising tuition costs that were making the dream unaffordable. While rising college tuition and postgraduate debt constitute a national crisis, their impact was particularly felt in California. The state's esteemed UC schools were tuition-free until the 1970s and very inexpensive into the 1990s. But after the state's economy began to decline around 2001, the UC Board of Regents raised tuition to make up for reduced state funding. Between 2003 and 2011, UC tuition more than doubled, skyrocketing 32 percent in 2009 alone. Balancing the UC budget on the backs of students finally reached a breaking point, and a powerful coalition of students, workers, and social justice activists mobilized to protect affordable college education in California.

Strong student opposition to tuition hikes at UC and CSU institutions (the latter, the network of state universities) first emerged after the steep 2009 increase. Connected to budget cuts in the UC system, this hike provoked what some described as "the biggest student protest for more than a generation." Faculty opposed to new work furloughs, students facing a proposed 30 percent tuition hike, and campus workers opposing cutbacks held large protests on UC campuses across the state. This was the first time that students had closely united with faculty and workers, and the 2009 protests proved a training ground for the broader reframing of the struggle. The largest protests occurred at UCLA and Berkeley, with students underscoring the fact that the state paid $49,000 per prison inmate but only $14,000 per UC student. As one leaflet put it, "If the state can lock us up, it can invest in our education for one-third of the cost."[11]

The fall 2009 protests did not stop the tuition hikes, but activists learned from the experience. UC regents and administrators, however, did not. After the regents voted in July 2011 to raise tuition by 9.6 percent on top of a previously approved 8 percent hike for that year, campus activists met with such statewide groups as the Alliance of Californians for Community Empowerment (ACCE) to plan a fall campaign. The goal was to connect student tuition increases to the state's need to raise more revenue, particularly from the wealthy. It was a powerful argument. Many feared that the UC system was becoming off-limits to students of working families that could not afford private colleges. The California Dream of social mobility was at stake, and the student campaign would go beyond the campus to address the state's larger failure to provide equal opportunity for all.

Ignoring the fallout over the recent increases, UC administrators proposed in September 2011 to raise tuition by 8 to 16 percent each year from 2012 to 2016. This generated widespread outrage and further convinced students that UC leaders were content to put the state's entire education funding shortfall on their backs. While the UC Board of

Regents initially rejected the administrators' proposed increase at their September meeting, they did not kill the proposal, but instead pushed back the vote to their November 16, 2011, meeting. If they thought this would allow anger over the administrators' September announcement to dissipate, they were wrong. Instead, the delay gave the growing coalition of students, workers, and other activists plenty of time to mobilize in anticipation of the November meeting, with major events scheduled for UC Berkeley and UC Davis in the preceding week.

In November 2011, large student protests occurred at UCLA and UC Berkeley and on fourteen other UC and CSU campuses. Coinciding with a high point for the Occupy movement, the protests framed the tuition hikes as part of the larger crisis of growing national income inequality and economic unfairness. Banks were targeted both for profiting from rising education costs and for displacing people from their homes through aggressive foreclosure practices. The fact that many UC regents were wealthy (appointees are often large campaign donors) became a major issue, as the regents were now defined as part of "the 1 percent." The protests sent the message that just as working people would not allow banks and the elite to unfairly deprive them of the American Dream of homeownership, students would not allow these forces to make college unaffordable.

Many of the campus protests included nonviolent civil disobedience. At some universities, students pitched tents and joined with other activists in "occupying" a particular campus area; their removal by campus police was criticized in some cases as unnecessarily rough. For example, Occupy Cal's anti–tuition hike rally at UC Berkeley on November 9 brought five to ten thousand activists to Sproul Plaza, and some campus and outside police responded by hitting peaceful protesters with batons and otherwise physically assaulting them. But as unjustified as such violence is, much of the public sees it as unavoidable in large protests. It took a shocking act of violence at UC Davis to put California's student protests on the national and even international map.

The Davis Outrage

Davis, California, is a small community outside the state capital of Sacramento. Perhaps best known for bike riding, a strong environmental consciousness, and a peaceful vibe, Davis is also known for its University of California campus, not known as an activist hotbed. But in November 2011, UC Davis became the national symbol of growing student resistance against tuition increases in California.

The trail of events at UC Davis began on November 15, the day preceding the scheduled Board of Regents meeting to consider UC's proposed tuition hikes. After a large rally, about fifty of the protesters marching to Mrak Hall, the UC Davis administration building, pitched two tents and camped out overnight. They remained there on November 16, when students from across the Bay Area joined anti-foreclosure activists in "occupying" the Bank of America in San Francisco's financial district. The protesters targeted the bank because one of the regents was on its board, which bolstered the activist argument that "the 1 percent" was behind both the tuition hikes and unnecessary foreclosures. The students intended to picket the UC Regents meeting in San Francisco that day, but the meeting was canceled due to the expected protest.

Whether the events in San Francisco on November 16 shaped what occurred at UC Davis on November 18 is not clear. But at 3:30 P.M., police in riot gear arrived and began removing tents and arresting protesters. Some of the activists began a sit-in, linking arms and refusing to move. This scene attracted additional students, who told police that they would not leave until activists already detained were released. Police refused this offer, resulting in the type of stalemate between police and activists that has routinely occurred in campus civil disobedience actions for decades. Yet in this case, the police treated the student protesters in much the same way racist southern sheriffs in the 1960s treated black students demanding civil rights—and joined their predecessors in creating national headlines.

At 4:00 P.M., two officers began spraying pepper spray directly in the faces of the sitting students. Cellphone cameras recorded the vicious attacks, which soon went viral. This publicity quickly turned the police response to the students' anti–tuition hike protests into an international news story. Eleven protesters received medical treatment, and two were hospitalized. This was not the first time police in the United States had misused pepper spray against activists linking arms and refusing to move: notoriously, they had done so during a September 25, 1997, protest by Earth First! in the office of Pacific Lumber, triggering a public backlash that helped save old-growth redwoods. But the adverse reaction here was multiplied because the victims were students peacefully protesting on their own campus.

The violence at UC Davis suddenly had the entire nation asking tough questions about what was happening at the University of California. James Fallows, national correspondent for the *Atlantic*, spoke for many in noting that his reaction to the eight-minute YouTube video of the incident "reminds me of grainy TV footage I saw as a kid, of black civil rights protestors being fire-hosed by Bull Connor's policemen in Alabama. Or of course the Tank Man in Tiananmen Square. Such images can have tremendous, lasting power." Joy Behar. on the popular daytime television talk show *The View,* asked, "What are we in, a fascist state now? A police state in this country? A lot of people watching are too young to remember Kent State . . . it's outrageous, this type of behavior!"[12]

Twitter and the entire array of social media tools were not available when Bull Connor was hosing down black students or when four Kent State students were murdered by campus police, but they were available in 2011. And while much of the post–pepper spray media discussion focused on patterns of excessive police violence, there was also considerable coverage of the underlying reasons for the protest.

THE POWER OF PROACTIVE ACTIVISM

UC Davis students did not try to provoke police violence. Nor did they expect that their protest would cast a national spotlight on rising California college tuition costs. But just as the excessive police response to the first Occupy New York City march across the Brooklyn Bridge helped build that movement (see chapter 1), the UC Davis events show how proactive tactics often cause opponents to make mistakes. Had the protesters not camped out on campus and simply gone home after the November 15 march and protests, the excessive response to their actions would not have occurred. And UC Davis officials, UC administrators, and the Board of Regents would not have found themselves on the defensive over repeatedly balancing budgets on students' backs.

Would the students' reframing of the historically "ivory tower" issue of tuition hikes into a broad rallying cry for social and economic justice have succeeded without the UC Davis incident? We can never know. But after increasing tuition year after year, the regents did not raise tuition from July 2011 through 2012. One reason was ongoing student pressure: from the fall of 2011 through 2012 the regents were unable to hold a single meeting not interrupted by protesters. Student activism ensured that preventing tuition hikes would be a key feature of Prop 30 on California's November 2012 ballot; within days of its passage, the UC Regents announced there would be no tuition increases for the balance of the school year. In January 2013, UC officials announced that there would be no hikes for the 2013–14 academic year, either.

In 2012 student pressure led to the enactment of Assembly Bill 970, which requires UC and CSU officials to consult with students at least thirty days before they publicly announce plans to increase tuition. The new law also imposes a ninety-day period between tuition hikes' approval and effective dates, and requires officials to justify fee increases and mitigate their impact on low-income students.

Charlie Eaton, a doctoral student in sociology and the financial secretary for the UC Student-Workers Union (United Auto Workers Local 2865), was among several activist-oriented students elected to union office in the spring of 2011. A former union organizer for health care workers, Eaton and his allies solidified the student-labor alliance both on and off campus and brought a movement-building spirit to the anti–tuition hike drive. Eaton sees the students' alliance with faculty and workers that began in 2009 as central to the campaign's success, noting that "when students are joined by faculty pulling out of classes and workers going on strike, it says to the public that something is seriously wrong with how California is funding its colleges and universities."[13]

As with student campaigns against sweatshops and for immigrant rights, the movement to limit UC tuition hikes overcame powerful obstacles to achieve success. While the struggle for affordable tuition is far from over, the progress in recent years has been remarkable. After nearly a decade in which they were left out of the process, students are now recognized as powerful players in education funding decisions—a tribute to their having broadened the appeal of their campaign.

THE WAR ON STUDENT ACTIVISM

As students struggle to create a world of greater social and economic fairness, powerful interests are not pleased. They may urge young people to "make a difference" in the lives of the less fortunate and to provide community service, but oppose students seeking systemic solutions by challenging corporate polluters or unscrupulous banks. Like the campus administrators who sought to deter student activism against tuition hikes, these powerful interests support campus idealism until it challenges their own business practices. And while today's students have not been victims of shootings like those at Kent State and Jackson State during the Vietnam War, campus activism is under attack.

Consider the case of the campus-based Public Interest Research Groups (PIRGs). When these groups emerged in the 1970s, they were widely supported as a great way for students to get involved in consumer and environmental issues. The PIRGs created a unique funding strategy that involved students voting to contribute by checking a box on their tuition payment. While some PIRG chapters also got funding through the traditional allocation of money to student groups, the groups' reliance on funding from those they served would seem to fit perfectly the Republican model of self-reliance and avoiding government-funded advocacy programs.

Yet by the 1990s the PIRGs had created a huge problem for themselves: they were too successful. As shown earlier in the discussion of their work on the Clean Air Act campaign, instead of confining their work to promoting campus recycling programs, student PIRG chapters were challenging powerful corporate interests. This focus was great for developing a new generation of progressive activists, but it brought challenges to the PIRGs' funding base. The many Republican governors elected in the 1994 GOP landslide appointed their corporate backers as trustees to state public educational institutions, and those trustees used their position to deny funding to the PIRGs. It no longer mattered that students sought to spend their own money to open new campus PIRG chapters or fund existing ones; these decisions were overruled either by school administrators or by the state trustees.

As a result, it became difficult during the 1990s for the PIRGs to expand to additional campuses in then-red states like Ohio and Colorado, despite student interest. Even now-ultrablue California had a Republican governor from 1983 to 1998 and from 2003 to 2010, which resulted in funding restrictions to the highly popular campus CALPIRG chapters.

Opposition to student activism increased even further when President George W. Bush helped send the economy into the ditch and put tax breaks for millionaires ahead of college funding. This made school administrators even more dependent on corporate and wealthy donors who did not want to fund institutions whose students were opposing their agendas.

This situation did not improve after President Obama's election in 2008. In fact, the war on student activism actually intensified. School officials seeking to impose college tuition hikes now faced a student population that had been promised "change" and was mobilizing to achieve it. And given that the economic slowdown forced states to cut college funding, administrators used the opportunity to eliminate the activist-oriented programs they had long opposed.

The Transformation of UC Santa Cruz

UC Santa Cruz would seem an unlikely arena for attacks on student activism, as its student body is among the most progressive of any public university. UCSC was created with the express purpose of providing an alternative to the educational experience offered by other UCs. Yet since the late 1990s, if not before, school administrators had been trying to transform the school into nearby Silicon Valley's educational partner. One of their longtime goals was eliminating the university's Community Studies Department, which was at the center of progressive student struggles both on campus and in the larger community. Community studies majors did fieldwork with Bay Area nonprofit organizations, gaining valuable experience and building connections with groups that would help them find postcollege employment. UCSC officials saw a department that allowed students to major in a curriculum focused on social change as conflicting with their new vision for the school, but their past efforts to close down the department had failed.

In 2010, California's fiscal crisis finally gave them this opportunity, as school officials claimed that budgetary imperatives required the department's closure. Closing Community Studies had minimal fiscal impact: Mike Rotkin, a popular longtime lecturer in the department and former mayor of Santa Cruz, was terminated but tenured professors continued teaching in other departments. Yet UCSC administrators used the budget crisis to achieve their longtime goal: facilitating UCSC's transformation from a progressive, activist bastion to an eager "partner" with high-tech companies seeking profit, not social change.

Battling Students in Santa Monica

Santa Cruz is not the only progressive bastion where school administrators seek to suppress student activism. In a city often described as the People's Republic of Santa Monica, school officials at Santa Monica College waged a relentless struggle in 2010 to prevent funding of a primarily Latino and African American CALPIRG chapter at the school.

In spring 2010 the school's students voted by a 62 percent margin for a $1.50 increase in the Associated Students fee specifically to fund CALPIRG. Affirming the students' will, the student government voted to allow students to fund a CALPIRG chapter. But the administration did not want the chapter, despite the training, internship, and postcollege employment opportunities it would provide for the school's many Latino and African American students.

So, as occurs on many campuses these days, administrators lobbied student representatives to change their vote. Among those leading the anti-CALPIRG effort was a woman with a large photograph of Barack Obama on her office wall. Students told her that Obama got his first activist experience at NYPIRG and had long promoted the type of work CALPIRG students perform. But she continued to oppose the chapter, and her intervention paid off. School administrators can provide students with valuable recommendations to graduate schools and employers, so it is understandable that those with no stake in the CALPIRG issue would not want to jeopardize this assistance over the issue. The administration's effort to sway student government at Santa Monica College succeeded, and in December 2010 the students' ability to fund CALPIRG by increasing student fees was revoked.

The Santa Monica College experience reflects a larger problem: CALPIRG has a major presence at the University of California campuses at Berkeley, Davis, Los Angeles, Santa Barbara, and Santa Cruz, but is denied opportunities to open chapters in the community colleges and state universities, where a far higher percentage of Latino and African American students attend. The primarily white and Asian American students attending UC schools have access to CALPIRG's free community organizing and activist training, but Latino and African American students primarily attending non-UC state colleges and universities do not get this opportunity. And this racially discriminatory suppression of activist training is occurring in a state where Latino voters keep Democrats in power.

University of Nike

The University of Oregon in Eugene once had a reputation similar to that of UC Santa Cruz as providing a noncorporate environment and having many students committed to activism. But that was before Nike founder Phil Knight became the school's chief private donor. Knight vowed to cut off funding when U of O joined an anti-sweatshop consortium, leading the school to quickly change course. Today, Knight's influence and the need to attract other private donors has made ridding the campus of groups that train and mobilize progressive student activists a priority.

I was on the Eugene campus in February 2011 when I came across the *Oregon Commentator,* a self-proclaimed "Conservative Journal of Opinion." Funded by the Associated Students of the University of Oregon (ASUO), its agenda is clear from its mission statement, printed on the inside cover: "We believe that the University is an important battleground in the 'war of ideas' and that the outcome of political battles of the future are, to a large degree, being determined on campuses today."

Winning this war of ideas means killing campus funding for OSPIRG, whose students combine work in food banks, homeless shelters, and community gardens with aggressive advocacy against corporate polluters, big banks, and other financial backers of the conservative movement. The lead editorial in the magazine's February 9, 2011, "Sex Issue" compared OSPIRG to "genital herpes," and claimed that OSPIRG's efforts to mobilize students for social justice are akin to spreading "gonorrhea of the throat."

The article "I OPPOSE OSPIRG" took up the entire back cover of the *Commentator*'s January 26, 2011, issue. The item featured interviews with the founder of the school's anti-abortion "Students for Life" chapter and with a student senator who continually bashes OSPIRG. University of Oregon students were funding this anti-progressive, anti–community service, anti-activist message instead of the activities of OSPIRG, which provides students with community service opportunities and has been a leading force for increased Pell grants and reduced textbook costs. Both benefit U of O students far more than the *Commentator*.

Why is a publicly supported university in a progressive city backing right-wing interests over OSPIRG, the only campus group that provides a training ground in organizing and activism? Because student funding is allocated by a student senate (the ASUO) elected by a small number of student voters disproportionately affiliated with fraternities and sororities. These representatives have every incentive to align with the school's administration, which has been hostile to OSPIRG since its former campus president Ben Unger publicly criticized Nike sweatshops in the 1990s. (After getting his start with OSPIRG, Unger was elected to the Oregon state legislature in 2012.)

The ASUO rejected OSPIRG funding for the third consecutive year in 2011, but student body president Amelie Rousseau supported OSPIRG and vetoed the budget. A newly elected student government then won support for OSPIRG's funding, but future battles are expected. The combined opposition from school administrators and ambitious student politicians eager to do their bidding forced OSPIRG to divert energy toward funding battles at a time when their activist members had no shortage of critical issues to mobilize around. In other words, instead of promoting students' participation in improving their community, the state, and the nation, U of O administrators sought to squelch such activism.

In addition to overt attacks on student activism, school administrators are more subtly discouraging such activities through allegedly neutral campus policies. This includes charging students high fees for using classrooms for evening meetings, imposing restrictions on the posting of event notices, and even prohibiting the use of chalk to announce events. In addition, students arrested for what authorities deem inappropriate campus activism are often prosecuted to the full extent of the law and are also subject to harsh academic disciplinary action.

Yet these recent efforts to deter student activism have largely failed. After the massive student participation in the 2008 Obama campaign, the media became convinced that this was a one-time deal and that student disengagement would return. Yet thanks to groups like the Student PIRGs' New Voters Project, student voter turnout in the November 2012 election increased to 19 percent of the electorate from 18 percent in 2008. In addition to ongoing campus activism against tuition hikes, young people continue to work for greater social and economic justice. The attacks on CALPIRG and UCSC's elimination of the Community Studies Department in 2010 both occurred in a year in which California students played a key role in defeating a Chevron-funded November ballot measure (Prop 23) designed to overturn the state's landmark climate-change law. School administrators will continue to battle campus activism, but students' idealism and commitment will continue to overcome.

Conclusion

New Activism for the Twenty-First Century

In Frank Capra's classic 1946 film, *It's a Wonderful Life,* Jimmy Stewart plays George Bailey, a character who comes to feel he has accomplished nothing in life and walks onto a bridge contemplating suicide. In the nick of time, an angel appears and shows him how poorly his town and family would have fared had he never been born. Bailey, realizing that he has made a positive impact on his world, renews his spirit and embraces life in a finale that has long brought tears to viewers' eyes.

When I wrote the original version of *The Activist's Handbook,* far too many activists had become distraught George Baileys bemoaning their perceived inability to make a difference in the world. The Reagan years of the 1980s and the 1994 Republican takeover of the House of Representatives left progressives in despair; many seemed to be lining up next to George Bailey on the bridge.

I tried to dispel this attitude by showing how activists in struggles across the nation had prevailed against seemingly insurmountable barriers by using specific tactics and strategies. And while I hope this new edition of the book also uplifts fallen activist spirits, activists in the second decade of the twenty-first century feel more confident in their ability to win allegedly unwinnable fights. I say this despite great social and economic unfairness in the United States and the increased potential of wealthy individuals and corporations to impact elections and the legislative process.

Today's activists feel more confident because the Internet has exposed a vast world of social change activism that traditional-media gatekeepers once excluded. Activists are more confident because, though they realize that conservative billionaires spent hundreds of millions of dollars in the 2012 national elections, their presidential candidate and nearly all of their United States Senate candidates in seriously contested races lost. Activists are confident because grassroots mobilizing has proved time and again that it can overcome big money, as so many examples in this book show.

Activists have reason for confidence. The gay rights movement has gone from pushing Democratic presidential primary candidates to back state recognition of same-sex "civil unions" in 2004, to getting President Barack Obama to publicly endorse gay marriage only eight years later. Obama went from opposing marriage equality at the start of 2012 to promoting it in his 2013 inaugural address. Immigrant rights activists thought they had lost their chance for comprehensive reform in the near term when 2012 began, but by 2013 a movement for enactment—inspired and fueled by young DREAM Activists—was stronger than ever. Green activists transformed a "done deal" to build the Keystone XL pipeline into a national grassroots campaign and a litmus test for the nation's commitment to combating climate change. And a small group of anarchists in New York City decrying "the 1 percent" had the audacity to launch a national debate about income inequality that still shapes public attitudes about the nation's commitment to economic fairness and equal opportunity for all. None of these achievements were easy. And activists and grassroots campaigns often fail regardless of the tactics or strategies used. But the power of activism to bring about greater social and economic fairness remains strong. As this book demonstrates, activists who create proactive agendas, establish fear-and-loathing relationships with elected officials, seek coalitions with ideologically diverse constituencies when necessary, strive to align the media with their cause, and understand how to use direct action and the courts can overcome all obstacles. And when such tactical activism does not succeed, it still maximizes the potential for victory.

The road to greater social and economic justice is not a straight line, and the path to real change is never easy. It took nearly a decade after Rosa Parks's historic action for the nation to pass the first major federal civil rights law. Cesar Chavez spent thirteen years organizing farmworkers before winning the nation's first Agricultural Labor Relations Act, and, only a year before this landmark victory, many had declared the farmworkers' movement a failure. Rarely does real change happen in the space of a few years, or through a single major struggle.

When Barack Obama won the presidency in November 2008, hopes for real change were high. But the difficulty of the road ahead soon became clear. It was not long before activists questioned Obama's commitment to real change, as well as his skill in surmounting political obstacles. Disappointment that more was not accomplished in President Obama's first two years led many Democrats and particularly young people to not vote in the 2010 midterm elections. This meager Democratic turnout gave Republicans control of the House and limited the president's ability to implement progressive change.

But many activists never gave up, and major gains for immigrant rights, gay marriage, and the environment occurred during the second half of Obama's first term. And with the president having won a second four-year term and aligning himself again with many progressive policies, activists have a chance to avoid the strategic mistakes of 2009–10 and to secure real and lasting change.

I am often critical of elected officials who campaign promising "change" but then become satisfied with the status quo upon taking office. Yet as this book demonstrates, progressive change is won by activists and their constituencies, not simply by elected officials. Activists must accept their own leadership role in the process and recognize that neither politicians nor political parties are the prime movers of progressive change.

Winning political power is like building a field of dreams: if activists and their constituencies build a strategically sound campaign or movement for social change, the elected officials will come. The Democratic Party wanted nothing to do with the civil rights movement for nearly a decade after Rosa Parks's refusal to move to the back of the bus; creation of the movement was necessary before politicians gave their support.

The character of George Bailey was created more than a decade before the famous bus ride of Rosa Parks. Had Bailey known the ramifications of Parks's act, he might never have doubted the value of his own life. Today's activists recognize that their participation in public life can make a critical difference in the world. By acting proactively and with tactical and strategic wisdom, social change activists can bring a degree of social and economic justice to the United States that has for too long been deferred.

Notes

CHAPTER 1

1. The VISTA program became an early target of the incoming Reagan administration transition team's plan to "defund the left." By 1982, VISTA-funded community-based organizing for social change had been nearly eliminated.

2. In the late 1970s, when the city briefly had district elections, the Tenderloin was split over two districts, with no progressive objecting. In 1987, when progressives attempted to restore district elections, there was a consensus that the Tenderloin should not be split, because it was seen as a distinct neighborhood.

3. "The Squeeze" and "Tenderloin Tango," *San Francisco Chronicle,* February 4–5, 1981.

4. Kalle Lasn of *Adbusters* had registered the web address OccupyWallSteet .org on June 9, but it was not serving the role of official website.

5. Nathan Schneider, "Who Will Occupy Wall Street on September 17?" *Adbusters,* September 14, 2011, http://www.adbusters.org/blogs/adbusters-blog/who-will-occupy-wall-street-september-17.html.

6. "Occupy Wall Street to Turn Manhattan into Tahrir Square," *IB Times New York,* September 17, 2011, http://newyork.ibtimes.com/articles/215511 /20110917/occupy-wall-street-new-york-saturday-protest.htm.

7. http://current.com/shows/countdown/videos/will-bunch-author-of-the-backlash-on-mainstream-medias-failure-to-cover-wall-street-protests.

8. Al Baker, Colin Moynihan, and Sarah Maslin Nir, "Police Arrest More Than 700 Protesters on Brooklyn Bridge," *New York Times,* October 1, 2011.

9. Cristian Salazar and Karen Zraick, "Obama Acknowledges Wall Street Protests as a Sign," *Bloomberg Businessweek,* October 6, 2011, http://www .businessweek.com/ap/financialnews/D9Q6UoO83.htm.

10. Richard Kim, "We Are All Human Microphones," *The Nation,* October 6, 2011.

11. Sean Captain, "The Demographics of Occupy Wall Street, *Fast Company,* October 19, 2011, http://www.fastcompany.com/1789018/occupy-wall-street-demographics-statistics.

12. Meredith Hoffman, "Protesters Debate What Demands, if Any, to Make," *New York Times,* October 16, 2011, A19.

13. Associated Press, "Riot Police Clear Out Downtown Occupy Oakland Camp," *New York Post,* November 14, 2011, http://www.nypost.com/p/news /national/police_clear_out_downtown_occupy_VRxdYCzNGeJdUDFr3mhk4 K#ixzz1vtfecp8g.

14. Chris Bowers, "Support for Occupy Wall Street Drops in New Poll," *Daily Kos,* November 16, 2011, http://www.dailykos.com/story/2011/11/16/1037042 /-Support-for-Occupy-Wall-Street-drops-in-nbsp-new-nbsp-poll.

15. Helen Kennedy, "Adbusters, the Occupy Wall Street Innovator, Says Movement Should Wind Down and Start Up in Spring," *New York Daily News,* November 15, 2011.

16. Michael S. Schmidt, "For Occupy Movement, a Challenge to Recapture Momentum," *New York Times,* April 1, 2012, 19.

17. John Knefel, "Media Get Bored with Occupy—and Inequality, Class Issues Fade along with Protest Coverage," Fairness and Accuracy in Reporting (FAIR), May 3, 2012, www.fair.org; Zaid Jilani, "CHART: Thanks to the 99 Percent Movement, Media Finally Covering Jobs Crisis and Marginalizing Deficit Hysteria," October 18, 2011, Think Progress, http://thinkprogress.org /special/2011/10/18/346892/chart-media-jobs-wall-street-ignoring-deficit-hysteria/.

18. Rich Morin, "Rising Share of Americans See Conflict between Rich and Poor," Pew Research Center, January 11, 2012, http://www.pewsocialtrends .org/2012/01/11/rising-share-of-americans-see-conflict-between-rich-and-poor/.

19. Malia Wollan, "Free Speech Is One Thing, Vagrants Another," *New York Times,* October 19, 2012.

20. Franklin Zimring discusses this latter point in *The City That Became Safe: New York's Lessons for Urban Crime and Its Control* (London: Oxford University Press, 2012).

CHAPTER 2

1. Mary Beth Rogers, *Cold Anger: A Story of Faith and Power Politics* (Denton: University of North Texas Press, 1990), 27.

2. Sonia Hernandez, quoted in Harry Boîte, *Community Is Possible: Repairing America's Roots* (New York: Harper & Row, 1984), 128.

3. Ibid., 169–70.

4. Cited in a Greenpeace flyer for the "Put People First, Not Polluters" bus tour.

5. Albert Gore, *Earth in the Balance: Ecology and the Human Spirit* (New York: Plume, 1993). "Gore Says Clinton Will Try to Halt Waste Incinerator," *New York Times,* December 6, 1992, D9. Browner subsequently disqualified

herself from decisions about the project because of her husband's employment with a national environmental group whose Ohio affiliate was "involved" in the dispute; "For Crusader against Waste Incinerator, a Bittersweet Victory," *New York Times,* May 19, 1993.

6. Will Nixon, "Up in Smoke," *In These Times,* March 21, 1994, p. 16.

7. Rick Hind, conversation with the author, October 21, 1994.

8. Mary McGrory, "Clinton's Smoke Blows Stacks," *Washington Post,* May 18, 1993; "Administration to Freeze Growth of Hazardous Waste Incinerators," *New York Times,* May 18, 1993, A1.

9. Hind quoted in Margaret Kriz, "Slow Burn," *National Journal,* April 3, 1993, p. 811.

10. The bill's enactment was motivated by Democratic senators' concern over retaining control of the Senate, because the Desert Protection Bill had become a litmus test for Feinstein's ability to "get things done" in Washington. "Environmental Movement Struggling as Clout Fades," *Los Angeles Times,* September 21, 1994.

11. Vicki Allen, "Green Groups Pressure Gore to Back Air Rule," Yahoo-Reuters, June 3, 1997, http://biz.yahoo.com/finance/97/06/03/y00002.

12. Ibid., Kathryn Holmann, conversation with the author, July 23, 1997.

13. Bill Nichols, "White House Quietly Seeks Common Ground," *USA Today,* June 5, 1997, 4A.

14. PIRG Electric Update, June 27, 1997. This internal document was transmitted to author by Gene Karpinski.

15. "Say No to Tar Sands Pipeline: Proposed Keystone XL Project Would Deliver Dirty Fuel at a High Cost," Natural Resources Defense Council report, March 2011, http://www.nrdc.org/land/tarsandspipeline.asp.

16. R.M. Arrieta, "Labor's Tar Sands Pipeline Dilemma," *In These Times,* August 26, 2011, http://www.inthesetimes.com/working/entry/11864/tar_sands_flap_and_labor_support/; Mark Guarino, "Hundreds Arrested Protesting Oil Pipeline," *Christian Science Monitor,* September 3, 2011, http://www.msnbc.msn.com/id/44386975/ns/us_news-christian_science_monitor/#.TxSdlErfZ1d.

17. John Broder, "Obama Abandons a Stricter Limit on Air Pollution," *New York Times,* September 3, 2011, A1; Julie Pace and Dina Cappiello, "Obama Halts EPA Regulation on Smog Standards, *Huffington Post,* September 2, 2011, http://www.huffingtonpost.com/2011/09/02/obama-halts-epa-regulation-smog-standards_n_946557.html; http://blog.algore.com/2011/09/confronting_disappointment.html.

18. Meteor Blades, "Jobs, Jobs, a Million Jobs, or a Couple Thousand Anyway," *Daily Kos,* January 19, 2012, http://www.dailykos.com/story/2012/01/19/1056497/-Open-Thread-for-Night-Owls-Jobs-jobs-a-million-jobs-or-a-couple-thousand-anyway.

19. Mike Elk, "Which Is More Likely to Rebuild the Labor Movement: Environmental Allies or 6,000 Temp Jobs?" *BeyondChron,* September 7, 2011, http://www.beyondchron.org/news/index.php?itemid=9491; Stacy A. Anderson, "Mark Ruffalo Backs Pipeline Protest near White House," Associated Press, November 7, 2011, http://www.suntimes.com/news/nation/8659302–418/mark-ruffalo-backs-pipeline-protest-near-white-house.html.

20. Michael Brune, "Keystone XL Victory Today, Clean Energy Tomorrow," SFGate.com, November 10, 2011, http://blog.sfgate.com/mbrune/2011/11/10/keystone-xl-tar-sands-energy-victory/.

21. Darren Samuelsohn, "Greens Call Out Keystone XL Deal," *Politico*, December 16, 2011, http://www.politico.com/news/stories/1211/70582.html#ixzz1k1NtSNsl.

22. "Bill McKibben Response to Expected State Department Rejection of Keystone XL Permit" (press release), January 18, 2012, http://www.350.org/en/media/jan18; John M. Broder and Dan Frosch, "Proposed Oil Pipeline Is Bogged Down by Politics," *New York Times*, January 19, 2012, A13; "Environmental Groups, Unions Support President Obama's Decision on Keystone XL Pipeline" (press release), Communications Workers of America, January 18, 2012, http://www.cwa-union.org/news/entry/environmental_groups_unions_support_presidents_decision_on_keystone_xl.

23. Julia Preston, "Obama to Push Immigration Bill as One Priority," *New York Times*, April 9, 2009, A1.

24. Rich Stolz, "Lessons for the Future of Immigration Reform," *Social Policy* 41 (Fall 2011): 4, 17.

25. Peter Wallsten, "Chief of Staff Draws Fire from Left as Obama Falters," *Wall Street Journal*, January 26, 2010, http://online.wsj.com/article/SB10001424052748703808904575025030384695158.html?mod=WSJ_latestheadlines#printMode; Sam Youngman, "White House Unloads Anger over Criticism from 'Professional Left,'" *The Hill*, August 10, 2010, http://thehill.com/homenews/administration/113431-white-house-unloads-on-professional-left).

26. Sofia Navas-Sharry, "Rep. Gutierrez and Others Arrested as They Protest 'One Million Deported under President Obama,'" America's Voice, July 27, 2011, http://americasvoiceonline.org/blog/entry/Rep._Gutierrez_and_Others_Arrested_Protesting_One_Million_Deportations/.

27. Associated Press, "Obama: Repeal of 'Don't Ask, Don't Tell' Possible," MSNBC.com, April 10, 2008, http://www.msnbc.msn.com/id/24046489/#.Tx7iKmGhGjc.

28. Matthew Yglesias, "Obama's 'Don't Ask, Don't Tell' Hypocrisy," *Daily Beast*, May 10, 2009, http://www.thedailybeast.com/articles/2009/05/10/obamas-dont-ask-dont-tell-hypocrisy.html

29. Aaron Belkin, Nathaniel Frank, Gregory M. Herek, Elizabeth L. Hillman, Diane H. Mazur, and Bridget J. Wilson, "How to End 'Don't Ask, Don't Tell': A Roadmap of Political, Legal, Regulatory, and Organizational Steps to Equal Treatment," Palm Center, University of California, Santa Barbara, May 2009, http://www.palmcenter.org/files/active/0/Executive%20Order%20on%20Gay%20Troops%20-%20final.pdf.

30. Bryan Bender, "Gay-Rights Groups Urge Reversal Now," *Boston Globe*, May 20, 2009, http://www.boston.com/news/nation/washington/articles/2009/05/20/continued_discharges_anger_dont_ask_dont_tell_critics/.

31. Mark Thompson, "Dismay over Obama's 'Don't Ask, Don't Tell' Turnabout," *Time*, June 9, 2009, http://www.time.com/time/nation/article/0,8599,1903545,00.html#ixzz1kKGuR8K5.

32. Christine Simmons, "Obama HRC Speech: 'I Will End Don't Ask, Don't Tell,' Says President Obama," *Huffington Post,* October 11, 2009, http://www.huffingtonpost.com/2009/10/10/obama-says-he-will-end-do_n_316524.html; "Obama at HRC: Recap of Blogger Comments," Lone Star Bear, October 11, 2009, http://lonestarbear.blogspot.com/2009/10/obama-at-hrc-recap-of-blogger-comments.html.

33. John Aravosis, "Where's the Beef?" Americablog, October 10, 2009, http://www.americablog.com/2009/10/wheres-the-beef.html.

34. Sam Stein, "DADT Repeal: Dems Move Forward with Plans," *Huffington Post,* March 18, 2010, http://www.huffingtonpost.com/2010/01/12/dems-move-forward-with-pl_n_420180.html.

35. Josh Gerstein, "President Obama Offers Little New in Speech to Gay Rights Activists at HRC Dinner," *Politico,* October 10, 2009, http://www.politico.com/news/stories/1009/28156.html.

36. "LGBT Legal and Advocacy Groups Decry Obama Administration's Defense of DOMA" (press release), ACLU, June 12, 2009, http://www.aclu.org/lgbt-rights_hiv-aids/lgbt-legal-and-advocacy-groups-decry-obama-administrations-defense-doma.

37. Abby Goodrich and John Schwartz, "Judge Topples U.S. Rejection of Gay Unions," *New York Times,* July 9, 2010, A1.

38. Joe Sudbay, "Transcript of Q and A with the President about DADT and Same-Sex Marriage," Americablog, October 27, 2010, http://gay.americablog.com/2010/10/transcript-of-q-and-with-president.html.

39. John Schwartz, "Gay Couples to Sue over U.S. Marriage Law," *New York Times,* November 9, 2010, A20; Charlie Savage, "Suits on Same-Sex Marriage May Force Administration to Take a Stand," *New York Times,* January 29, 2011, A14.

40. Kerry Eleveld, "Obama: 'Prepared to Implement,'" *The Advocate,* December 22, 2010, http://www.advocate.com/news/news-features/2010/12/22/exclusive-interview-president-barack-obama-dadt.

41. Charlie Savage and Sheryl Gay Stolberg, "In Shift, U.S. Says Marriage Act Blocks Gay Rights," *New York Times,* February 23, 2011, A1; Charlie Savage, "Suits on Same-Sex Marriage May Force Administration to Take a Stand," *New York Times,* January 29, 2011, A14.

42. Chris Johnson, "Justice Dept. Brief against DOMA Lauded as 'Watershed Moment,'" *Washington Blade,* July 6, 2011, http://www.washingtonblade.com/2011/07/06/justice-dept-brief-against-doma-lauded-as-watershed-moment/.

CHAPTER 3

1. William Greider, *Who Will Tell the People? The Betrayal of American Democracy* (New York: Simon and Schuster, 1992), 234.

2. Ibid., 235.

3. Unless otherwise noted, the events and chronology of the Brooklyn Navy Yard incinerator fight were provided to the author by Larry Shapiro, Arthur

Kell, and Martin Brennan of NYPIRG in various conversations and correspondence during 1994 and from fact sheets prepared by NYPIRG.

4. *New York Newsday,* "Brooklyn Sunday" supplement, February 20, 1994.

5. Luis Garden Acosta, conversation with the author, November 20, 1994.

6. Both the Satmars and the Latinos of Williamsburg supported Dinkins in 1989, so people openly wondered at the time about Dinkins's political wisdom in sacrificing their support for a project chiefly advocated by Wall Street and the *New York Times.* The Satmars strongly supported Giuliani in 1993, and Dinkins's narrow defeat is partially attributable to his switch to a pro-incinerator position.

7. A fifty-ton-per-day medical waste incinerator had recently been built in the South Bronx. The opening of the North River Sewage Treatment Plant in West Harlem in 1986 was soon followed by complaints of foul odors and respiratory problems from the area's predominantly African American residents. The plant was built in Harlem after the affluent, mostly white Upper West Side organized successfully to defeat construction in that neighborhood.

8. Arthur Kell of NYPIRG, correspondence with the author, July 28, 1994.

9. "Dinkins Cools on Incinerator," *New York Daily News,* March 24, 1992.

10. Luis Garden Acosta, conversation with the author, November 20, 1994.

11. "Race to Pollute," *Newsday,* Brooklyn edition, October 6, 1992.

12. The WWW comprised several religious leaders affiliated with the Catholic Church and individual activists unaffiliated with the Latino or Hasidic communities.

13. "Race to Pollute."

14. Shapiro of NYPIRG, quoted in "Activists Attack Incinerator, Cogeneration Plant," *Staten Island Advance,* October 30, 1992, A7.

15. "Grave Site May Be under Proposed Incinerator," *New York Times,* December 27, 1992, p. 32.

16. Photos of the march may be found in "Paying Tribute to Heroes of Revolutionary War," *Brooklyn Heights Courier,* July 12–25, 1993.

17. "Incinerator Burns Marchers," *New York Newsday,* January 15, 1993; photo caption in "Environmental Concerns Unite a Neighborhood," *New York Times,* January 15, 1993.

18. All quotations in this paragraph are from "Groups Want Hearings on Navy Yard Incinerator," *Legislative Gazette* (Albany, New York), June 14, 1993. It was only later that Garden Acosta learned that the incinerator was actually a fifty-five-story monstrosity (conversation with Garden Acosta, November 20, 1994).

19. Correspondence with Larry Shapiro, June 10, 1994. "There's the Rubbish," *New York Newsday,* Brooklyn Sunday supplement, February 20, 1994, says that in 1989 Giuliani had considered incineration projects "a necessity."

20. "No-Show by Mayor Angers Those at Fort Greene Forum," *The Phoenix* (Brooklyn), September 27–October 4, 1993.

21. "Incinerator Again Testing New Mayor," *New York Times,* February 27, 1994.

22. Ibid.

23. Ibid.

24. All quotations in this paragraph are from "State Ignores Navy Yard Toxins," *New York Daily News,* March 20, 1994.

25. "Hasidic and Hispanic Residents in Williamsburg Try to Forge a New Unity," *New York Times,* September 18, 1994; conversation with Garden Acosta, November 20, 1994.

26. David Niederman, conversation with the author, November 11, 1994; "Hasidic and Hispanic Residents in Williamsburg Try to Forge a New Unity."

27. Conversation with Garden Acosta, November 20, 1994.

28. Correspondence with Kell, July 28, 1994.

CHAPTER 4

1. "Paying a Question in Ballot Initiatives," *New York Times,* August 20, 1994; "Hiram Johnson Please Call Home," *San Francisco Chronicle,* September 10, 1994.

2. See Margaret Brodkin and Coleman Advocates for Children and Youth, *From Sand Boxes to Ballot Boxes: San Francisco's Landmark Campaign to Fund Children's Services* (San Francisco: Brodkin and Coleman Advocates for Children and Youth, 1994), 90. The book was funded by the Charles Stewart Mott Foundation and is available from the author.

3. Saul Alinsky, *Rules for Radicals* (New York: Vintage, 1972), 12–13.

4. Official opposition ballot argument, *California Voter Handbook,* November 1990.

5. Technically, the measure was a referendum put on the ballot by landlords after it was signed by the mayor into law. Everyone knew that legislative passage of vacancy control would become subject to a referendum. By pushing to enact vacancy control in early 1991, tenant advocates were, in essence, choosing to put an initiative on the November 1991 ballot. Tenant advocates were in the same position as if they had used the initiative route directly.

6. Our opposition's campaign manager, Jack Davis, had never previously lost a rent control–related campaign. Davis received the lion's share of credit for masterminding Frank Jordan's upset victory over Art Agnos in the 1991 San Francisco mayor's race.

7. Alinsky, *Rules for Radicals,* xviii.

8. Thomas Ferguson and Joel Rogers, *Right Turn: The Decline of Democrats and the Future of American Politics* (New York: Hill and Wang, 1986).

9. Lydia Chávez, *The Color Bind: California's Battle to End Affirmative Action* (Berkeley: University of California Press, 1998).

CHAPTER 5

1. Ben Bagdikian, *The Media Monopoly,* 4th ed. (Boston: Beacon Press, 1992), 15, 47–48.

2. "Our City's Shame," *San Francisco Chronicle,* December 6, 1982, A1.

3. I dealt extensively with the producer on a story in which he sought to support his thesis that there was enough low-cost housing available for all of the homeless staying in shelters. It became obvious that his commitment to his

thesis overshadowed any journalistic obligation to report the facts. The resulting two-part series was so confusing that its message was lost.

4. Randy Shaw, *Reclaiming America: Nike, Clean Air, and the New National Activism* (Berkeley: University of California Press, 1999), 35–37.

5. City Hall–, statehouse-, or U.S. Capitol–based reporters often do such favors for the executive branch in exchange for priority access on major stories.

6. Jude Wanniski, *The Way the World Works: How Economies Fail—and Succeed,* 3rd ed. (Morristown, N.J.: Polyconomics, 1989).

7. Michael Winerip, "Amid a Federal Education Inquiry, an Unsettling Sight," *New York Times,* February 26, 2012, A10.

8. Diane Ravitch, "Shame on Michelle Rhee," *Daily Beast,* March 29, 2011, http://www.thedailybeast.com/articles/2011/03/29/michelle-rhees-cheating-scandal-diane-ravitch-blasts-education-reform-star.html.

9. Joy Resmovits, "America's Education Reform Lobby Makes Its Presence Known at the Voting Booth," *Huffington Post,* November 22, 2011, http://www.huffingtonpost.com/2011/11/21/education-reform-money-elections_n_1105686.html.

10. "The Rhee Miracle Examined Again—by Cohort," GFBrandenburg's Blog, January 31, 2011, http://gfbrandenburg.wordpress.com/2011/01/31/the-rhee-miracle-examined-again-by-cohort/

11. Randy Shaw, "Anti–Teacher Union 'Reformers' Hoisted on Own Petard," *BeyondChron,* August 23, 2011, http://www.beyondchron.org/news/index.php?itemid=9455.

CHAPTER 6

1. Change.org's utility for such campaigns may soon be reduced. In October 2012 it announced that it would allow corporate advertising, Republican Party solicitations, anti-abortion and anti-union ads, and other far-from-progressive sponsorships.

2. Matthew Kavanagh, "Kony 2012: Does Social Media Oversimplify?" *LA Progressive,* March 22, 2012, http://www.laprogressive.com/kony-2012-social-media-wrong/?utm_source=LA%20Progressive%20Newsletter&utm_campaign=3bc6b23596-LAP_News_19_July_2011_Live7_18_2011&utm_medium=email.

3. Brian Stelter, "From Flash to Fizzle," *New York Times,* April 15, 2012, Sunday Review, p. 5.

4. For more on new media and Wisconsin, see John Nichols, *Uprising* (New York: Nation Books, 2012), 107–15.

5. Joe Trippi, *The Revolution Will Not Be Televised* (New York: Harper Collins, 2004), 96–98, 104.

6. Kos, "Jon Tester and the DREAM Act," *Daily Kos,* December 18, 2010, http://www.dailykos.com/story/2010/12/18/929996/-Jon-Tester-and-the-DREAM-Act. Tester narrowly won reelection without Netroots support in 2012.

7. Malcolm Gladwell, "Small Change," *New Yorker,* October 4, 2010.

8. Mike Gaworecki, "Social Media: Organizing Tool and a 'Space of Liberty' in Post-Revolution Egypt?" *Social Policy* 41, no. 4 (Winter 2011): 66–69.

CHAPTER 7

1. Many books describe the conditions giving rise to ACT UP. I have relied primarily on the following: Bruce Nussbaum, *Good Intentions: How Big Business and the Medical Establishment Are Corrupting the Fight against AIDS* (New York: Atlantic Monthly, 1990); Robert M. Wachter, *The Fragile Coalition: Scientists, Activists, and AIDS* (New York: St. Martin's Press, 1991); Douglas Crimp and Adam Rolston, *AIDS Demo Graphics* (Seattle: Bay Press, 1990); Jonathan Kwitny, *Acceptable Risks* (New York: Simon and Schuster 1992); Randy Shilts, *And the Band Played On: Politics, People and the AIDS Epidemic* (New York: St. Martin's Press, 1987); and Larry Kramer, *Reports from the Holocaust* (New York: St. Martin's Press, 1989).

2. Nussbaum, *Good Intentions*, 129–30, 139–40, 142–43.

3. Wachter, *Fragile Coalition*, 59; Crimp and Rolston, *AIDS Demo Graphics*, 26–27.

4. Crimp and Rolston, *AIDS Demo Graphics*, 14–15.

5. Nussbaum, *Good Intentions*, 187.

6. Many activists wrongly assume that media outlets have a collective memory or that editors are capable of making the obvious linkage between events; a quick response can ensure that the same reporter stays on the story and perhaps convinces his or her editor to grant space for a follow-up report.

7. ACT UP member Laura Thomas, conversation with the author, June 7, 1994.

8. Nussbaum, *Good Intentions*, 204–6; Crimp and Rolston, *AIDS Demo Graphics*, 76–77, 80–81.

9. "AIDS Blockade Halts Morning Commuters," *San Francisco Chronicle*, February 1, 1989, A1.

10. "Read This or Else," *San Francisco Examiner*, February 1, 1989, A3; "AIDS Blockade Halts Morning Commuters."

11. Wachter, *Fragile Coalition*, 62–63.

12. Crimp and Rolston, *AIDS Demo Graphics*, 131–41.

13. "AIDS Protests at Churches," *San Francisco Chronicle*, December 18, 1989, A4.

14. Crimp and Rolston, *AIDS Demo Graphics*, 137.

15. Wachter, *Fragile Coalition*, 20.

16. Nussbaum, *Good Intentions*, 278–79.

17. House Resolution 4370, introduced in 1993, would have cost $2 billion over five years. It won only twenty-one cosponsors in the House and went nowhere.

18. "AIDS Vaccine," *East Bay Express* (Berkeley), August 5, 1994, 1.

19. Ibid.

20. Figures from the U.S. Public Health Service, cited in "Kansas City ACT-UP Chapter May Shut Its Doors for Good," *San Francisco Chronicle*, January 16, 1995; "Larry Kramer's Roar Turns to Contented Purr," *New York Times*, January 12, 1995, B1.

21. Unless otherwise noted, the events and chronology of the Section 504 struggle were provided by disability rights activists Kitty Cone and Judy Heumann in various conversations and correspondence during 1994.

22. "Handicapped Use Protests to Push HEW to Implement '73 Bias Law," *New York Times,* April 29, 1977, 12; and "Equity for Disabled Likely to Be Costly," ibid., May 1, 1977.

23. "HEW Protest by Handicapped," *San Francisco Chronicle,* April 6, 1977; "Handicapped Call Off D.C. Demonstration," ibid., April 7, 1977.

24. The only change made to the original version of Section 504 was an attorney general's opinion clarifying that alcoholics and drug addicts were covered by the act as long as they were otherwise qualified for the job or program involved (Joseph A. Califano, Jr., *Governing America* [New York: Simon and Schuster, 1981], 261). "Equity for Disabled Likely to Be Costly."

25. William Dietrich, *The Final Forest: The Battle for the Last Great Trees of the Pacific Northwest* (New York: Simon and Schuster, 1992), 154 (Friedman quote).

26. Rachel L. Swarns, "Bill on Illegal Immigrant Aid Draws Fire," *New York Times,* December 30, 2005; White House, Office of the Press Secretary, "President Applauds House for Passing Immigration Reform Bill," press release, December 16, 2005, www.whitehouse.gov/news/releases/2005/12/20051216–13.html; U.S. Congress, House, *Congressional Record,* December 16, 2005, HI1952.

27. "The Gospel vs. H.R. 4437," editorial, *New York Times,* March 3, 2006; Sensenbrenner quoted in David Broder, "Bush Provided Spark,"

28. Niraj Warikoo, "Latinos Voice Opposition: Thousands Protest Immigration Proposal," *Detroit Free Press,* March 28, 2006; Myung Oak Kim, "Service Workers Demand Their Voice Be Heard," *Rocky Mountain News,* June 5, 2006, www.rockymoutainnews.com/drmn/local/article/0,1299, DRMN_15_4750959,00.html.

29. Amy Goodman and Juan Gonzalez, "Immigrant Rights Protests Rock the Country; Up to 2 Million Take to the Streets in the Largest Wave of Demonstrations in U.S. History," *Democracy Now,* April 11, 2006, www.democracynow .org/article.pl?sid+06/04/11/1426231.

30. Goodman and Gonzalez, "Immigrant Rights Protests Rock the Country"; Scott Gold, "Student Protests Echo the '60s, but with a High-Tech Buzz," *Los Angeles Times,* March 31, 2006; Harold Meyerson, "The Smartest Movement," *LA Weekly,* April 12, 2006; Teresa Watanabe and Hector Becerra, "How DJs Put 500,000 Marchers in Motion," *Los Angeles Times,* March 28, 2006; Teresa Watanabe and Nicole Gaouette, *Los Angeles Times,* March 28, 2006; "Next: Converting the Energy of Protest to Political Clout," *Los Angeles Times,* May 2, 2006.

31. Quoted in Randy Shaw, *Beyond the Fields: Cesar Chavez, the UFW, and the Struggle for Justice in the 21st Century* (Berkeley: University of California Press, 2008), 232.

32. For crowd estimates in this and the following two paragraphs, see Xóchitl Bada, Jonathan Fox, Andrew D Selee, and Mauricio Sánchez Álvarez, *Invisible No More: Mexican Migrant Civic Participation in the United States* (Washington, D.C.: Mexico Institute, 2006); Clare Bayard, "A Catalogue of Resistance: Immigrant-Led Human Rights Mobilizations, Spring 2006," libcom.org, May 12, 2006 http://libcom.org/forums/north-america/immigrant-led-human-rights-mobilizations-spring-2006–12052006; Goodman and Gonzalez, "Immigrant Rights Protests Rock the Country."

33. "Rallies across U.S. Call for Illegal Immigrant Rights," CNN.com, April 10, 2006, www.cnn.com/2006/POLITICS/04/10/immigration/index.html?iref= newsearch.

34. Bada et al., *Invisible No More;* Bayard, "A Catalogue of Resistance."

35. Alex Isenstadt, "Town Halls Gone Wild," *Politico,* July 31, 2009, http://www.politico.com/news/stories/0709/25646.html.

36. Ibid.

37. Dan Eggen and Philip Rucker, "Conservative Mainstays and Fledgling Advocacy Groups Drive Health-Reform Opposition," *Washington Post,* August 16, 2009, http://www.washingtonpost.com/wp-dyn/content/article/2009/08/15 /AR2009081502696.html.

38. Mark Jurkowitz, "PEJ News Coverage Index, August 3–9, 2009: Town Hall Showdowns Fuel Health Care Coverage," Journalism.org, Pew Research Center's Project for Excellence in Journalism, http://www.journalism.org /index_report/pej_news_coverage_index_august_39_2009.

39. Ibid.

40. Brian Beutler, "Tea Party Town Hall Strategy: 'Rattle Them,' 'Stand Up And Shout,'" Talking Points Memo, August 3, 2009, http://tpmdc .talkingpointsmemo.com/2009/08/tea-party-town-hall-strategy-rattle-them-stand-up-and-shout.php.

41. For a full analysis of media coverage of the Tea Party, see Theda Skocpol and Vanessa Williamson, *The Tea Party and the Remaking of Republican Conservatism* (New York: Oxford University Press, 2012).

CHAPTER 8

1. Self-identified progressive elected officials often prefer delaying tactics to casting a publicly recorded vote against a progressive constituency. A vote to further "study" an issue can allow the public clamor for action to evaporate.

2. The case title is *Whitfield v. Board of Supervisors* (1991) 227 Cal.App. 3d 451; 277 Cal.Rptr. 815.

3. "Wal-Mart Sex Discrimination Class Action Plaintiffs Urge Supreme Court to Uphold Historic Civil Rights and Workers' Laws in Brief Filed Today," PR Newswire, February 22, 2011, http://www.prnewswire.com/news-releases/wal-mart-sex-discrimination-class-action-plaintiffs-urge-supreme-court-to-uphold-historic-civil-rights-and-workers-laws-in-brief-filed-today-116669074.html.

4. The Supreme Court's decision is set forth in *Perry v. Perez* (2012) 132 S.Ct. 934. Adam Liptak, "Justices' Texas Redistricting Ruling Likely to Help G.O.P.," *New York Times,* January 21, 2012, A1; Manny Fernandez, "Federal Judges Approve Final Texas Redistricting Maps," *New York Times,* February 29, 2012, A8; Manny Fernandez, "Federal Court Finds Texas Voting Maps Discriminatory," *New York Times,* August 29, 2012, A3.

5. *In re Marriage Cases* (2008), 43 Cal.4th 757.

6. Taylor Branch, *Parting the Waters: America in the King Years, 1954–63* (New York: Simon and Schuster, 1988).

7. Friction also occurred because, in reaction to the success of King's Montgomery bus boycott, Alabama officials punitively "outlawed" the NAACP in

their state, costing the organization a large segment of its dues-paying membership. See Branch, *Parting the Waters,* 186–87.

8. See http://www.juliangross.net/docs/CBA_Handbook.pdf.

9. West quoted in "Dearborn Project Withdrawn, but CBA Model Carries On," Puget Sound Sage, April 24, 2009, http://www.pugetsoundsage.org /article.php?id=195.

CHAPTER 9

1. Donald Katz, *Just Do It: The Nike Spirit in the Corporate World* (New York: Random House, 1994), ix.

2. "Nike Update" and "Duke Anti-Sweatshop Policy," email messages to author from Campaign for Labor Rights, November 3 and 5, 1997.

3. Max White, interview with author, June 1, 1997. White is a founder of the Portland-based Justice Do It! Jeff Manning, "Nike Battles Back, but Activists Hold the High Ground," *Portland Oregonian,* October 10, 1997, p. 1.

4. David Gonzalez, "Latin Sweatshops Pressed by U.S. Campus Power," *New York Times,* April 4, 2003, http://www.nytimes.com/2003/04/04 /international/americas/04LABO.html.

5. Alan Scher Zagier, "Russell Shifts Course on Honduran Union Workers," *Los Angeles Times,* November 18, 2009.

6. Dan Nejfelt, "Bold Faith Type: Ola Kaso's Inspiring Testimony at Sen. Durbin's DREAM Act Hearing," Faith in Public Life, June 28, 2011, http:// www.faithinpubliclife.org/blog/ola_kasos_inspiring_testimony/; Karen K. Narasaki, "DREAM Act Is an Acute Issue for Asian Americans," *The Hill,* December 17, 2010, http://thehill.com/blogs/congress-blog/civil-rights/134295- dream-act-is-an-acute-issue-for-asian-americans.

7. Devin Dwyer, "Defying Cops and Klan, Immigrants Trek 1,500 Miles to Washington," ABC News, April 30, 2010, http://abcnews.go.com/Politics /illegal-immigrants-seek-reform-1500-mile-trek-dc/story?id=10499173# .T_n3L3DfZ1d.

8. Matt Barreto and Latino Decisions, "Why the DREAM Act Will Matter in 2012," March 1, 2011, *BeyondChron,* http://www.beyondchron.org/news /index.php?itemid=8941.

9. John Ingold, "Immigration Activists Stage Sit-In at Denver Obama Office," *Denver Post,* June 5, 2012, http://www.denverpost.com/breakingnews /ci_20791243/immigration-activists-stage-sit-at-denver-obama-office.

10. Julia Preston and John H. Cushman, Jr., "Obama to Permit Young Migrants to Remain in U.S.," *New York Times,* June 16, 2012, A1.

11. Mary O'Hara, "University of California Campuses Erupt into Protest," *The Guardian* (UK), September 24, 2009, http://www.guardian.co.uk /world/2009/sep/24/california-university-berkeley-budget-protest.

12. James Fallows, "The Moral Power of an Image," *Atlantic,* November 20, 2011, http://www.theatlantic.com/national/archive/2011/11/the-moral- power-of-an-image-uc-davis-reactions/248778/.

13. Charlie Eaton, interview with the author, September 7, 2012.

Index